Melanchthon
in Europe

Texts and Studies in Reformation and Post-Reformation Thought

General Editor
Prof. Richard A. Muller, Calvin Theological Seminary

Editorial Board
Prof. Irena Backus, University of Geneva
Prof. A. N. S. Lane, London Bible College
Prof. Susan E. Schreiner, University of Chicago
Prof. David C. Steinmetz, Duke University
Prof. John L. Thompson, Fuller Theological Seminary
Prof. Willem J. van Asselt, University of Utrecht
Prof. Timothy J. Wengert, The Lutheran Theological Seminary at
   Philadelphia
Prof. Henry Zwaanstra, Calvin Theological Seminary

Caspar Olevianus, *A Firm Foundation: An Aid to Interpreting the Heidelberg
Catechism,* translated, with an introduction by Lyle D. Bierma.
John Calvin, *The Bondage and Liberation of the Will: A Defence of the Orthodox
Doctrine of Human Choice against Pighius,* edited by A. N. S. Lane,
translated by G. I. Davies.
*Law and Gospel: Philip Melanchthon's Debate with John Agricola of Eisleben over
Poenitentia,* by Timothy J. Wengert.
Martin Luther as Prophet, Teacher, and Hero: Images of the Reformer, 1520–1620,
by Robert Kolb.
Melanchthon in Europe: His Work and Influence beyond Wittenberg, edited by
Karin Maag.

Melanchthon in Europe

His Work and Influence beyond Wittenberg

Edited by
Karin Maag

paternoster

Baker Books

A Division of Baker Book House Co
Grand Rapids, Michigan 49516

© 1999 by Karin Maag

Published by Baker Books
a division of Baker Book House Company
P.O. Box 6287, Grand Rapids, MI 49516-6287

and

Paternoster Press
P.O. Box 300, Carlisle, Cumbria CA3 0QS
United Kingdom

Printed in the United States of America

Library of Congress Cataloging-in-Publication Data

Melanchthon in Europe : his work and influence beyond Wittenberg / edited by Karin
   Maag.
      p.   cm. — (Texts and studies in Reformation and post-Reformation
thought)
    Includes bibliographical references and index.
    ISBN 0-8010-2223-1 (pbk.)
    1. Melanchthon, Philipp, 1497–1560. I. Maag, Karin. II. Series.
  BR339.M47 1999
  270.6'092—DC21
                                                  99-31488

British Library Cataloging-in-Publication Data

A catalogue record for this book is available from the British Library.

ISBN 0-85364-976-6

Table of Contents

9 8351

Series Preface

The heritage of the Reformation is of profound importance to the church in the present day. Yet there remain many significant gaps in our knowledge of the intellectual development of Protestantism in the sixteenth century, and there are not a few myths about the theology of the Protestant orthodox writers of the late sixteenth and the seventeenth centuries. These gaps and myths, frequently caused by ignorance of the scope of a particular thinker's work, by negative theological judgments passed on the theology of the Reformers or their successors by later generations, or by an intellectual imperialism of the present that singles out some thinkers and ignores others regardless of their relative significance to their own times, stand in the way of a substantive encounter with this important period in our history. Understanding and appropriation of that heritage can occur only through the publication of significant works—monographs and sound, scholarly translations—that present the breadth and detail of the thought of the Reformers and their successors.

Texts and Studies in Reformation and Post-Reformation Thought proposes to make available such works a Caspar Olevianus's *Firm Foundation*, Theodore Beza's *Table of Predestination*, and Jerome Zanchi's *Confession of Faith,* together with significant monogrphs ont raditional Reformed theology, under the guidance of an editorial board of recognozed scholars in the field. Major older works, like Heppe's *Reformed Dogmatics*, will be reprinted or reissued with new introductions. These works, moreover, are intended to address two groups: an academic and a confessional or churchly audience. The series recognizes the need for careful, scholarly treatment of the Reformation and of the era of Protestant orthodoxy, given the continuing presence of misunderstandings particularly of the later era in both the scholarly and the popular literature as well as the recent interest in reappraising the relationship of the Reformation to Protestant orthodoxy. In addition, however, the series hopes to provide the church at large with worthy documents from its rich heritage and thereby to support and to stimulate interest in the roots of the Protestant tradition.

Richard A. Muller

Preface

The essays in this volume are a reflection of the growing interest among historians for Philip Melanchthon. Four contributors presented their papers at a Melanchthon Colloquium organized by the Meeter Center in Grand Rapids in October 1997, while the other four presented their work in various sessions at the 1997 Sixteenth Century Studies Conference in Atlanta. We are delighted that they agreed to contribute to this volume, and that Richard Muller has accepted it into his series with the Meeter Center's imprint. We also wish to thank Jim Wever and Baker Book House for their work in bringing this volume to publication. Thanks are also due to our student worker, Noelle Barkema, for help at the proofreading stage, and to the technical staff of the Information Technology Center, especially Nancy Zylstra, for help with computer problems. My personal thanks as editor go to Susan Schmurr, the Meeter Center Administrative Aide, who patiently worked at formatting, inserting changes, and making all the necessary adjustments to the document.

Karin Maag,
H. Henry Meeter Center for Calvin Studies
Grand Rapids, December 1998

Notes on Contributors

Lyle Bierma is Professor of Theology at Reformed Bible College in Grand Rapids, Michigan. His main research interests lie in German Calvinism of the later sixteenth century.

Amy Nelson Burnett is Associate Professor and Graduate Chair in History at the University of Nebraska-Lincoln. Her main research interests lie in the Protestant Reformation in Basle.

Dezso Buzogany is Professor at the Protestant Theological Institute in Cluj, Romania. The theme of his research is Melanchthon's contribution as an educator.

Bruce Gordon is a Lecturer in Modern History at the University of St. Andrews in Scotland, and Associate Director of the St. Andrews Reformation Studies Institute. His main research interests are the Reformation in Switzerland and Italy.

Nicole Kuropka is a Ph.D. research student at the Kirchliche Hochschule Wuppertal, Germany. Her main area of research is Melanchthon's reinterpretation of rhetoric. She currently holds a fellowship at the Institute for European Studies in Mainz, Germany.

Karin Maag is the Director of the H. Henry Meeter Center for Calvin Studies, and Associate Professor in History at Calvin College in Grand Rapids, Michigan. Her research interests include higher education in the Reformation and the training of Reformed ministers in the sixteenth century.

Richard Muller is Professor of Historical Theology at Calvin Theological Seminary. His research focuses on Calvin and Reformed theology.

John Schneider is Professor of Religion and Theology at Calvin College in Grand Rapids, Michigan. His main research focus is on Melanchthon as a commentator on the Scriptures and teacher of Protestant Christian Doctrine.

Timothy Wengert is Professor of the History of Christianity at the Lutheran Theological Seminary in Philadelphia. His research focuses primarily on German Reformation history and the Lutheran confessions.

Abbreviations

ARG	*Archiv für Reformationsgeschichte*
BKS	*Die Bekentnissschriften der evangelisch-lutherischen Kirche.* 10th ed. Göttingen: Vandenhoeck and Ruprecht, 1986.
BPKG	*Blätter für Pfälzische Kirchengeschichte*
CO	*Ioannis Calvini Opera Quae Supersunt Omnia.* Edited by Wilhelm Baum, E. Cunitz, and E. Reuss. 59 vols. Brunswick: A. Schwetschke, 1863–97
CR	Philip Melanchthon. *Corpus Reformatorum. Philippi Melanchthonis opera quae supersunt omnia.* Edited by Karl Bretschneider and Heinrich Bindseil. 28 vols. Halle: A. Schwetschke and Sons, 1834–60.
ET	*Evangelische Theologie*
LJ	*Lutherjahrbuch*
LW	Conrad Bergendorff, ed. *Luther's Works.* Philadelphia: Muhlenberg, 1958.
MBW	Philip Melanchthon. *Melanchthons Briefwechsel: Kritische und kommentierte Gesamtausgabe.* Edited by Heinz Scheible. 10 vols. to date. Stuttgart-Bad Cannstatt: Frommann-Holzboog, 1977–.
MSA	Philip Melanchthon. *Melanchthons Werke in Auswahl. [Studienausgabe.]* Edited by Robert Stupperich. 7 vols. Gütersloh: Gerd Mohn, 1951–75.
OS	Peter Barth and Wilhelm Niesel, eds. *Joannnis Calvini Opera Selecta.* Munich: Kaiser, 1952.
SCJ	*Sixteenth Century Journal*
WA	Martin Luther. *Luthers Werke. Kritische Gesamtausgabe [Schriften]* 65 vols. Weimar: H. Böhlau, 1883–1993.
WABr	Martin Luther. *Luthers Werke. Kritische Gesamtausgabe. Briefwechsel.* 18 vols. Weimar: H. Böhlau, 1930–85.
ZKG	*Zeitschrift für Kirchengeschichte*
ZThK	*Zeitschrift für Theologie und Kirche*

Introduction

The year 1997 marked the 500th anniversary of the birth of the German Reformer and educator Philip Melanchthon. Many events, conferences and colloquia were held during this year to mark the occasion and to present studies on Melanchthon to the international scholarly community.

This volume examines various aspects of Melanchthon's work in the context of his day. Before analyzing the various historical approaches which have characterized Melanchthon studies, however, a brief biographical sketch of Melanchthon may prove helpful.

Born in 1497, Melanchthon was the eldest son of an armourer, Georg Schwartzerdt, who worked for various nobles and princes, including his patron, the Elector Palatine. Thus, Melanchthon's family was part of the growing number of relatively affluent artisans, who could hence afford to provide a good education to their sons. Significantly for his future intellectual career, Melanchthon's mentor was the leading German Hebraist, Johann Reuchlin. After the early death of Melanchthon's father and grandfather in 1508, it was largely thanks to Reuchlin's influence and encouragement that Melanchthon was able to go from the Latin school in Pforzheim to enroll in the universities of Heidelberg and Tübingen. He received his Bachelor of Arts degree from Heidelberg in 1511, at fourteen years old, which was not unusual for the period, when boys barely entering their teens were sent to study humanities at a university. One must remember that the arts courses were considered very much as preparation for more advanced studies in the faculties of law, medicine, and theology. In 1514, Melanchthon received the Masters of Arts degree from Tübingen.[1]

Reuchlin's support continued to be beneficial for Melanchthon following his years in Tübingen, as it was thanks to his mentor that the young man obtained the post of professor of Greek at the relatively new university of Wittenberg, which had been founded in 1502. Indeed, Frederick the Wise, Elector of Saxony, had wanted to appoint Reuchlin to the new created post of Greek professor in 1518. Reuchlin, however, de-

---

1. Heinz Scheible, *Melanchthon: eine Biographie* (Munich: Verlag C. H. Beck, 1997), 13–27. For a biography in English, see Clyde Manschreck, *Melanchthon, the Quiet Reformer* (New York: Abingdon Press, 1958)

clined, recommending Melanchthon instead.[2] From 1518 on, therefore, Melanchthon taught in Wittenberg's university, a post which he retained until his death in 1560. In the early years, while lecturing in the arts faculty, he continued his own studies in theology, attending lectures given by professors from the theology faculty, including Martin Luther. In 1519, Melanchthon obtained his Bachelor of Theology degree, allowing him to teach in theology as well as in arts.[3]

As Melanchthon pursued his theological work, he deepened his awareness and commitment to the Reformation message as articulated by Luther. Concrete examples of Melanchthon's commitment to the new religious order include his marriage in 1520 to Katharina Krapp from Wittenberg, and his participation in Wittenberg communion services during which both the bread and the wine were distributed to the faithful, as early as September 1521.[4]

Most of Melanchthon's subsequent career was spent in Wittenberg, although his experience in the field of education increasingly led authorities elsewhere to call upon him for advice regarding their schools and universities. In 1524, for instance, Melanchthon spent two months in Nüremberg, helping the city to put together the ordinances and curriculum for its Latin school.[5] Melanchthon's educational expertise was also brought to light in his written works, in particular in his *Loci Communes*, first published in 1521. This work, intended for theology students and pastors, provided a method for understanding and analyzing the Scriptures by gathering together the themes that each passage of Scripture dealt with and organizing these themes in a suitable manner. Thus, Melanchthon's method combined biblical exegesis, rhetorical analysis, and logic into a usable whole.[6]

Melanchthon also served on many visitation committees, inspecting the state of religious belief and practice throughout the rural areas of Saxony. His main work outside Wittenberg, however, was as a member of Protestant delegations to disputations and colloquies throughout the Holy Roman Empire. Melanchthon accompanied Luther to the Leipzig disputation in 1519 and to the Colloquy of Marburg in 1529 and was also

---

2. John Schneider, *Philip Melanchthon's rhetorical construal of Biblical authority:* Oratio Sacra (Lewiston, Edwin Mellen Press, 1990), 51–52.

3. Scheible, *Melanchthon*, 28–33.

4. *Ibid.*, 38, 63.

5. J. F. Collange, 'Philippe Melancthon et Jean Sturm, humanistes et pédagogues de la Réforme', *Revue d'Histoire et de Philosophie Religieuse* 68 (1988) 10.

6. Scheible, *Melanchthon*, 140–42; Schneider, *Oratio Sacra*, 205–10.

the leading Protestant representative at the Regensburg colloquy in 1541.[7] The fact that meetings like that of Regensburg brought together the more moderate elements both among the Lutherans and the Catholics, has at times led to suspicion of Melanchthon's genuine and firm commitment to Luther's stance. Yet it is clear from Melanchthon's own writings that he was not prepared to accept deviations from what he saw as the fundamentals of the Reformation. Indeed, it was at the Colloquy of Regensburg that Melanchthon refused to consider any further negotiation on the role of the Church and the place given to human authority through the ecclesiastical structures headed by the Pope. For Melanchthon, any further realignment of the Lutheran position closer to the Catholic one would put the Lutherans in danger of jeopardizing their understanding of the Church.[8]

From the mid-1540s until his death in 1560, Melanchthon's life and work were increasingly overshadowed by internal conflict with other Lutherans, who felt that he did not follow Luther's path faithfully enough. Melanchthon's noted moderation, his participation in colloquies with Catholics and the Reformed, and the absence of support from Luther himself following his death in 1547 meant that Melanchthon was vulnerable to such attacks. His opponents, including Andreas Osiander, Matthias Flacius Illyricus and Nicolas Gallus, all accused him of moving away from Luther's teachings to varying degrees.[9] Paradoxically, their attacks do show how significant Melanchthon was for the Lutheran Reformation, since his opponents perceived him as such a serious threat. His death in 1560 did not put an end to the controversies among the Lutherans, as moderates and hard-liners continued to support their own interpretation of key doctrines as being the correct one.[10]

The attention currently focused on Melanchthon is long overdue. As Luther's second in command and later successor (albeit amid some opposition, as described above), over the years Melanchthon has suffered a similar historical fate to other second generation Reformers such as Theodore Beza in Geneva and Heinrich Bullinger in Zurich. As associates and successors to the leading trio of Luther, Calvin and Zwingli,

---

7. Scheible, *Melanchthon*, 82–83, 58, 104–5, 132–33.

8. Timothy Wengert, 'The Day Philip Melanchthon got mad' in *Lutheran Quarterly* 5 (1991), 419–33.

9. Scheible, *Melanchthon*, 200ff, 196ff, 221–23.

10. Ernst Koch, 'Auseinandersetzungen um die Autorität von Philipp Melanchthon in Kursachsen im Vorfeld der Konkordienformel von 1577' in *Lutherjahrbuch* 59 (1992), 128–59.

men like Melanchthon have long had their own legacy scrutinized in terms of their faithfulness to the inheritance of their predecessor, rather than being evaluated in the light of their own work.[11]

In response to such analyses, other scholars have sought to carve out an entirely separate domain for Melanchthon, particularly as regards his work as a humanist. In doing so, these historians have helped to bring to light his unique contribution to the intellectual endeavors of his own time. In this context, Deszo Buzogany's integrative contribution to this volume on Melanchthon's work as a humanist and a Reformer seeks to bridge the gap between the theological and philosophical approaches taken by Melanchthon, particularly in his teaching on dialectics at Wittenberg.[12] Nicole Kuropka takes a similar approach in her chapter on Melanchthon's use of rhetoric, highlighting his successful combination of rhetorical models and practice both from the classical world and from Scripture.[13] The integration of Melanchthon's humanist background with his theology, particularly through his study of rhetoric, is also emphasized by John Schneider in his contribution. Schneider argues strongly for the internal coherence of Melanchthon's intellectual approach throughout his career.[14]

Others have sought to reestablish Melanchthon's role as a figure of international stature in his own time, thus moving Melanchthon studies beyond the walls of Wittenberg. In doing so, these scholars have underlined once again that the German Reformation did come to an end with Luther's death in 1547, nor was it set in stone forever after. Indeed, the roots of Melanchthon's conflict with Luther's more hard-line followers was surely due to the ongoing process of change in the German Reformation, particularly in the light of the ever firmer establishment of competing confessional groups. Yet assessing Melanchthon's influence and impact among his contemporaries is not always straightforward. Aside from the Catholic Church from which they had split, the Lutherans' main rivals during Melanchthon's lifetime were the Reformed, based primarily in the Swiss lands and in Geneva. In this context, Melanchthon's contacts with the Zwinglians and Calvinists are of particular interest. The chapters by Amy Nelson Burnett and Bruce Gordon in this volume help to analyse the encounters between Melanchthon and the Swiss

---

11. See John Schneider's analysis of this approach in his *Oratio Sacra*, 4.

12. See Chapter 4, below.

13. See Chapter 8, below.

14. See Chapter 7, below.

Reformed, while Timothy Wengert's contribution on Melanchthon and Calvin provides a corrective to earlier analyses of the relations between the two men.[15] Moving beyond the realm of contact with individuals, Lyle Bierma's article examines the extent of Melanchthon's influence on the text and doctrine of the Calvinist Heidelberg Catechism, and in a similar vein, Richard Muller's chapter takes a closer look at one particular aspect of the contact between Melanchthon and Calvin, namely the German Reformer's influence on Calvin's most famous work.[16] Setting Melanchthon in the European context of his time helps to erase the image of Melanchthon as a pale copy of Luther, and helps to restore his position as a major Reformer in his own right.

15. See Chapters 1, 2 and 3, below.
16. See Chapters 5 and 6, below.

1

"We Will Feast Together in Heaven Forever": The Epistolary Friendship of John Calvin and Philip Melanchthon

Timothy Wengert

In 1842, as the ninth and final volume of Melanchthon's correspondence in the *Corpus Reformatorum* rolled off the Schwetschke presses in Halle, researchers had at their disposal only six letters between the leading Reformers in Wittenberg and Geneva.[1] Within a generation the number had grown considerably as the addendum to Melanchthon's correspondence, edited by Heinrich Bindseil and published in 1874, contributed fourteen and Calvin's correspondence in the *Corpus Reformatorum* an additional four.[2] Counting descriptions of one letter and one conversation with Melanchthon contained in letters to William Farel and the mention of three lost letters among letters of Melanchthon and Calvin, we can

---

1. MBW 3245 (CR 5:107–9; =CO 11:539–42), MBW 3886 (CR 5:734–39; =CO 6:621–24), MBW 6576 (CR 7:1085f.; =CO 14:368f.), MBW 7306 (CR 8:362f.; =CO 15:268f.), MBW 7489 (CR 8:482f.; =CO 15:615f.), and MBW 8384 (CR 9:328f.; =CO 16:659).

2. Bindseil's work, *Philippi Melanchthonis epistolae, iudicia, consilia, testimonia aliorumque ad eum epistolae quae in Corpore Reformatorum desiderantur* (Halle: Schwetschke, 1874), appeared in the midst of the publication of Calvin's correspondence and contained MBW 3157 (Bds. 165–69; =CO 6:229–32), MBW 3169 (Bds. 169–71, =CO 11:515–17), MBW 3803 (Bds. 214–18; =CO 12:9–12), MBW 3884 (Bds. 479f., not in CR 40), MBW 3885 (Bds. 219f.; =CO 12:61f.), MBW 3928 (Bds. 221–23; =CO 12:98–100), MBW 5830 (Bds. 310–13; =CO 13:593–96), MBW 6655 (Bds. 331–35; =CO 14:414–18), MBW 7273 (Bds. 364f.; =CO 15:215–17), MBW 7424 (Bds. 372–74; =CO 15:488f.), MBW 7562 (Bds. 379f.; =CO 15:737f.), MBW 7957 (Bds. 396–98; =CO 16:280–82), MBW 8293 (Bds. 417–19; =CO 16:556), and MBW 8782 (Bds. 435–38; =CO 17:384–86). The corresponding portions of Calvin's correspondence (CO 10–17), published by Schwetschke between 1871 and 1877, also included MBW 2366 (CO 11:17f.), MBW 3273 (CO 11:594f.), MBW 3531 (CO 11:696–98), and MBW 8331 (CO 16:604f.).

now document twenty-nine exchanges between these two pillars of the Reformation.[3]

The publication of this wealth of new sources on the relation between Melanchthon and Calvin led to several writings at the time, none more important than an article by Philip Schaff in the *Papers of the American Society of Church History* in 1891, entitled "The Friendship of Calvin and Melanchthon." This article, which formed the basis of comments in Schaff's multi-volume *History of the Christian Church*, has had continuous influence over the past century, notably in an article by James T. Hickman, "The Friendship of Melanchthon and Calvin."[4] Both Schaff and Hickman argue that Melanchthon and Calvin had established a true friendship and, despite certain differences in theology, enjoyed fundamental agreement in the faith.

In fact, the *topos* of friendship is used to explain away many of the theological tensions between the two men. Schaff begins his address, "When God has a great work to do in his kingdom on earth he trains and associates congenial agents of different gifts, but of one spirit and aim, to carry out his purposes."[5] And near the end of his article, Hickman exclaims "This friendship demonstrates the possibility of harmony in spite of theological differences."[6] The ecumenical agenda of both writers is not hard to discern.

By far the most thorough assessment of the relationship of Calvin and Melanchthon was produced by Willem Nijenhuis.[7] Here, too, an ecu-

---

3. Calvin's letters to Farel are described in MBW 2103 (CO 10:276–80) and MBW 2152 (CO 10/2:322–32); mention of now lost letters are found in MBW 3169 (where Calvin referred to a letter written by Melanchthon around October 1542), MBW 3273 (where Melanchthon referred to a letter written by Calvin around June 1543 and brought by Johannes Sturm of Strasbourg to Melanchthon in Bonn), and MBW 8331 (where Calvin mentioned two letters sent "inter paucos dies," one of which was MBW 8293).

4. *Westminster Theological Journal* 38 (1976): 152–65. Besides Schaff's work, Hickman depends on John T. McNeill, Williston Walker, and Clyde Manschreck.

5. Philip Schaff, "The Friendship of Calvin and Melanchthon," in *Papers of the American Society of Church History*, 4 (1892): 143–63. Another early study was by Emile Doumergue, *Jean Calvin: Les hommes et les choses de son temps*, vol. 2 (Lausanne: G. Bridel, 1902), 545–61.

6. Hickman, "Friendship," 164.

7. Willem Nijenhuis, *Calvinus oecumenicus: Calvijn en de eenheid der kerk in het licht van zijn briefwisseling*, Kerkhistorische Studien, 8 ('s-Gravenhage: Martinus Nijhoff, 1959), 12–14, 131–99. Other, narrower studies include Rodolphe Peter, "Calvin, traducteur de Mélanchthon," in *Horizons européens de la Réforme en Alsace*, ed. Marijn de Kroon and

menical agenda may be seen, although the careful historical work makes this a far more balanced contribution. Nijenhuis views Calvin's correspondence with Melanchthon from within the larger framework of discussions with the Lutherans and divides Calvin's relations into several epochs (before Luther's death and before and after the Consensus Tigurinus).[8] In the end, however, Nijenhuis concludes that Calvin's correspondence witnesses to his "total personal dedication to the Church of Christ and its unity."[9]

The present study, by placing the correspondence between Melanchthon and Calvin within the context of Renaissance letter-writing etiquette and the theological struggles of the day, challenges older visions of an ecumenical friendship and uncovers the profound tensions between these two Reformers. To use the word "friendship" (especially without modifiers) to describe any historical relationship poses complicated historiographical problems. By calling any two historical figures "friends," historians often seek to overcome psychological and theological differences using classical, even biblical, *topoi*. The friendship of David and Jonathan (or Achilles and Ajax), like the conversion of St. Paul, possesses only limited usefulness as a category for historical research. Nevertheless, this commonplace has particularly plagued recent research on Melanchthon. On the one hand, to insure Melanchthon's commitment to humanism, scholars have declared Melanchthon and Erasmus friends—despite the fact that almost every letter exchanged between them includes biting criticism of the recipient.[10] On the other, scholars eager to unite Melanchthon's theology with Luther's have also declared them friends.[11] Ignoring for the moment the twentieth-century American habit of calling anyone with whom one has conversed for more than two minutes a friend—if the word friendship is carefully defined as intimate

---

Marc Lienhard (Strasbourg: Istra, 1980), 119–33, and Danièle Fischer, "Calvin et la Confession d'Augsbourg," in *Calvinus ecclesiae Genevensis custos*, ed. Wilhelm Neuser (Frankfurt am Main: Peter Lang, 1984), 245–71.

8. See Nijenhuis, *Calvinus*, 131–41, 141–54, 154–99, respectively, where the final section is subdivided into periods of polemic (1549–1556), working toward a colloquy (1556–1559), and resignation (1559–1564). The present research uncovered similar shifts.

9. Ibid., 314, quoting from the English summary.

10. See Timothy J. Wengert, *Human Freedom, Christian Righteousness: Philip Melanchthon's Exegetical Dispute with Erasmus of Rotterdam* (New York: Oxford University Press, 1997).

11. See the criticism by Heinz Scheible, "Luther and Melanchthon," *Lutheran Quarterly*, n.s., 4 (1990): 317–39.

attachment, esteem, and affection between two people, then perhaps only Joachim Camerarius, Veit Dietrich, and Caspar Cruciger, Sr. qualify as Melanchthon's friends.[12]

The relation between Calvin and Melanchthon, on the contrary, was no friendship in this sense. Instead, it was what one might more properly call an epistolary friendship, that is, a literary fiction imposed by the authors themselves, especially Calvin, onto a very complex web of interactions, not all of which were friendly. At first reading, Melanchthon's early declaration of affection ("I love you from my soul and I pray that Christ may rule you")[13] and Calvin's equally enthusiastic description of his relation to Melanchthon seem to describe an intimate friendship. Calvin wrote: "We are sustained by that blessed hope, to which your letters recall us: we will feast together in heaven forever, where we will enjoy our love and friendship."[14] Such professions, however, were the staple of Renaissance letters and were based upon classical models and biblical norms.[15] Historians must not confuse professions of intimacy for the actual, intimate sharing of one's thoughts and feelings, especially when reading the correspondence of the sixteenth century, where expressions of affections were the rule. Moreover, when we place such powerful

---

12. Camerarius was Melanchthon's first biographer and an early publisher of his correspondence. He exchanged more letters with Melanchthon than anyone else. See Timothy J. Wengert, "'With Friends Like This . . .': The Biography of Philip Melanchthon by Joachim Camerarius," in *The Rhetorics of Life-Writing in Early Modern Europe: Forms of Biography from Cassandra Fedele to Louis XIV*, ed. Thomas F. Mayer and D. R. Woolf (Ann Arbor: University of Michigan, 1995), 115–31. Veit Dietrich was a student of Melanchthon and preacher in Nuremberg. Caspar Cruciger, also one of Melanchthon's students, taught at the University of Wittenberg. For him see Timothy J. Wengert, "Caspar Cruciger (1504–1548): The Case of the Disappearing Reformer," *The Sixteenth Century Journal* 20 (1989): 417–41. For other important students of Melanchthon see *Melanchthon in seinen Schülern*, Wolfenbütteler Forschungen, 73, ed. Heinz Scheible, (Wiesbaden: Harrassowitz Verlag, 1997).

13. MBW 2366 (CO 11:17). "Te ex animo amo et precor Christum ut te gubernet."

14. MBW 3169 (CO 11:515), dated 16 February 1543: "Sustineamur beata illa spe, ad quam nos literae tuae revocant: in coelis nos simul perpetuo victuros: ubi amore amicitiaque nostra fruemur."

15. See Danièle Fischer, "Calvin et la Confession d'Augsbourg," 248. No self-respecting biblical scholar would transform St. Paul's expressions of love for his congregations into intimate friendships. Even sixteenth-century exegetes understood the rules governing friendly letters. See Timothy J. Wengert, "Georg Major (1502–1574): Defender of Wittenberg's Faith and Melanchthonian Exegete," in Heinz Scheible, ed., *Melanchthon in seinen Schülern*, 150–51, regarding Major's understanding of Philippians as a friendly letter.

metaphors as "feasting together in heaven" within the context of the eucharistic debates, then another construction of such comments becomes possible It must also never be forgotten that, with rare exceptions, Renaissance letters were public events, meant to be shared with others.[16] Thus they contained public affections not private ones.

Even the oft-quoted reminiscence of Calvin regarding the recently departed Melanchthon must be seen strictly within the Renaissance and Reformation framework, where it appeared. Calvin wrote:

> O Philip Melanchthon! I appeal to thee who now livest with Christ in the bosom of God, and there art waiting for us till we shall be gathered with thee to that blessed rest. A hundred times when worn out with labors and oppressed with so many troubles, didst thou repose thy head familiarly on my breast and say: 'Would that I could die in this bosom!' Since then I have a thousand times wished that it had been granted to us to live together; for certainly thou wouldst thus have had more courage for the inevitable contest, and been stronger to despise envy, and to count as nothing all accusations. In this manner, also, the malice of many would have been restrained who, from thy gentleness which they call weakness, gathered audacity for their attacks.[17]

In fact, Calvin was alluding to certain strains in their relationship: Meanchthon's supposed tendency to capitulate and his failure to support Calvin directly, Calvin's presumed strength, and the maliciousness of Melanchthon's accusers. However, coming as it did within a tract on the eucharist, it was also Calvin's attempt to depict Melanchthon as a supporter of the Genevan's eucharistic theology, something he never was in his own lifetime.[18]

16. Two examples of this were Calvin's letter of 21 April 1544 (MBW 3531), which Melanchthon sent to Joachim Camerarius in Leipzig with instructions to distribute to others (MBW 3588; CR 5:415–16), and Melanchthon's memorandum of 17 April 1545 (MBW 3886; CO 6:621–24), which ended up in the Netherlands through the offices of Francis Dryander (MBW 3955; CR 5:794–95).

17. Cited without reference in Schaff, "The Friendship," 160. It is found in CO 9:461–62, taken from Calvin's "On the True Partaking of the Flesh and Blood of Christ" (1561).

18. Danièle Fischer, "Calvin et la Confession d'Augsbourg," 247–52, provides a partial list of their disagreements (including predestination, the Lord's Supper, adiaphora, Lutheran ceremonies) and mentions Melanchthon's praise for Castellio and Calvin's frustration at the Wittenberger's indecision. See below for further analysis of these issues.

The twenty-nine known exchanges between Calvin and Melanchthon provide a window for examining a highly charged relationship over a twenty-year span, during which many of the basic contours of the Protestant churches and their theology were debated. Such expressions of affection remind us that the principals were themselves passionate, committed individuals, for whom companionship, harmony, and truth defined existence. By maintaining a correspondence, both men hoped to gain something from the other while maintaining at least the semblance of peace between them for the sake of the church.

I. First Encounters

Under what circumstances did this epistolary friendship arise? Martin Bucer probably fostered the relationship between Melanchthon and the newly arrived French refugee, Calvin; the Wittenberg Concord of 1536 (on which both Melanchthon and Bucer labored) created the necessary theological peace under which it could develop. Calvin arrived in Strasbourg during September 1538 at Bucer's insistence in order to serve the French-speaking congregation there.[19] By October he could report to Farel contacts with Melanchthon over the then raging issue of church property.[20] Four months later the same issue and the question of church discipline were discussed. Here Calvin also described for Melanchthon his understanding of the Lord's Supper.[21]

When Calvin arrived in Strasbourg its clergy had already signed the Wittenberg Concord. They agreed that Christ was not absent from the Supper, that the bread and wine were not empty symbols and that, distinguishing the earthly and heavenly aspects of the Supper, "with the bread and wine the body and blood of Christ are truly and essentially present, offered, and received." While rejecting transubstantiation, they also held that "with the bread the body of Christ is truly present and truly offered." The worthiness of the recipient did not determine the presence of Christ in the Supper.[22] It is in the light of this agreement that Calvin's second edition of the *Institutes*, published in 1539, must be

19. For these biographical details, see T. H. L. Parker, *John Calvin: A Biography* (Philadelphia: Westminster, 1975).

20. MBW 2103 (CO 10:276–80). Cf. MBW 1853 (CR 3:288–90), dated 24 February 1537, where Melanchthon argued the case before the rapacious Philip of Hesse.

21. MBW 2152 (CO 10/2:322–32).

22. StL 17:2087f. See Mark U. Edwards, *Luther and the False Brethren* (Stanford: Stanford University Press, 1975), 149–55.

read.[23] No wonder Luther had such kind words for Calvin's "Reply to Sadoleto"![24] "Consider the nobility of Luther," Calvin reported to Farel. According to Melanchthon's report, when someone tried to induce Luther to criticize Calvin's position on the Lord's Supper in the "Reply," Luther read the passages and praised Calvin despite them.[25] By this time Melanchthon and Calvin had met in Frankfurt am Main and had discussed, among other things, the Lord's Supper.[26] This encounter may well have convinced Melanchthon that Calvin held to the Wittenberg

23. See Danièle Fischer, "Calvin et la Confession d'Augsbourg," 254–55, for an analysis of Calvin's preface, where he makes direct mention of the Concord. From the text itself see, for example, Inst. IV.xvii.7, where he rejects those who "make us partakers of the Spirit only," or IV.xvii.10, where he insists that "unless a man means to call God a deceiver, he would never dare assert that an empty symbol is set forth by him" and then concludes in IV.xvii.18 that "under the symbol of bread we shall be fed by his body, under the symbol of wine we shall separately drink his blood, to enjoy him at last in his wholeness." It was for Calvin "as if" Christ were present and a communion bestowed "by the power of his Spirit," but it was a communion with Christ nevertheless. In IV.xvii.40 he dealt with the *manducatio infidelium*.

24. WABr 8:568–70, a letter to Bucer dated 14 October 1539; here 569,29–30: "Bene vale, et salutabis D. Iohannem Sturmium et Ioh. Caluinum reverenter, quorum libellos cum singulari voluptate legi." MBW 2289 (WABr 8:562–66) included the elector's suggestion to publish it in Saxony.

25. This was reported by Melanchthon to Bucer via the messenger. See MBW 2290 (CO 10/2:432), dated 14 October 1539. The passage from the "Reply to Sadoleto" may have been this (translated in *John Calvin and Jacopo Sadoleto: A Reformation Debate*, ed. John C. Olin [New York: Harper, 1966], 70–71) : "In the case of the Eucharist, you blame us for attempting to confine the Lord of the universe . . . within the corners of a corporeal nature with its circumscribed boundaries. What end, pray, will there be to calumny? We have always distinctly testified, that not only the divine power of Christ, but His essence also, is diffused over all, and defined by no limits, and yet you hesitate not to upbraid us with confining it within the corners of corporeal nature! How so? Because we are unwilling with you to chain down His body to earthly elements. But had you any regard for sincerity, assuredly you are not ignorant how great a difference there is between the two things—between removing the local presence of Christ's body from bread, and circumscribing His spiritual power within bodily limits." Calvin went on to say, "We loudly proclaim the communion of flesh and blood, which is exhibited to believers in the Supper; and we distinctly show that that flesh is truly meat, and that blood truly drink—that the soul, not contented with an imaginary conception, enjoys them in very truth. That presence of Christ, by which we are engrafted in Him, we by no means exclude from the Supper, nor shroud in darkness. . . ."

26. MBW 2152 (CO 10/2:322–32), in a report to Farel dated 16 March 1539. Calvin expressed his respect for Melanchthon's exegesis and style and their differences in method in the preface to his commentary on Romans (dated 18 October 1539 to Simon Grynacus; CO 10:402–406). His comments on Melanchthon's neglect of passages may have referred not only to the *Commentarii* of 1532 but to the *Dispositio* of 1530.

Concord in principle,[27] and it encouraged Calvin to believe that Melanchthon approved of his understanding of the Lord's Supper.[28]

It is in the context of this encounter and these expressions of approval that the expressions of love must be placed. On the single most important issue dividing Protestants, Melanchthon and Calvin seemed, at this time anyway, to be united. Under the banner of that unity they then met in Worms and Regensburg for the colloquy with the Catholic representatives in 1540–41. Melanchthon's correspondence touched on Calvin in two instances: once when they collaborated on a letter to Francis I and once when they wrote letters of consolation to the father of the recently deceased Louis de Richebourg.[29] At Regensburg Calvin first became familiar with the Confessio Augustana Variata, the emended version of the Augsburg Confession written by Melanchthon to take the Wittenberg Concord into consideration.[30]

II. Free Will and Predestination

With Calvin's return to Geneva in September 1541, the correspondence between the two men, scarcely begun, suffered something of a break-

27. The question of Calvin's subscription to the Concord or to the Augsburg Confession, especially the *Variata* edited by Melanchthon for the 1541 Regensburg Colloquy, is a complicated one and best dealt with by Danièle Fischer, "Calvin et la Confession d'Augsbourg," 253–54. Fischer, citing CO 9:841–46, concludes that Calvin "affirma haut et clair, que les positions eucharistiques de son *Institution Chrétienne* de 1539 n'allaient absolument pas à l'encontre de celles de la *Formule de Concorde*."

28. Nijenhuis, *Calvinus oecumenicus*, 12, points to Calvin's comments to Farel (MBW 2152) and summarizes, "Hij deelt aan Farel mede, dat er overeenstemming bestaat tussen Melanchthon en hemzelf inzake de avondmaalsleer."

29. See MBW 2703 (CR 4:327f.), dated 23 May 1541, and MBW 2683 (CR 4:239–41; cf. CO 11:188–94), dated April 1541. For Calvin's contributions at the colloquies, see Wilhelm H. Neuser, *Calvins Beitrag zu den Religionsgesprächen von Haguenau, Worms und Regensburg* (Neukirchen: Erziehungsverein, 1969). Calvin was not pleased with Bucer and Melanchthon's compromise language on the eucharist. See Parker, *John Calvin*, 135.

30. See Danièle Fischer, "Calvin et la Confession d'Augsbourg," and the literature cited there. Despite Fischer's questioning (263) whether Calvin formally subscribed to the Variata, his language (CO 16:430: "Nec vero Augustanum Confessio repudio, cui pridem volens ac libens subscripsi, sicuti eam autor ipse interpretatus est") seems to indicate he did. The key word is "pridem" (long ago) and probably referred to the period just before his return to Geneva in 1541. The final phrase, "sicuti eam autor ipse interpretatus est," is a clear reference to the Variata, which even Melanchthon's *Corpus doctrinae* of 1560 viewed as an exposition of the original. For the later discussion of the Lord's Supper, see below.

down as much because of logistical problems in communication as anything else. A now lost letter sent by Melanchthon from Wittenberg in October 1542 took four months to arrive in Geneva.[31] Calvin made up for these delays by writing his first public letter to Melanchthon: the preface to *The Bondage and Liberation of the Will*, his attack on the Catholic theologian Pighius.[32]

Calvin could hardly have been ignorant of Melanchthon's (and, he had to assume, Wittenberg's) shift on the issue of human bondage from Luther's 1525 attack against Erasmus in *De servo arbitrio*—Pighius himself had pointed it out.[33] Indeed, the eighteenth article of the Augsburg Confession emphasized a distinction between freedom in civil matters and weakness in spiritual things,[34] and the second edition of Melanchthon's *Loci communes* of 1535 spoke of three causes for salvation (the Word, the Holy Spirit and the human will [*voluntas*]) and glossed over predestination.[35] Thus, Calvin, in prosecuting his case against Pighius, sought to reclaim the authority of Melanchthon, whose own opinion on the topic was unclear. Calvin dedicated this book to Melanchthon, "because it contains a defence of the godly and sound teaching of which you are not only a most zealous supporter, but a distinguished and very brave champion."[36] Calvin proceeded to compare his brevity and clarity to Melanchthon's own, but again as an argument in favor of Calvin's own treatment of this topic—one which Melanchthon had, so to speak, declared off limits in the 1535 *Loci*.[37] Calvin even suggested that Melanch-

---

31. Cf. MBW 3169 (CO 11:515–17), from Calvin, dated 16 February 1543.

32. CO 6:229–404. The preface was probably written in January 1543. See the arguments in MBW 3157.

33. CO 6:250–51 (ET 28–29).

34. CA XVIII (BKS, 73–74). The small changes in the Variata underscore that God commands and forces carnal people to civil righteousness through the law.

35. CR 21:376, 428, 450–53.

36. CO 6:229–30 (ET, 3).

37. CO 6:229–30 (ET, 3–4): "The kind of defense which I employ is straightforward and honest. For as much as you shrink from crafty, sidelong devices in argument which serve to draw darkness over things which are otherwise clear and open, in short from all pretence and sophistry, so you are pleased by an unembellished and frank clarity which, without any concealment, sets a subject before the eyes and explains it. This quality of yours has often stirred in me great admiration, just because it is so rarely found, for, although you are outstanding for your amazing insight, you still rank nothing above straightforwardness." For Melanchthon's comments on the subject, see CR 21:373, where on the issue of the free will (*liberum arbitrium*) Melanchthon stated, "Non quaeritur de arcano Dei consilio gubernantis omnia; non quaeritur de praedestina-

thon had urged him to refute Pighius.[38] Thus, this preface is a delightful example of the shrewdness of Renaissance polemics, where, because shifts in thought were a sign of weakness, the enemy of my enemy, who scarcely agrees with me, must be made my friend.

In the body of the text, Calvin for the first time referred to Melanchthon's moderation. However, this must not simply be taken at face value. On the contrary, as we shall see, Calvin employed this (Stoic) category consistently in order to ameliorate real differences between himself and Melanchthon. What better way to overcome divisions in a polemical situation than to invoke a favorite humanist virtue. In point of fact at two crucial points Melanchthon and Calvin disagreed. For one thing, Melanchthon began his discussion of human freedom and bondage in the distinction between human and divine righteousness. For another, he divided all questions of divine causality from predestination—discussing the former under God's governance and the latter under the gospel.[39]

Melanchthon's thank you note for the tract was sent on 11 May 1543 from Bonn, where he was assisting Bucer in the ill-fated attempt to reform the archdiocese of Cologne.[40] His response is a lesson in Renaissance diplomacy. He first thanked Calvin for complimenting his simplicity. However, just as Calvin had employed an appeal to similarity in style to gain Melanchthon's approbation for Calvin's approaching a subject declared off limits in the *Loci*, Melanchthon now took the compliment to attack the subject of Calvin's book. Calvin ought to use his gifts—as Melanchthon claimed he himself did—for explaining important evangelical doctrines (such as the teaching of the Son of God, human sin, repentance and faith, prayer, and the church) and not for intricate disputations.[41]

Turning to the topic of predestination itself, he then quoted his Tübingen teacher, Francis Kircher from Stadion (hence: Stadianus), who taught that divine providence and contingency could never be satisfacto-

---

tione; non agitur de omnibus contingentibus." Given this debate, Melanchthon's later comments in the third edition of the *Loci* could be construed as a correction of his Genevan correspondent.

38. CO 6:229–30 (ET, 4): "Besides I remember that you once assigned me the task of writing something to restrain Pighius's insolence if he should continue to challenge us."

39. Both of these distinctions formed the heart of later Lutheran comments on predestination and free will in the Formula of Concord.

40. MBW 3245 (CR 5:107–9; =CO 11:539–42). He mentioned that he had not yet received the book but had looked at a copy in Bucer's possession.

41. CR 5:108. He cited Paul's exhortation to Timothy in 1 Timothy 4:14.

rily balanced. Out of regard for the weak, Melanchthon argued that David's guilt was his own fault, not God's, and that he also retained the Holy Spirit by the action of his will [*voluntas*]. Having refuted Calvin's arguments, Melanchthon then prevented open warfare with this clever conclusion: "I do not write these things as if handing down to you, a most erudite and skilful person in the exercise of piety, some dictates. Indeed, I know that these things harmonize with your ideas. However, mine are cruder, accommodated to use."[42] Here Melanchthon had turned Calvin's reference to moderation on its head. This virtue had at its heart the Christian concern for the weak and simple and an avoidance of sophistry. But it was not simply a humanist virtue but rather a pointed theological argument and hermeneutical tool for recognizing the limits of erudition. Thus, in Melanchthon's eyes Calvin's approach—for all its biblical sincerity—was by its very subtlety speculative.

The very next letter from Melanchthon's pen (Calvin's intervening response is lost) reiterated the two reformers' fundamental disagreement on the question of predestination. Here, however, Melanchthon asserted that at least the two agreed on their understanding of the power of original sin.[43] It seems that for Melanchthon the disagreement on predestination was secondary and should not hinder their underlying support of the gospel.

Calvin not only knew differences existed between him and Melanchthon, he did something about them in another public letter, one that Melanchthon did not see and could not have read: the 1546 preface to the French translation of Melanchthon's third edition of the *Loci communes*. In the first place, Calvin acknowledged Melanchthon's avoidance of subtleties. He was a man "of profound wisdom, who did not wish to enter into subtle disputes." His only regard was for the edification of his readers. "The greatest simplicity is the highest virtue when dealing with Christian doctrine."[44]

---

42. CR 5:109. That is, to use among the *rudes*. Erasmus had similarly complained that Melanchthon had wasted his talents, but he urged him to turn from theology back to the humanities. Here the debate is over how to teach in the church, not whether to teach there.

43. MBW 3273 (CO 11:594f.), dated 12 July 1543 and sent from Melanchthon in Bonn to Calvin in Strasbourg.

44. CO 9:848. "Et de faict, ce qui est bien à priser, ie voy que l'auteur, estant homme de profond savoir, n'a pas voulu entrer en disputes subtiles, ne traiter les matieres d'un artifice tant haut qu'il luy eut esté facile de faire, mais s'est abaissé tant qu'il a peu, n'ayant esgard qu'à la seule edification. C'est certes la façon et le style que

As an example Calvin mentioned first the doctrine of the freedom of the will, which Melanchthon discussed only in terms of Christian salvation. Calvin explained that Melanchthon allowed for "civil" freedom in "things below" so as to emphasize God's grace. By forewarning the readers about Melanchthon's intention, Calvin hoped that they would not be scandalized when reading the *Loci*.[45] Second, Calvin turned to predestination. Again Melanchthon wanted, according to Calvin, to avoid all curiosity by dealing only with those things that needed to be known about the subject. Finally, Calvin noted that Melanchthon employed the same approach for the sacraments. He concluded that by understanding Melanchthon's modesty the reader could truly profit from this book.[46]

This clever introduction accepted Melanchthon's own defense of his approach to these articles of faith as outlined in their private correspondence—but to Calvin's theological advantage. By emphasizing Melanchthon's modesty, Calvin actually made room for his own, opposing positions without thereby having to refute Melanchthon. Melanchthon's reserve, which in Melanchthon's view arose from not only pastoral concerns (Calvin acknowledged that) but also theological insight into the limits of theological discourse, became in Calvin's hands a psychological or literary shortcoming, which Calvin had to warn the readers about in order that they might still profit from Melanchthon's work.

Even this subtle construing of Melanchthon's theology, however, did not prevent Melanchthon's position on predestination from becoming caught up in a Genevan dispute. In 1551 Jerome Bolsec and Jean Trolliet had crossed Calvin on the question of predestination, resulting in the arrest of Bolsec in October.[47] When the matter came before the city council, Trolliet appealed in his written defense to Melanchthon's position as outlined in the French translation of the *Loci*.[48] Calvin, in turn,

---

nous aurions tous à tenir: sinon que les adversaires nous contraignissent par leurs cavillations à nous destourner de ce train. Tant y a que la plus grande simplicité est la plus grande vertu à traicter la doctrine Chrestienne."

45. CO 9:849. "Mais si a il esté bon d'en advertir les lecteurs, afin que nul ne fust scandalizé de peu de chose, voyant l'intention de l'auteur."

46. CO 9:850. "Quant les lecteurs garderont une telle modestie à iuger du livre qu'a eu l'auteur en le composant, tout ira bien, et n'y aura rien qui les empesche à y profiter beaucoup."

47. For details, see Parker, *John Calvin*, 112–16.

48. CO 14:374–77. Jerome Bolsec was also involved.

was forced publicly to explain the discrepancy between his position and Melanchthon's.[49]

Like Melanchthon, Calvin insisted God was not the author of sin. However, Calvin also admitted that he diverged from Melanchthon on this point.

> Melanchthon, being a timid man, and not wanting to give curious folk a reason for inquiring too deeply into the secrets of God, accommodated himself too much to people's common understanding. He has desired more to accommodate to people's common sense. In the present case he has by these means spoken more as a philosopher than a theologian.[50]

Moreover, Calvin insisted that he had letters from Melanchthon that proved his case. He also insisted that if Melanchthon's statements were accorded such authority, then, in accord with the *Loci communes*, a third sacrament, confession, would also have to be reinstated in Geneva.[51]

Here Calvin viewed Melanchthon's theology, in its refusal to probe God's mysteries revealed in Scripture, as having succumbed to philosophical speculation. This hermeneutical divide appeared already in Calvin's letter of 1 January 1552 to Lelio Sozzini, who had urged restraint on Calvin in these matters. Calvin succinctly outlined his position: he abhorred paradoxes, he insisted on professing what he had learned from the Word of God, and he found comfort in the Word's simple teaching.[52]

What was Melanchthon's reaction to Calvin's approach? In a private letter to his friend Camerarius, dated 1 February 1552, he reported on the debate in Geneva concerning "Stoic necessity" and the arrest of Bolsec.[53] He also knew of Sozzini's admonition. The Zurich theologians, Melanchthon commented, were milder. On the same day he wrote to his son-in-law, Caspar Peucer, "O what a terrible matter! The teaching of

---

49. CO 381–82, dated 6 October 1552.

50. CO 11:381. Cest que Melancthon [sic], estant homme craintif, pour ne point donner occasion a gens curieux de trop senquerir des secrets de Dieu, sest voulu par trop accommoder au sens commun des hommes. Et par ce moyen a plus parle en philosophe quen theologien, quant a la cause presente." Melanchthon had demonstrated this by referring to Plato's authority. At the same time, Calvin praised Melanchthon's wisdom, virtue, and faithful work for the gospel.

51. CO 11:382.

52. CO 14:229–30.

53. MBW 6322 (CR 7:930–31). He nicknamed Calvin "Zeno."

salvation is obscured by disputations foreign to it."[54] Thus for Melanchthon the dispute itself, not the content of the doctrine, indicated the importation of philosophy into theology.

In a letter of 28 November 1552 Calvin informed Melanchthon of the dispute and the *Loci's* role in it.[55] He insisted that he had not attacked Melanchthon directly and thereby headed off any public dispute with the Wittenberg Reformer. On the question of predestination itself, Calvin acquiesced to Melanchthon's emphasis on the universality of God's promise (cf. the 1543 edition of the *Loci*, CR 21:451) but at the same time insisted that the efficacy of that promise was limited to those with the gift of faith. Calvin also noted Melanchthon's objection to the Consensus Tigurinus on this point (article 16). In closing comments that were also aimed at preventing a public dispute, Calvin praised Melanchthon's moderation while stressing that only face-to-face conversation could resolve this potential conflict.[56] When Melanchthon failed to respond to this letter, Calvin sent yet another appeal for understanding on this issue.[57] By then, however, the most pressing issue had become the Lord's Supper.

Later in their correspondence this issue surfaced only tangentially. When Calvin complained about Melanchthon's silence on the Lord's Supper, Melanchthon responded by vowing to take up the fight in matters central to the faith—which he explained meant answering the attacks on him by Nicholas Gallus and others on original sin and free will (something that indirectly would have implicated Calvin as well).[58] Shortly thereafter Justus Velsius in Frankfurt am Main railed against Calvin and the godlessness of his denial of free will.[59] Calvin, also in Frankfurt at the time, reported the same thing to Melanchthon, pleaded

54. MBW 6324 (CR 7:931–32). "O rem miseram! Doctrina salutaris obscuratur peregrinis disputationibus."

55. MBW 6655 (CO 14:414–18). He was responding directly to MBW 6576 (CO 14:368–69), dated 1 October 1552, in which Melanchthon had resumed their correspondence.

56. CO 14:417–18. "Notus est mihi tuus candor, perspecta ingenuitas et moderatio: pietas vero angelis et toti mundo testata est. Ergo facile, ut spero, tota ea res inter nos expediretur." The appeal to face-to-face conversation in Renaissance letters must always be understood as an attempt to avoid a public dispute.

57. MBW 7273 (CO 15:215–17), dated 27 August 1554. His frustration with Melanchthon was aptly expressed in two other letters from the same time to Vermigli and Sleidan (CO 15:219–21). His charge: Melanchthon was too influenced by philosophy.

58. MBW 7489 (CR 8:482–83; =CO 15:615–16), dated 12 May 1555.

59. MBW 7958 (Hartfelder, ZKG 12 [1891]: 205–6), dated 17 September 1556.

with the Wittenberg Reformer to come to his defense, and commiserated with him over the attacks of the Flacians.[60] Despite appeals from both sides, Melanchthon said nothing.

III. Adiaphora

The correspondence between Calvin and Melanchthon occurred in fits and starts. After an initial spurt from 1538 to 1545, the next letter was written in 1550. After a hiatus of two years, the correspondence picked up again briefly during 1552 but then stopped until 1554. Another brief flurry at that time again was broken off, despite Calvin's attempts to restart it, until 1557. These four breaks point not so much to missing letters as to Melanchthon's pique—witnessed to in three instances within the correspondence itself. In 1545 Calvin urged Melanchthon to go public on his understanding of the Lord's Supper.[61] The result? Silence. In 1550 Calvin wrote a pointed letter upbraiding Melanchthon for his stance on adiaphora.[62] The result? Not only silence but a rumor that Melanchthon had ripped the letter up—the sixteenth-century equivalent of hanging up on someone.[63] After 1552 Melanchthon refused to respond immediately to Calvin's challenge on predestination and the Lord's Supper.[64] When Calvin again urged Melanchthon to be forthcoming about his position on the Lord's Supper, the older man did not respond for three years.[65]

One of the sharpest exchanges in their correspondence revolved around the question of adiaphora, indifferent matters in church practice. To begin with the Reformers seemed united on this issue. Calvin, plagued with people unwilling to change church practices, asked Melanchthon for his and Luther's opinions of his recently published tracts, *De vitandis superstitionibus* and *Excusatio ad Pseudo-Nicodemitas*.[66] Melanch-

---

60. MBW 7957 (CO 16:280–82), dated 17 September 1556.

61. MBW 3928 (CO 12:98–100), dated 28 June 1545.

62. MBW 5830 (CO 13:593–96), dated 19 June 1550.

63. MBW 6655 (CO 14:414–18), dated 28 November 1552. Melanchthon blamed unreliable couriers (MBW 6576; CO 14:368–69).

64. MBW 7273 (CO 15:215–17), dated 27 August 1554.

65. Calvin's challenge came in MBW 7562 (CO 15:737–38), dated 23 August 1555. In a letter dated 3 August 1557, MBW 8293 (CO 16:556–58), he complained about not having heard from Melanchthon for three years.

66. CO 6:537–614. MBW 3803 (CO 12:9–12), dated 21 January 1545. See Francis Higman, "The Question of Nicodemism," in *Calvinus Ecclesiae Genevensis Custos*, ed. Wilhelm Neuser (Frankfurt am Main: Peter Lang, 1984), 165–70.

thon responded by refusing to give the tracts to Luther (given the looming controversy over the Lord's Supper with Zurich) and shared instead his own opinion alone.[67] The resulting memorandum, published in Calvin's 1550 edition of *De vitandis superstitionibus*, linked necessary practices to the first commandment and thereby (contrary to Luther's grudging toleration of transubstantiation in a letter to the Italian evangelicals)[68] rejected adoration of and processions with the bread in the Mass. Adiaphora embraced all those practices which, while subject to abuse, could nevertheless be tolerated within the church. Melanchthon's memo also included special advice against the Anabaptists, against the sophistic excuses of the Nicodemites, against the hasty rush toward martyrdom, and in favor of clear witness to the gospel among the churches in exile.[69]

Upon receiving this letter, Calvin immediately conveyed his thanks to Melanchthon.[70] Less than a month later, Jacob Bording wrote to Melanchthon from Antwerp, asking for specific advice in his situation, given Melanchthon's general advice to Calvin. Melanchthon's response demonstrates how central *moderatio* was for his theological program.[71] He refused to give advice because of its danger to the weak. "Advice for the firm [in faith] is harder and sharper, for the young recruits and those unable to fight, who must be drawn and not frightened off, milder. As St. Paul commands [in Romans 14:1]. . . As a rule I follow this principle in such advice."[72] The specific need of the individual for the gospel outweighed the possibility of giving general rules for dealing with this issue.

In 1547 the evangelical princes suffered defeat at the hands of the imperial forces, aided by the "Judas of Meissen," Maurice of Saxony.[73] When it became clear that the triumphant emperor intended to impose

67. MBW 3884 (Bds. 479–80), Melanchthon's first draft of the letter, and MBW 3885 (CO 12:61–62), dated 17 April 1545.

68. WABr 10:330–31. Luther's comments in Melanchthon's view contradicted the Wittenberg Concord.

69. MBW 3886 (CR 5:734–39; =CO 6:621–24), dated 17 April 1545.

70. MBW 3928 (CO 12:98–100), dated 28 June 1545. He did, however, admit to some differences. P. 100: "Tametsi enim paululum est discriminis in particulis quibusdam, de re tamen ipsa optime inter nos convenit."

71. MBW 3955 (CR 5:794–95), dated 17 July 1545.

72. CR 5:794: "Consilia de firmis duriora καὶ ἀκριβέστερα, tyronibus et imbellibus leviora, qui provehendi sunt non deterrendi, ut Paulus iubet . . . Hanc fere rationem in his consiliis sequor."

73. For this material, see my article on "Adiaphora" in the *Oxford Encyclopedia of the Reformation* and the literature cited there.

the interim agreement on religious practices—passed at the diet in Augsburg in 1548 and hence nicknamed the "Augsburg Interim," which only allowed the Protestants married priests and communion in two kinds—Maurice and his advisors, including the recently reconstituted faculty of the University of Wittenberg, struggled to formulate an evangelical response that avoided the direct imposition of the hated Interim in Saxon lands. The resulting document, which staked out a moderate position on the Lord's Supper and justification, allowed the reinstitution of certain "indifferent" Roman practices.

When this proposal, to which the electors of Brandenburg and Saxony had agreed in principle but which never came to a vote by the Saxon estates meeting in Leipzig (this despite its being named the "Leipzig Interim"), became public in late 1548, it and its principal author, Philip Melanchthon, were attacked in various circles. Already in January 1549 Georg Buchholzer of Berlin sent a friendly inquiry to Melanchthon on the matter after having heard it read out publicly by John Agricola of Eisleben, chief theological advisor to the Brandenburg court and co-author of the Augsburg Interim. A more serious challenge arose from Lutheran theologians holed up in Magdeburg, including Matthias Flacius and Nicholas von Amsdorf. They argued that in a time of persecution things that normally were adiaphora could not be changed; such times demanded instead confession of faith. This became the first in a series of disputes to rock Lutheranism at least until the Formula of Concord brought some semblance of peace in 1580.

At the height of this initial storm of controversy, John Calvin also staked out his position. First, he wrote against the Augsburg Interim itself.[74] We know from Melanchthon's correspondence that a copy of Calvin's work on the subject reached him in early 1549.[75] When in mid-1549 Melanchthon became embroiled in the adiaphoristic controversy, Calvin sent Melanchthon a less than friendly letter. He expressed his sadness over the controversy and invoked their friendship as the basis for his admonition to Melanchthon, who had to shoulder some of the blame for the dispute.[76] He summarized Melanchthon's position this way: "This is

---

74. CO 7:547–674: "Interim Adultero-Germanum: cui adiecta est vera Christianae pacificationis et ecclesiae reformandae ratio."

75. MBW 5434 (CR 7:328–30), a letter to Joachim Moller in Celle dated 4 February 1549.

76. MBW 5830 (CO 13:593–96), dated 19 June 1550. "In libera admonitione veri amici officio fungar."

the sum of your defense: only the purity of doctrine is retained; concerning external things one must not fight stubbornly."[77] Such struggles, Calvin noted, were foreign to Melanchthon's *modestia*. However, Calvin insisted that so many things ought not be conceded to the papists because they contradict God's Word and capitulation simply gives more ammunition to the enemy. Calling on the blood of the martyrs and the example of St. Paul, Calvin attempted to overcome Melanchthon's timidity. "Who would be so insane as to hold everything to such an extreme as to neglect the heart of the gospel?"[78] No wonder this surprisingly sharp rebuke, arriving in Wittenberg in the midst of his paper war with the so-called Magdeburg Consistory, evoked silence and sparked the rumor (at the very least) that Melanchthon had ripped the letter up. When the correspondence resumed, Calvin was always quick to express his sorrow at the attacks from the Flacians, perhaps as an indirect way of mitigating the severity of his earlier remarks.

IV. The Lord's Supper

By far the most dominant theme in this correspondence was the Lord's Supper and its attendant controversies. Each Reformer played an important role in the eucharistic theology and political maneuvering of the other. After initial harmony on the issue described above, problems first surfaced in relation to the second public dispute over the Lord's Supper between Luther and the Zurich theologians, which began in 1543.[79] A harsh condemnation of Zwingli by Luther in a letter to the printer Christopher Froschauer led to equally harsh threats from Zurich.

Calvin reported Bullinger's complaints to Melanchthon and urged him to restrain his belligerent colleague.[80] At the same time both Bucer and Melanchthon, fearful that the Wittenberg Concord might collapse, sought to restore calm among the warring parties. However, Luther was also rumored to be writing against Bucer and Melanchthon in his so-

---

77. CO 41:594. "Haec tuae defensionis summa est, modo retineatur doctrinae puritas, de rebus externis non esse pertinaciter dimicandum."

78. Co 41:595. "Cuius dementiae est, sic ad extremum tueri omnia, ut totius evangelii summa negligatur?"

79. For this debate, see Timothy J. Wengert, "Luther and Melanchthon, Melanchthon and Luther," *Luther-Jahrbuch* 65 (1998).

80. MBW 3531 (CO 11:696–98), dated 21 April 1544. To demonstrate the seriousness of the problem to Camerarius, Melanchthon sent him a copy of Calvin's letter (MBW 3588).

called "Shorter Confession" on the Lord's Supper. Calvin's next letter to Melanchthon, which contained copies of his writings against the Nicodemites, questioned whether a letter from him should be given to Luther (it was not) and described Calvin's upset with Luther's tract and Andreas Osiander's even sharper attack. In this connection even Calvin could invoke the virtue of moderation. "That man's [Osiander's] petulance displeases me . . . so that I desire instead moderation, prudence and even sanity."[81] He also mentioned he was working to calm Bullinger. In Melanchthon's response he suggested he needed Calvin's advice more than Calvin needed his, and he mentioned for the first time the threat of exile.[82]

Calvin immediately replied by criticizing the Zurich Confession as a poor defense of Zwingli.[83] He also criticized Luther's bombast. The Reformer had placed the church in a danger that had to be countered. In this context Calvin then urged Melanchthon to go public with his understanding of the Lord's Supper.[84] It would seem that this demand, coupled with the dislocations of the Smalcald War, Calvin's signing of the Consensus Tigurinus, and his rebuke of Melanchthon's position on adiaphora in 1550, contributed to Melanchthon's seven-year silence.

The subsequent mention of the Lord's Supper occurred in the middle of the next controversy over that doctrine: the dispute between Calvin and Joachim Westphal.[85] Again Calvin begged Melanchthon for a public word on the dispute. He also described his agreement with Luther's sacramentology in these terms. "In baptism the efficacious Spirit is present in order to wash and regenerate us. The Holy Supper is a spiri-

81. MBW 3803 (CO 12:9–12), dated 21 January 1545. Zurich's pastors responded with the Zurich Confession.

82. MBW 3884 (Bds. 479–80) and MBW 3885 (CO 12:61–62), dated 17 April 1545. Initially Melanchthon used this threat in anticipation of Luther's attack on him (which never materialized) in the "Shorter Confession" and stated it arose at his brother George's suggestion. By this time it had become a part of his ideal of moderation.

83. MBW 3928 (CO 12:98–100), dated 28 June 1545. The Confession was "puerilis, quum in multis pertinaciter magis quam erudite." Bucer, too, was not pleased, claiming that it was an attempt to twist the Wittenberg Concord in such a way as to set Bucer against Luther. See MBW 3854.

84. CO 12:99. "Ad hanc ergo plenam et solidam mentis tuae explicationem forte viam tibi patefacere nunc vult Deus, ne perpetuo haereant dubii, qui ab autoritate tua pendent, quos scis esse quam plurimos." The Wittenberg *Reformatio*, written by Melanchthon, did as much. However, its eucharistic theology would hardly have pleased Calvin.

85. See Parker, *John Calvin*, 137–39.

tual banquet in which we truly feed upon the flesh and blood of Christ."[86] Here is Calvin's construal of the Wittenberg Concord.

In response Melanchthon expressed his support of Calvin's Trinitarian defense and his treatment of Servetus.[87] He claimed that people were attacking Calvin out of hatred for him, Melanchthon. He expected exile and hoped to speak with Calvin, "whom I know to be a lover of the truth."[88] This final comment, in the nuanced language of the time, must be understood as indicating to Calvin that the two men in fact differed on this doctrine. It mirrored precisely Calvin's own earlier language regarding predestination. It meant Melanchthon would not attack Calvin publicly, but it precluded his support.

Calvin realized what the score was. In his response he thanked Melanchthon for his support on Servetus and expressed the hope that Melanchthon had not taken his admonition (to speak out publicly on the Lord's Supper) badly. He was convinced they could work out an agreement on predestination.[89] This did not, however, prevent Calvin from demanding Melanchthon's public support on the doctrine of the Lord's Supper. He knew Melanchthon's mind! Moreover, Zurich had already responded.[90]

Melanchthon knew all along the public nature of these letters and how Calvin was likely to use his support. He steadfastly turned aside Calvin's request (Calvin could judge his own opponents and their theatrics) and prayed for the divided church.[91] But he also corrected Calvin's mis-

86. MBW 7273 (CO 15:215–17), dated 27 August 1554, here 217. "In Baptismo adesse Spiritus efficaciam, ut nos abluat, et regeneret. Sacram Coenam spirituale esse epulum, in quo vere Christi carne et sanguine pascimur." (The johannine language ["flesh of Christ"] indicates a very different understanding of Christ's presence than that in Wittenberg.) To get on Melanchthon's good side, Calvin also announced his willingness to discuss the issue of predestination and described his own hurt at the unfair attacks on Melanchthon by the "Osiandrists" in the question of justification.

87. MBW 7306 (CO 15:268–69), dated 14 October 1554. This approval was a constant theme throughout his correspondence of the time. See MBW 7558 (CR 8:523–24), to Heinrich Bullinger dated 20 August 1555, and MBW 8185 (CR 9:131–35), a public letter dated 10 April 1557.

88. CO 15:269: "quem scio amantem esse veritatis."

89. MBW 7424 (CO 15:488–89), dated 5 March 1555. The language (which could be construed as questioning Melanchthon's sincerity) is striking: "ut de gratuita piorum electione sincerior quam antehac docendi formam inter nos mutuo conveniunt."

90. CO 15:488–89. *"Peri tes artolateias* pridem interior animi tui sensus mihi cognitus est, quem etiam non dissimulas in tuis literis. Sed mihi displicet tua ista nimia tarditas. Nunc iudicium tuum avidissime exspecto."

91. MBW 7489 (CO 15:615–16), dated 12 May 1555.

taken impression of his silence. He was prepared to respond directly to attacks where the gospel was at stake,[92] and he rejected Calvin's connection of his silence with a fear of exile or other dangers.[93] Calvin agreed that the opponents just wanted to fight, but he urged Melanchthon (borrowing phrases from the *Te Deum*) to join the chorus of the company of angels and the holy fathers in support of the church.[94] The result was three years of silence on Melanchthon's part.

Melanchthon was unwillingly caught in the middle of this controversy. At the same time as Calvin was urging him to speak out, others on the opposite side of the dispute were doing the same. Already in 1555 Johann Stigel begged Melanchthon to answer Calvin's attacks on Luther.[95] In a response to a request from Christopher Stathmion, a pastor at the Coburg, Melanchthon outlined his basic position.[96] He has often been asked about the "sure and certain form of the words" (*de forma certa verborum*). He rejected Osiander's claim that the bread is God and insisted rather on the Pauline use of *koinonia* in I Corinthians 10:16.

He clearly understood the differences between his and Calvin's theology, even describing how in Poland some followed Calvin's books while others preferred to order the church "according to the norm of our confession" (*iuxta normam confessionis nostrae*).[97] By this time Calvin's second response to Westphal had been printed.[98] It appealed directly to Melanchthon's description of Luther's support for Calvin (in connection with the "Reply to Sadoleto").[99] Melanchthon's (less than honest) response to Andrew Misenus in Altenburg a year later insisted that he had never said what Calvin claimed and that he had not read all that Calvin had written.[100] He again appealed for the use of sure forms of speech

92. Here he referred to Gallus' attack on free will, to which he promised to respond "simply and without ambiguity."

93. CO 15:616: "Nec in hac senecta pertimesco exsilia et alia pericula." Calvin's posthumous *laudatio* cited by Schaff would not have gained Melanchthon's approval.

94. MBW 7562 (CO 15:737–38), dated 23 August 1555.

95. MBW 7656 (CR 8:621), dated 1 December 1555.

96. MBW 7883 (CR 8:790–91), dated 4 July 1556.

97. MBW 8164 (CR 9:788), dated 23 March 1557. This may be based upon reports like that of Johann Crato in Breslau (MBW 6544).

98. CO 9:41–120, "Secunda Defensio piae et orthodoxae de sacramentis fidei contra Ioachimi Westphali Calumnias." The preface is dated 5 January 1556.

99. CO 9:52. "Quin etiam Lutherus ipse quum scripta mea inspexisset, quale de me iudicium fecerit, mihi per testes idoneos probare non difficile erit. Sed mihi unus pro multis erit Philippus Melanchthon."

100. MBW 8092 (CR 9:18–19), dated mid-January 1557.

and rejected the Bremen city council's use in its condemnation of Hardenburg of such novel phrases as "the bread is the essential body of Christ." "Who has spoken this way? We say: 'With the bread the body of Christ is consumed.'"[101] This refusal to equate the bread with Christ's body, which Melanchthon construed as an invitation to bread worship, marked his entire eucharistic theology.[102] Christ's presence was with the bread and occurred during the proper use of the elements, not before or after. He contented himself with the sure and certain forms of speaking found in Paul.

This same search for "certain forms of speaking" appeared even near the end of Melanchthon's life. When some Hungarian evangelicals inquired about the Lord's Supper after one of their colleagues, Christopher Reuter, had written against Zwingli and Calvin, Melanchthon responded by pointing them to his statements in the *Examen ordinandorum* to prove that he himself was not a Calvinist. He refused to accept the book in order not to become sucked in to the conflict and emphasized that the presence of Christ was associated with its proper use, not with processions or adoration of the host.[103] Even Georg Buchholzer, while using what Melanchthon said in the *Examen* to prove Melanchthon was not a Calvinist, had pleaded with Melanchthon for a clearer public statement.[104]

In 1557 another flurry of letters surrounded the publication of Calvin's final response to Westphal and the impending colloquy in Worms.[105] Now Calvin urged Melanchthon to convince the princes to in-

---

101. CR 9:18–19. "Nuper huc Senatus Bremensis misit legatos. Erat propositio his verbis scripta: panis est essentiale corpus Christi. Quis sic locutus est? Dicimus: cum pane sumi corpus Christi."

102. It also meant that he would reject the notion of ubiquity.

103. MBW 9075 (unpublished), dated 27 September 1559 (cf. MBW 9123), and Melanchthon's response in MBW 9218 (CR 9:1038–39), dated 4 February 1560.

104. MBW 8996 (in G. Kawerau, *Johann Agricola von Eisleben: Ein Beitrag zur Reformationsgeschichte* (Berlin: Wilhelm Hertz, 1881), 347–49). In the *Examen,* published in 1552, Melanchthon asked what is distributed and received in the Lord's Supper. He answered: "Warer Leib und Blut des HErrn Jhesu Christ. Der hat diese nießung eingesetzt, das er bezeuget, das er warhafftiglich und wesentlich bey uns und in uns sein wil und wil in den bekerten wonen, jnen seine güter mitteilen und in jnen krefftig sein. Wie er spricht Joh. 15[:4]. 'Bleibet in mir und ich in Euch.'"

105. MBW 8293 (CO 16:556–58), dated 3 August 1557, a lost letter, and MBW 8331 (CO 16:604–5), dated 8 September 1557. Calvin's tract, "Ultima admonitio ad Joachimum Westphalum," is published in CO 9:137–252 and called on Melanchthon for support.

vite the Swiss to a religious colloquy or to hold one of his own.[106] Melanchthon finally responded in October.[107] He described the departure of the Gnesio-Lutheran party, praised the people sent by Calvin (a party that included Budacus and Beza) and prayed for the church. He did not publicly support Calvin.

However, in a speech to the evangelical delegates at Worms delivered a month earlier, Melanchthon, while condemning Westphal's use of "new and unusual language" to defend transubstantiation and a localized presence of Christ's body within the bread, added that Calvin's language also needed further explanation—a sure sign that Melanchthon realized their views did not coincide.[108] It was also a sign that he stood closer to Calvin than to Westphal on this issue as far as the language itself was concerned. Melanchthon insisted that any discussion of Christ's presence in the Lord's Supper had to be limited to biblical expressions (especially 1 Corinthians 10:16) and patristic usage.[109]

Despite this moderation, or perhaps because of it, Calvin's patience had finally reached the breaking point. In his last letter from their correspondence, dated 19 November 1558, he drew a parallel between attacks on Geneva by Spain and France with Melanchthon's theological enemies and with Calvin's opponents within Geneva and without (especially Westphal).[110] He then directly criticized Melanchthon's silence in the Lord's Supper controversy. Although he sought an unbroken friendship, he was hurt by the fact that Hubert Languet was spreading rumors (to Sebastian Castellio's delight) about Melanchthon's criticism of Calvin's

---

106. Melanchthon had suggested as much to John Laski (MBW 7926 and MBW 7960).

107. MBW 8384 (CR 9:328–29; =CO 16:659), dated 8 October 1557. Cf. MBW 8380 to Heinrich Bullinger.

108. MBW 8332 (unpublished), dated 9 September 1557.

109. In that way his last public word on the subject, the "Iudicium de coena domini" of 1560, also demanded of Heshuss in Heidelberg the same restraint. See MSA 6:484–86, where his concerns remained the language ("de una forma verborum"), transubstantiation ("Non dicit, mutari naturam panis"), and the restriction of Christ's presence to its proper use and not "extra sumptionem." Christ is present "non propter panem sed propter hominem." He also accepted the use of the term symbol because of patristic testimony. Heshuss's simple rejection of this term was criticized because of the way it set Heshuss himself up as an unassailable authority ("quae est igitur tanta auctoritas Heshusii").

110. MBW 8782 (CO 17:384–86).

teaching.[111] Only Melanchthon's death prevented a public breach and allowed for Calvin's less than realistic eulogy in 1561.

V. Exegesis

The correspondence between Calvin and Melanchthon also included an exegetical component. In the letter that was supposed to have accompanied the gift of Calvin's treatise on Pighius, he requested from Melanchthon a copy of his commentary on Daniel.[112] Apparently Melanchthon fulfilled that request, for in a letter sent the following year Calvin praised the Daniel commentary he had received.[113] Such praise was by no means disingenuous. In 1555 a French translation of Melanchthon's work was published in Geneva and included Calvin's own introduction to Daniel as well. Given these clear historical connections, it is quite disappointing that modern scholars have not seen fit to compare these two exegetes on this work. Both understood they were living in the last days; both tried, under the influence of Luther's own apocalyptic expectations, to interpret Daniel's visions for contemporary society.[114] It is unfortunate that with few exceptions investigation of Melanchthon's influence over Calvin's exegesis has been limited by Calvin's remarks in the preface to his commentary on Romans, in which he complains about Melanchthon's tendency to skip over verses when using the *loci* method in biblical interpretation.[115] In fact, the Reformers often read and used one another's exegetical insights.

111. In his postscript to three sermons against Castellio from 1562, Calvin could angrily charge (CO 58:202): "Quant à Melancthon, si ce rustre ne s'arreste point à lui comme il le proteste, mais à l'Evangile, comment prouvera-il par l'Evangile que Dieu n'ordonne point de ses creatures?"

112. MBW 3169 (CO 11:515–17), dated 16 February 1543. Apparently the books were not ready in time for the Frankfurt book fair and were thus delayed.

113. MBW 3531 (CO 11:698), dated 21 April 1544. "Testor hoc tibi, nullo me huius aetatis scripto hactenus ita fuisse delectatum." For background on this commentary, see Hans Volz, "Beiträge zu Melanchthons und Calvins Auslegungen des Propheten Daniel," ZKG 67 (1955/6):93–118.

114. This spilled over into their correspondence. See, for example, Melanchthon's letter to Calvin on 12 July 1543 (MBW 3273; CO 11:594), where Melanchthon wrote: ". . . [commende]s filio Dei, quem Daniel inquit [in ex]tremo tempore dissipaturum ecclesiae [devast]atorem esse."

115. CO 10:402–6, dated 22 October 1539, addressed to Simon Grynaeus. Calvin's comments could possibly also refer to Melanchthon's *Dispositio* on Romans (CR 15:443–92) from 1530. For one of the only treatments of Melanchthon's influence on Calvin, see Richard Muller, "'Scimus enim quod les spiritualis est': Melanchthon and Calvin on

This did not mean they always agreed in such matters. For example, attached to a private letter written in 1543 to Joachim Camerarius, Melanchthon sent a copy of his *Unterschied des Alten und Neuen Testaments* with instructions to give it to Bernard Ziegler, so that he might better discern the differences between Melanchthon and Calvin on this point.[116] This action indicates an important hermeneutical divide between the two Reformers. Melanchthon's law-gospel hermeneutic clearly contradicted, in his own eyes, the salvation-historical approach of his Genevan correspondent. It continues to divide Christians today.

VI. Conclusions

Predestination, church practices, free will, the Lord's Supper: the topics of Melanchthon and Calvin's correspondence touched on many of the burning issues of the day. Given the penchant for polemic in that day and ours, their epistolary friendship, for all its weaknesses, provides an interesting model for theological discourse. Moderation and respect helped set a tone for discussion that allowed conversation to continue throughout their careers. They were not best friends; they were fierce, committed Christians, who struggled to right the church amid a stormy sea of troubles and who understood the importance of the other man's help in this endeavor.

These letters also reveal the limits of such conversation. In the end Calvin misconstrued Melanchthon's moderation, as did many of his more vociferous opponents, and attempted to spur him on, especially in the questions of the Lord's Supper and predestination, to debate what in Melanchthon's mind was undebatable. The strict limitation that Melanchthon imposed on himself and his correspondents was, in his view at least, a biblical one. He refused to invent new language to describe Christ's eucharistic presence, and thus tolerated Calvin's view; he refused to speculate about the relation between divine causation and salvation. This moderation was thus not a character flaw, nor did it arise out of genuine fear in the face of persecution. It was a stubborn refusal to venture beyond the biblical and patristic witness in theological discourse. But Melanchthon also linked this moderation to one of Lutheranism's enduring hallmarks: the central concern for how the distinction between law and gospel provides comfort to the terrified conscience.

the Interpretation of Romans 7:14–23," in *Melanchthon and the Commentary*, ed. M. Patrick Graham and Timothy J. Wengert (Sheffield, Sheffield Academic Press, 1997).

116. MBW 3387 (CR 5:243), dated 7 December 1543.

Calvin also developed a radically biblical theology. However, he insisted that the biblical witness itself set the limits not just of terminology but of content and that therefore any comfort had to be found within the totality of that witness. What appeared to Melanchthon as speculation was for Calvin faithfulness. And Melanchthon's *moderatio,* for all its appeal, could only be construed by Calvin as timidity or, worse yet, the result of philosophical scruples. It is finally this hermeneutical divide that continues to mark the differences between these two great streams of the Protestant tradition and between their ablest spokesmen.

2

Wary Allies: Melanchthon and the Swiss Reformers

Bruce Gordon

In his preface to the 1578 Basel edition of Sebastian Castellio's *Dialogos Quatuor*, in which the Savoyard treated the subjects of predestination, election, free will and faith, Fausto Sozzini wrote:

> Theodor Bibliander and Philip Melanchthon came after Erasmus, and Melanchthon was one of those who, having been ignited by the fire of Luther, clung to him (Luther) to the extent that he would not even approach Erasmus. Indeed he treated Erasmus as an adversary, choosing to buttress Luther's arguments with his own writings until he recognized his error and began to alter his work. When the opportunity arose, he (Melanchthon) strenuously propagated his own views in opposition to Luther, thereby recalling many souls from (Luther's) mendacious teaching. Bibliander through his whole life defended with perseverance the goodness of the human will in contrast to Peter Martyr, who held to another position, though he preferred to withdraw behind a wall and not interpret scripture in public on the grounds that he wished to keep silent, or for some reason, to dissemble.[1]

Sozzini's curious conjunction of Melanchthon with Bibliander, a man who openly espoused universalism against Calvin's teaching on predestination, presents us with something of the central paradox of Melanchthon's relationships with the Swiss churches.[2] Simply put, Melanchthon was different things to different people. To begin to reconstruct how Melanchthon was received and understood by the Swiss, his reputation, extensive epistolary contacts and the dissemination of his writings must be considered within the varied contexts of the Swiss reformation. That Melanchthon found a range of receptive audiences among the Swiss

---

1. *Sebastiani Castellionis Dialogi III* Aresdorffi 1578 fol. 3r–4v.
2. On Fausto Sozzini, see Zbigniew Ogonawski, "Socinus, 1539–1604" in Jill Rait (ed), *Shapers of Religious Traditions in Germany, Switzerland and Poland, 1560–1600* (New Haven: Yale University Press 1981), 195–209.

owes much to the common intellectual heritage whose roots lay in the life and work of Erasmus in Basel.[3] Melanchthon's importance to the Swiss was symbolic as well as intellectual; he was appropriated by the Swiss churches and their critics, both explicit and implicit. Through this conscription he was understood to stand for a range of causes: belief in free will, religious tolerance, a Reformed teaching on the Eucharist, and for moderation among the rabid supporters of Luther. The incoherence of Melanchthon's image among the Swiss owed much to the circumstances of his life as well as his temperament. Reading through the body of Melanchthon's letters to the Swiss one has to sort through the politeness and elegance of humanist epistolary forms to gain a glimpse of the complex concerns which lay underneath. It was in Melanchthon's nature to be diffident and the historian must use care in apportioning relative weight to his letters.

Melanchthon's contribution to the Swiss reformation was considerable and varied. Intellectually, he influenced a whole generation of theologians and educators. His works were standard texts of theological education, and he was for the Swiss the great humanist; yet this humanism, the bond which united him to so many scholars among the Swiss, also served as a mask behind which Melanchthon could conceal himself. Fausto Sozzini's uncle Lelio, who was later to espouse anti-trinitarianism, was his pupil, and like many of those learned refugees who took refuge in the Swiss cities of Basel and Zurich, he looked to Melanchthon as his mentor in opposing the theological doctrines enshrined by the established churches. Melanchthon for his part was extremely solicitous of Lelio, always asking for news of his activities. Whilst these "heretics" invoked the name of Melanchthon, their adversaries, men like Heinrich Bullinger, Ludwig Lavater and John Calvin looked to Melanchthon for support of a very different, and rather more political nature. Conrad Gesner and Peter Martyr, further, lauded Melanchthon as the man who had brought Aristotle into the Protestant intellectual world. For Ludwig Lavater, it was not Melanchthon's espousal of free will, but rather the verity of his position on the Lord's Supper, and his willingness to suffer at Luther's hands, which confirmed his place among the reformed brethren. Yet, despite this panoply of relations, Swiss of all ilk were in the end deeply disappointed by Melanchthon, for their hopes had been great that he

---

3. A good summary of Erasmus' time in Basel is to be found in R. J. Schoeck, *Erasmus of Europe: Prince of Humanists 1501–1536* (Edinburgh: Edinburgh University Press, 1993), 320–36.

would abandon Lutheran Germany and settle among those who regarded themselves as being theologically and intellectually his friends.

The broader context for the Swiss view of Melanchthon is to be found in the curious situation of the Swiss reformation in the decades following Zwingli's violent death in 1531. It can be argued that much of the subsequent course of the Swiss reformation was an attempt to come to terms with Luther's quarrel with Zwingli over the Eucharist in the 1520s. The theological issues of this subject have been thoroughly investigated and need no repetition here, but what remains to be examined is how deeply this division informed the Swiss mentality of the second generation.[4] The Swiss never recovered from their rejection by Luther. His repudiation left them alienated and vulnerable, and throughout the remaining decades of the sixteenth century they sought ways of recovering a relationship with the German Lutheran churches.[5] Yet these attempts were fraught with ambivalence and ambiguity. All Protestants understood the necessity of confessional as well as political unity in the face of the Habsburg Catholic threat. Indeed, many of the leading churchmen in the Swiss lands were displaced Germans (Simon Grynaeus, Sebastian Münster and Wolfgang Musculus), and the bonds of humanism stretched across frontiers. Nevertheless, the Swiss held fast to the memory of Huldrych Zwingli; they felt threatened and intimidated by the larger, more dominant Lutheran churches. Common cause in the Reformation clashed with wounded pride to create a labyrinth through which no one could pass with ease. It is against this backdrop of delicate sensitivities and political realities as well as sincere theological hopes that any consideration of Melanchthon's exchanges with the Swiss must be placed.

Johannes Oecolampadius, a fellow German, was one of Melanchthon's earliest contacts in the Swiss Confederation. He wrote first in July 1519 to report on the Leipzig Disputation.[6] Melanchthon held Oecolampadius in the highest regard, praising the Basel reformer years after his death. Their correspondence in the 1520s was frequent and intense, yet the strains of the Zwingli/Luther divide soon started to show. As early as

---

4. A particularly useful account of the quarrel is found in Mark U. Edwards, *Luther and the False Brethren* (Stanford: Stanford University Press, 1975), 82–111.

5. Bruce Gordon, "Calvin and the Swiss Reformed Churches," in A Duke, G. Lewis and A.D.M. Pettegree (eds) *Calvinism in Europe 1540–1620* (Cambridge: Cambridge University Press, 1994), 64–82.

6. *MBW* 59. On Oecolampadius the standard work remains the two-volume study by Ernst Staehelin, *Briefe und Akten zum Leben Oekolampads* (Leipzig: Heinsius, 1927).

1524 Melanchthon expressed to Oecolampadius his reservations about the iconoclasm in Zurich[7] and by 1525 he was defending Luther's position on the presence of Christ in the Eucharist.[8] As the storm clouds of sacramental conflict began to gather in 1525 Oecolampadius penned a moving testament to his friendship with Melanchthon.[9] In this letter Oecolampadius wrote describing how his friends had either abandoned him or were forced into exile; his parents were suffering miserably; his home city of Weinsberg had been destroyed; Erasmus had withdrawn his friendship. Against all of this he appealed to Melanchthon's love. Oecolampadius continued to offer friendship to Melanchthon, for he saw in him the best hope of averting disaster in the sacramental debate. He sent Melanchthon editions of his works with the protestation that there was ground for agreement.[10]

Melanchthon's reply from 25 April 1529 set the tone for much of his future correspondence with the Swiss reformers. His silence, he wrote, was on account of the ferocity of the sacramental debate.[11] Although pained by the division, Melanchthon resolutely defended the Wittenberg position, arguing that it had the weight of patristic authority.[12] Oecolampadius' reply to this letter, which he wrote in August 1529, formed a robust rejection of Melanchthon's sacramental position.[13] The one position which he shared with Melanchthon was the desire for a colloquy to resolve the matter. Thus, at least from the perspectives of the two friends Melanchthon and Oecolampadius, the road to Marburg was paved with good intentions. Despite their differences, however, Melanchthon continued to honour Oecolampadius long after his death in 1531, and ten years later he wrote of how he treasured Oecolampadius' gift of Agricola's *Dialectic*.[14] Oecolampadius was the type of man with whom Melanchthon most enjoyed contact: irenic, scholarly and moderate in temperament.

Perhaps the warmest relationship Melanchthon had with a reformer in the Swiss lands was with another German scholar of great distinction living in Basel, Simon Grynaeus. The two young men had studied to-

---

7. *MBW* 345. 30 September 1524.
8. *MBW* 370. 12 January 1525.
9. *MBW* 429. 15 November 1525.
10. See letters *MBW* 686 and 766.
11. *MBW* 775.
12. Ibid.
13. *MBW* 812.
14. *MBW* 2780.

gether in the Latin school in Pforzheim, and Grynaeus had belonged to Melanchthon's circle in Wittenberg during the 1520s.[15] Grynaeus remains one of the key figures of the early reformation awaiting scholarly attention; a task rendered virtually impossible, regrettably, by his unreadable hand. Having been recalled to Basel after the death of Oecolampadius, Grynaeus struggled through the 1530s, alongside Oswald Myconius, to reconcile Zwinglian and Lutheran theological positions. The correspondence between Melanchthon and Grynaeus resonates with the warmth of close friendship. On 1 March 1534 Grynaeus wrote:

> Your plan finally to liberate yourself from the endless political activities and to retreat to yourself and to make time for your studies and home I would hold to be a very good thing, if only I could believe that you could finally make a decision. Your good nature has led to the point that you do not have enough time for every noble goal, because you try to be everything to everyone. In good conscience and by God I assure you once again in all honesty of what I have thought and said; it would have been a more secure and enduring gain for your home if you had followed the counsel and desires of learned men and dedicated yourself more to scholarship than politics.[16]

In the same letter Grynaeus advised Melanchthon to go to England, but only if Henry VIII should invite him, for he alone could lead the nascent evangelical movement which was taking shape there. Melanchthon did write to Henry on 17 August 1535 enclosing a copy of his *Loci communes*, which was delivered to the King by Alesius.[17] One of Gyrynaeus' sources of information was his contact with Thomas Cranmer.[18] In the meanwhile, however, Grynaeus welcomed the news that Melanchthon was returning to Heidelberg.[19]

Grynaeus' pastoral concern for Melanchthon reflected his own preference for the world of the mind over political activism. Nevertheless, Grynaeus was a linchpin in the formation of an international web of

---

15. The best survey article on Grynaeus is Peter Bietenholz's contribution on the scholar in his *Contemporaries of Erasmus: A Biographical Register of the Renaissance and Reformation*, 3 vols (Toronto: University of Toronto Press, 1986) II. 142–46.

16. *MBW* 1413.

17. *MBW* 1607. Henry replied on 1 October 1535 thanking Melanchthon and saying that Cranmer would provide the news from England.

18. Diarmaid MacCulloch, *Thomas Cranmer. A Life* (New Haven: Yale University Press, 1996), esp. 60–68 and 173–74.

19. Ibid.

contacts among reformers. Grynaeus's international reputation was grounded in his status as one of the leading scholars of his day; Melanchthon in his preface to the 1541 edition of his works printed by Johannes Herwagen in Basel praised Grynaeus as the embodiment of the principles of learning which he most admired.[20] Melanchthon was not alone in acknowledging his debt to Grynaeus, for the Basel scholar's crucial support of Calvin in the mid 1530s established the credentials of the French exile in Basel, Zurich and Geneva.[21] Further, his patronage of Simon Sulzer proved an important moment in the development of Lutheran thought within the Swiss Confederation.[22] On 26 March 1538, after the bitter division between the Swiss and the Lutherans over the Wittenberg Concord, Grynaeus wrote to Melanchthon:

> The bearer of this letter is a pious and learned young man, who with burning zeal and in the hope of seeing you has traveled to Wittenberg. I ask you, please facilitate a discussion with him. In the matter of the published Concord he is not unsympathetic, and I ask you to use your powers of persuasion to win him to Christ and the Church. He is well thought of among his own people and it is certain that he will receive a prominent position in Bern. Your reputation in the Lord is so great, that all the best wish now to get to know you. As with all our other matters, it is best that you hear from him.[23]

Less than a month later Melanchthon wrote a letter to Viet Dietrich in Nuremberg recommending the young Sulzer.[24]

The intimacy of Melanchthon's relationship with Grynaeus was not continued with the latter's successor in Basel, Oswald Myconius, who led

---

20. *MBW* 2799. It was in this same preface that Melanchthon honored the memory of Oecolampadius.

21. In the dedication to his *Commentary on the Epistle to the Romans,* Calvin wrote that he and Grynaeus had worked together on scriptural exegesis. As Ganoczy points out, Grynaeus was primarily a philologist and Calvin the theologian, but Grynaeus' influence on Calvin during his stay in Basel in the 1530s made a lasting impression. Alexandre Ganoczy, *The Young Calvin*, trans. D. Foxgrover and Wade Provo (Philadelphia: Westminster Press, 1987), 92.

22. The most useful recent article on Sulzer is Amy Nelson Burnett, "Simon Sulzer and the Consequences of the 1563 Strasbourg Consensus in Switzerland," *ARG*, 83 (1992), 154–79.

23. *MBW* 2009.

24. The letter is dated 23 April 1538. *MBW* 2021.

the church until his death in 1553.[25] Myconius attempted to retain Basel's position of openness to both the Zwinglian and Lutheran camps, but in the increasingly polarized world of the 1530s this role proved untenable. Heinrich Bullinger, whose position as spokesman for the Swiss churches became evident in the debates of the mid 1530s, thought little of the man from Lucerne. In Bullinger's eyes Myconius' wriggling was no less lacking in probity than the conciliatory efforts of the despised Martin Bucer. In 1544, when matters between Zurich and Wittenberg reached a nadir, Myconius wrote to Melanchthon describing the personal abuse poured upon his head by the Zwinglians.[26] He spoke of how he had been branded a "Bucerian", "Lutheran" and a "traitor." Myconius' appeal to Melanchthon was based on his belief that the two shared positions on the Eucharist. In the letter he detailed his rejection of both Luther's view of ubiquity as well as the Zwinglian separation of the body from the divinity of Christ. The principal problem, as Myconius saw it, was that Swiss resentment of Luther was so great that nothing less than uncritical support for Zwingli would free him from vilification.[27]

Myconius was not a great mind, and his theological endeavours rightly drew little admiration, but his letter to Melanchthon is an important expression of the dilemma which confronted any outsider dealing with the Swiss: the legacy of Zwingli. The guardian of Zwingli's memory was his successor Heinrich Bullinger, a man whose relationships with foreign reformers were colored by his need to balance conflicting forces within both the Zurich and Swiss churches. His contact with Melanchthon began in the turbulent years of the early 1530s when Bullinger wrote expressing his hope that despite the poor reputation enjoyed by the Swiss in Wittenberg it might be possible for the two men to become friends.[28] Melanchthon's friendly reply in June of the following year marked the beginning of an exchange which would last more than twenty years.[29] It was a fraternal relationship which weathered a variety

---

25. W. Brändly, "Oswald Myconius in Basel," *Zwingliana* 11 (1959), 183–92.

26. 9 June 1544. *MBW* 3580.

27. As late as 1538 Bullinger wrote to Melanchthon providing documentation which proved, he believed, that Zwingli was not responsible for the Second Kappel War. The letter from Bullinger to Melanchthon is dated 31 August, 1538. *MBW* 2087.

28. 31 August 1535. *MBW* 1617.

29. 1 June 1536. *MBW* 1758.

of storms, large and small, without ever becoming especially close.[30] The texture of their friendship reflected their cautious yet kindly dispositions. Melanchthon lacked Calvin's perseverance in drawing Bullinger into a more open relationship, though it must be added that he never needed Bullinger in the way the Genevan reformer did. Fundamentally, Bullinger admired Melanchthon's didactic skills, and he entrusted the *Praeceptor Germaniae* with the education of many young sons of the Zurich church. This confidence in Melanchthon as teacher ran parallel to Bullinger's reservations about some of Melanchthon's theological positions.

A recurring theme in Bullinger's correspondence with Melanchthon was how the students returning to Zurich from Wittenberg praised the reception they had received from Melanchthon. This pedagogical relationship was a lifeline to the Swiss churches, and Melanchthon's good will was essential. With the exception of Basel, whose status among the Swiss churches was quite uncertain, there were few places to which the churches of Zurich, Bern and Schaffhausen could send their young men for a proper Protestant education.[31] Melanchthon established a reputation as a congenial host, open to those who had made the journey north. This was to have important implications for the development of Protestant culture in the Swiss Confederation. In Bern Johann Heinrich Meyer, who had been an enthusiastic pupil of Melanchthon in Wittenberg, led the *Untere Schule* for many years, and was succeeded by Eberhard Rümlang, who had likewise studied under Melanchthon.[32] In the Prophezei, first in Zurich and then from 1533 in Bern Melanchthon's *Rhetoric* became a cornerstone of the educational programme.[33] Melanchthon's influence upon the educational system in the Protestant Swiss states was so considerable that the Bernese council considered calling him to Lausanne in 1558 after the departure of Pierre Viret.[34]

This concern for education led to a touching episode at the end of Melanchthon's life when Bullinger sent his son Heinrich to Wittenberg to study. The elder Bullinger wrote to Melanchthon on 22 August 1555

30. For a concise overview of Bullinger's correspondence with Melanchthon, see Rainer Henrich's lecture for the colloquium celebrating the centenary of the Zwingliverein. The text of the lecture is available on the web at www.unizh.ch/irg/mela.html

31. On education in the Protestant areas of the Swiss Confederation, see Karin Maag, *Seminary or University? The Genevan Academy and Reformed Higher Education, 1560–1620* (Aldershot: Ashgate Publication Company, 1995).

32. Kurt Guggisberg, *Bernische Kirchengeschichte* (Bern: P. Haupt, 1958), 174.

33. Ibid., 167.

34. Ibid., 221.

asking whether Melanchthon might provide accommodation in his own home for his son, for which he would gladly pay.[35] In an aside which tells something of how the epistolary relationship among the reformers worked at this point, Bullinger wrote that he would leave it to Calvin to report on the other news of importance.[36] In March of the following year, Bullinger wrote again thanking Melanchthon for the kind reception he had offered his son. The letter closed with the usual greetings from Zurich colleagues, with special mention of Lelio Sozzini, Melanchthon's former pupil now residing in the Swiss city.

Although it was not unusual for Swiss students to reside with Melanchthon, the letter of 1556 offers an insight into how Bullinger made use of his son's proximity to Melanchthon to cultivate relations. In the letter of 13 March 1556 he mentioned that he was sending Melanchthon, through the young Heinrich, a copy of his *Summa christenlicher Religion* for his approbation.[37] The gift of a book was part of the normal exchange between scholars and churchmen, a tradition which had gone so horribly wrong in 1544 with Luther's response to the gift of a Zurich Bible, but it highlights the respect in which Melanchthon continued to be held despite the polemical vicissitudes of the 1530s and 40s. It was a relationship which was built on the Swiss assumption that left to himself Melanchthon would support their theological positions. It was the bitterest of blows, therefore, when in April 1557 Melanchthon put his name to a document at the Worms Colloquy which explicitly condemned Zwingli's theology.[38]

Bullinger was well aware that the life of a sixteenth-century church leader involved the delicate balance of the public and private. His own experience with the Zurich magistrates taught him very early on that the requirements of the church's temporal masters did not square with the spiritual injunctions of the scriptures. Church leaders had to weigh up biblical and mundane concerns, and essential to this was the limitation of differences and disagreements between reformers to private correspondence. Bullinger understood from Melanchthon's work that the Wittenberg reformer's positions on the Eucharist and predestination were tantalizingly close to his own.[39] Bullinger saw in Melanchthon's treatment of

35. *MBW* 7561.
36. Ibid.
37. *MBW* 7747.
38. Gordon, "Calvin and the Swiss Reformed Churches," 79.
39. As Craig Farmer has recently argued, Melanchthon's use of the word "exhibere" in the 1540 "Variata," which was intended in a spirit of unity, did not please

predestination a similar rejection of Calvin's position on double predestination, which the Zurich reformer felt made God the author of evil.[40]

Such debates, however, were not for public consumption, and just as Bullinger was prepared to leave matters unstated in order to bolster Calvin's position in Geneva, he was mindful of the circumstances in which Melanchthon had to live and work. Bullinger had to play to a variety of audiences: his political masters, those who venerated the memory of Zwingli and the forces among the Swiss arguing for the renewal of the French alliance. These essentially Swiss concerns had to be considered alongside the growing imperative for a broader unified front among Protestants in Europe. This was brought into sharp relief by the stirrings of the Catholic church in Italy in the early 1540s and the return of Charles V to his German lands in 1543. These closely related fronts forced upon the Swiss the need to confront once again the Luther question.

It was against this background that we see Bullinger turn to Melanchthon as mediator in the 1540s. When the Swiss were grossly offended by Luther's refusal of the Bible sent to him by Froschauer in 1543 Melanchthon had to assuage their outrage.[41] In the troubled years of 1544/45, when the relationship between Melanchthon and Luther became particularly tense Bullinger worked with Calvin, as Wilhelm Neuser has shown, to bring Melanchthon to the Swiss Confederation.[42] Melanchthon had intimated to friends such as Musculus in Augsburg that he would soon have to leave Wittenberg, and the rumours began to fly along Protestant communication lines.[43] Bullinger made offers to

Bullinger. Craig S Farmer, "Eucharistic Exhibition and Sacramental Presence in the New Testamtent Commentaries of Wolfgang Musculus," in Rudolf Dellsperger, Rudolf Freudenberger and Wolfgang Weber (eds), *Wolfgang Musculus (1497–1563) und die oberdeutsche Reformation* (Berlin: Akademie Verlag, 1997), 304–5.

40. Cornelius P. Venema, "Heinrich Bullinger's Correspondence on Calvin's Doctrine of Predestination 1551–1553," *SCJ* 17 (1986), 435–50.

41. Luther's letter to Froschauer is found in WAB 10 384–88 n.3908. The letter is dated 31 August 1543. Melanchthon wrote to Bucer on 4 November 1543 arguing that the best response to the insult was silence.

42. W.H. Neuser, "Die Versuche Bullingers, Calvins und die Strasburger, Melanchthon zum Fortgang von Wittenberg zu bewegen," in U. Gäbler and E. Herkenrath (eds), *Heinrich Bullinger 1504–1575. Gesammelte Aufsätze zum 400. Todestag* (2 vols., Zurich: Theologischer Verlag, 1975), 35–55.

43. On 12 August 1544 Melanchthon wrote to Wolfgang Musculus in Augsburg that Luther had reopened the sacramental quarrel and that he (Melanchthon) would likely have to leave Wittenberg. Eight days earlier Luther had vented on Melanchthon his anger over the Eucharistic teaching in the "Cologne Reformation," written by Mel-

Melanchthon of what he could expect in Zurich, but it is evident that the Zurich church leader soon lost interest in attracting such a rich prize to his city. Although the epistolary relationship between Bullinger and Melanchthon continued until 1559, two years after the fatal blow of the document signed at the Worms Colloquy, it remained at the level of the polite exchange of texts and information. While Bullinger's letters continued to express hopes of confessional unity, the Antistes of Zurich did not refrain from drawing attention to points of doctrine on which the two men parted company. In particular Melanchthon's espousal of free will and private confession stuck in Bullinger's throat. The overall tone of the correspondence is of shared theological beliefs tempered by a realization that historical circumstances would prevent them from ever coming together. Melanchthon and Bullinger were prisoners to the devastating quarrel between Luther and Zwingli, and neither could do much about it.

Nevertheless, the Swiss had another purpose for Melanchthon. The high regard in which the Swiss theologians held Melanchthon found expression in the first historical accounts of the Reformation to be penned by Zwinglian writers; having failed to recruit him in life, the leaders of the Zurich church sought to appropriate his memory. In the 1564 edition of his *Historia vom dem Streit in des Herrern Nachtmal*, a translation of the Latin text printed the previous year, Ludwig Lavater accorded Melanchthon a place of honour in the visceral story of the sacramental quarrel.[44] Lavater mentions Melanchthon only a couple of times, but on each occasion the effect of the invocation is to lend crucial support to the Zurich cause. A case in point is Lavater's rendering of Melanchthon's letter to Bullinger of 1544:

> You will perhaps already have received my letter in which I describe the dreadful text of Luther's in which he renews the war over the Lord's Supper . . . Our enemies will rejoice, particularly those who practice

---

anchthon and Bucer. Hans Scheible, "Wolfgang Musculus und Philipp Melanchthon," in Rudolf Dellsperger, Rudolf Freudenberger and Wolfgang Weber (eds), *Wolfgang Musculus (1497–1563) und die oberdeutsche Reformation* (Berlin: Akademie Verlag, 1997), 194–95.

44. Ludwig Lavater, *Historia/||oder Geschicht/||von dem ursprung und fürgang der grossen zwyspaltung/|| so sich zwüschend D. Martin Luthern an|| ein/ und Huldrychen Zwinglio am anderen|| teil/* . . . (Zurich, 1564).

monkish superstition and seek ever to divide our church, something which especially pains me.[45]

Following Melanchthon's death Lavater provided a moving account in which the Wittenberger was given his place in the Zwinglian pantheon.

> In the month of April Philip Melanchthon departed this life (sorely missed by all godfearing people), a man who in all forms of learning was a modest person and a highly regarded teacher. He laboured daily to an old age through illness and sorrow. This man had long had a close relationship with the Zwinglians. With both Bullinger and Calvin, among others, he kept a friendly correspondence. Various quarrels gave him grounds for wishing to come to Zurich or Geneva on account of agreement on the teaching of the Lord's Supper. As a result of this, amongst other things, his students, not only those whom he taught during his life but also posthumously through his works have fallen into dispute and hatred. Melanchthon had predicted that the matter of the Lord's Supper would give birth to a dreadful war.[46]

Lavater's historical account of Melanchthon is important for a number of reasons. The paucity of references to Melanchthon in the *Historia* suggests that from the Swiss perspective he did not play a crucial role. The emphasis in the text, however, is not upon what he said or did, but rather upon what he stood for in the debate. In Lavater's reconstruction of the sacramental debate there is a conscious shaping of Melanchthon as a figure who was deeply sensitive to the Zwinglian cause. In the passages quoted above the language of a martyrology pulsates through the phrasing: he was a man of truth surrounded by mendacious creatures who soon fell out after his death. Melanchthon is spoken of in terms of a prophet, the man who predicted the terrible strife to come, and as a righteous man who had suffered for the faith. If the cautious relationship between Bullinger and Melanchthon revealed in their correspondence gives us an insight into the complex web of interconfessional relations, the Melanchthon of Swiss history writing, in the hands of Bullinger's friend and colleague Lavater, is stripped of ambivalence and ambiguity. In death Melanchthon, for the leaders of the Swiss churches, became "one of us."

45. Ibid., 86.
46. Ibid., 127–28.

If Melanchthon's reception among the Swiss church leaders was cautious and equivocal, the protean character of his reputation is underlined by the radically opposing ways in which he was interpreted by groups wishing to claim his patronage. For the many Italian theologians resident in the Swiss Confederation Melanchthon was a champion of free will, a man who represented toleration and true Gospel principles against the increasingly ecclesiastical and doctrinally precise established churches in Zurich, Bern, Basel and Geneva.[47] Against this view was an important group of theologians, many of them Italian and humanist scholars, who praised Melanchthon for bringing the logical rigour of Aristotle into Protestant thought.

Oswald Myconius' letter to Melanchthon of 14 June 1550 contains a warm recommendation of Lelio Sozzini to Melanchthon. Sozzini arrived in Wittenberg in July of 1550 and remained for just under one year.[48] The extent of Melanchthon's influence on Sozzini is difficult to measure, for it was not until after Sozzini's departure from Wittenberg for Italy that he became more associated with the ideas of Servetus. Nevertheless, Melanchthon was clearly taken with this man whose energies on behalf of the Reformed cause in Eastern Europe he so admired. Without doubt Lelio was Melanchton's most important link to the Italian scholars in Basel.

Melanchthon's reputation among the Italians, primarily those located in Basel, was grounded in the high esteem in which they held his *Loci communes*. In December 1549 Celio Curione took up correspondence with Melanchthon by recommending Pietro Paulo Vergerio, a fellow exile, who was looking for a post.[49] Curione expressed his gratitude for the work of the Wittenberg reformer, claiming, as the Italians often did when writing to the northern reformers, that he had been converted to the evangelical cause by reading one of his texts, in this case the *Loci communes*.[50] Curione (1503–69) was an important figure in Basel. A humanist and schoolteacher by training, he taught in the university, although his family remained in a precarious financial situation.[51] The

---

47. See George Huntston Williams, *The Radical Reformation*, 3rd edition (Kirksville, Mo.: Sixteenth Century Journal Publishers, 1992). His chapter, "Radical Italian Evangelicals in Swiss exile" (943–90) provides useful biographical sketches of the key figures.

48. *MBW* 5826.

49. *MBW* 5705.

50. Williams, *Radical Reformation*, 953.

51. Curione had fled Italy in 1542 and as early as 1549 he was suspected in Basel of denying the divinity of Christ. According to Williams he remained a firm friend of

common link between the two men appears to have been Lelio Sozzini, who seems to have informed Melanchthon of Curione's work.

Curione was an active correspondent with Melanchthon during the 1550s, as he was with Bullinger in Zurich. On 1 May 1551 Melanchthon wrote to Curione praising him for his work, commenting on how the unity of the educated within the church was essential to its survival.[52] Three years later he wrote to again to Curione praising the Basel humanist for his work on Cicero which had been printed by Oporinus in 1553.[53] Melanchthon for his part seems to have been content to keep the relationship at the level of humanist exchange. In 1557 Curione wrote to say that he had seen a copy of a letter written by Melanchthon to Martin Görlitz in 1530 condeming the Swiss reformers as Zwinglians.[54] The letter had been reprinted by Westphal during his attack on Calvin, and Curione sought to explain Melanchthon's remarks by asserting that the letter was a forgery, as it did not square with Melanchthon's other Eucharistic statements.[55] This optimistic interpretation received no reply from Melanchthon and when Curione wrote a year later on 31 August 1558 he drew attention to the silence from Wittenberg, though he said he would continue to send students. Once again Melanchthon's wish to parry questions which strayed beyond the fraternal bonds of humanism was brought into relief.

This emphasis on the unity of humanist scholars in the service of the church formed a central theme in Melanchthon's most controversial contact with the Basel circle. This was Melanchthon's letter to Sebastian Castellio of 1 November 1557.[56] It was at this point that Calvin and his supporters were most furiously vilifying Castellio. Castellio's link to Melanchthon was rather indirect, for, unlike Sozzini, he had not studied in Wittenberg. The connection appears to have been through Francisco de Enzinas, who was Castellio's closest friend during the Basel years 1545–48

Bernardino Ochino and defended himself as being an Erasmian in questions of religious liberty. Williams, *Radical Reformation*, 955. In 1557, the same year that Castellio was examined, Curione was brought to trial for his notes on Girbaldi's *De vera cognitione Dei*. Curione excused himself on the grounds that his notes were purely grammatical. The definitive work remains Markus Kutter, *Celio Secondo Curione* (Basel: Helbing & Lichtenhahn, 1955).

52. *MBW* 6008.
53. 1 May 1554. *MBW* 7164.
54. 1 September 1557. *MBW* 8325.
55. Ibid.
56. *MBW* 8414.

and again in 1549. Enzinas had been a protégé of Melanchthon in Wittenberg where he had been encouraged to translate the New Testament into Spanish.[57] As Hans Guggisberg has argued, Melanchthon was the one German reformer with whom Castellio had any contact.[58] Indeed, Castellio, reflecting perhaps Melanchthon's general position among the Italian and Spanish exiles in Basel, portrayed Melanchthon as an advocate of toleration and an opponent of the death penalty for heretics.[59] In *De Haereticis* Melanchthon is frequently referred to as an opponent of the doctrine of predestination propounded by Calvin; the two men are clearly set against one another in the work.[60]

Melanchthon's letter to Castellio was most likely the result of Hubert Languet, a close friend of Melanchthon's who spent a considerable amount of time in Basel during 1557, and who enjoyed good relations with both prominent families and printers in the Rhenish city.[61] Languet and the irenic Catholic Georgius Cassander both spoke very highly of Castellio to Melanchthon, despite the rapacious attacks of Beza and Calvin on the Savoyard.[62] Melanchthon's letter to Castellio was a triumph of

---

57. Enzinas lived with Melanchthon after his matriculation in Wittenberg in 1541. It was during his time in Melanchthon's house that he began translating the New Testament from Greek into Spanish. Edward Boehmer, *Bibliotheca Wiffeniana Spanish Reformers of Two Centuries from 1520*, 2 vols. (New York: B. Franklin, 1962) I. 131–84. There is also a helpful article on Enzinas by Constance J. Mathers in Hans Hillerbrand (ed), *The Oxford Encyclopedia of the Reformation* 4 vols (Oxford: Oxford University Press, 1996), II, 50–51.

58. Hans R. Guggisberg, *Sebastian Castellio, 1515–1563 Humanist und Verteidiger der religiösen Toleranz* (Göttingen: Vandenhoeck & Ruprecht, 1997), 140.

59. It should be noted that in 1557 Melanchthon signed a memorandum agreeing with the execution of Servetus. Roland Bainton, *Concerning Heretics*, (rpt. New York: Octagon Books, 1965), 58.

60. Ibid., 142–43.

61. Languet wrote to Melanchthon on 8 June 1557 reporting the he had found Basel delightful. He was full of praise for the publishing house of Oporinus, a man whom he described as being as selfless as Melanchthon himself. Languet also reported on the numbers of Spanish and French troops he had seen on his journey to Basel. He noted that the Germans and the Swiss were very much for Henry II of France. *MBW* 8248.

62. The letter came in the same year that Castellio had to defend his views on predestination before the university and magistrate of Basel. The Basel Antistes at this point was none other than Simon Sulzer, whose good will ensured that Castellio survived the ordeal. See Peter G. Bietenholtz, *Basle and France in the Sixteenth Century. The Basle Humanists and Printers in Their Contacts with Francophone Culture* (Geneva: Librarie Droz, 1971), 125.

humanist diplomacy. No mention is made of the theological positions (predestination, free will, the death penalty for heretics) which Castellio attributed to Melanchthon. Instead, the letter addresses Castellio as a fellow humanist, a man to be greatly praised for his work on sacred scripture; Melanchthon thought highly of Castellio's Latin Bible. In addition, Melanchthon wrote of Castellio's tribulations, commentating that he too had suffered terribly from the religious quarrels. In conclusion, Melanchthon offered Castellio his eternal friendship and expressed the hope that they would one day meet. They never did. The letter was never repeated, but this did little to militate against the fury which flared in Geneva. Calvin heard of the letter in April of 1558 and immediately jumped to the conclusion that Melanchthon had betrayed the Reformed churches.[63] How could the man, Calvin wondered, who had supported them in the Servetus case now express his sympathies for the archfiend Castellio?

Melanchthon's relations with Castellio and more importantly with the Italian exiles within the Swiss churches provide a window on his overall standing among the Swiss. Men like Curione, Lelio Sozzini, Camilio Renato and later Bernardino Ochino were resolute in their veneration of Zwingli, whom they regarded as the pure voice of reform.[64] Although, for the most part, these men lived and worked within the context of the Swiss Reformed churches in the cities of Basel, Zurich and Bern, they clearly harboured deep-set reservations about the theological direction of Zwingli's successors. Bullinger, and even more Calvin, they believed, had abandoned Zwingli's biblical language and were moving the church towards a reaffirmation of tradition and philosophy. Their horror at the drift towards orthodoxy among the Swiss churches was deepened by their own experiences in Italy: most had fled their native land in the early 1540s when the Catholic church began to move against religious dissent. Their whole conception of reform was grounded more in principles of *sola scriptura* than ecclesiology.

These men saw in Melanchthon's writings the voice of a humanist scholar who interpreted the Bible after the spirit of Erasmus. They also saw in Melanchthon a man who could be held up against Calvin in the matters of predestination and free will. Yet, in order to do this whilst

63. Guggisberg, *Sebastian Castellio*, 164–65.
64. This subject is covered in the doctoral dissertation of Mark Taplin, "The Italian Reformers and the Zurich Church," (University of St Andrews Ph.D. dissertation, 1998).

preserving good relations with the Wittenberg reformer they had to dis semble, to disguise the true radicalness of their theological positions. Bernardino Ochino did this through the use of the dialogue. In his dia logue it is the opposing interlocutor who actually represents Ochino's own views, and although he gives way in the end, it is clear that his have been the more forceful arguments.[65] Melanchthon also provided these exiles with a model of dissimulation, a *modus vivendi* in a world of creep ing doctrinal exactitude. The story is not without its ironies. Whilst the leaders of the reformed churches were attempting to draw Melanchthon into their camp, his tribulations in Wittenberg provided many of the re ligious exiles in the Swiss cities with a sense of meaning for their strug gles with the establishment. Melanchthon the Nicodemite was a vener ated figure.

For the humanist-minded Italian exiles Melanchthon was the true heir of Erasmus, an opponent of the increasing trend towards systematic theology. But for many in the intellectual community among the Swiss Melanchthon was admired for the polar opposite qualities. From the middle of the sixteenth century onwards one of the dominant questions for the Swiss was the issue of natural theology, the relationship between revelation and reason.[66] The slow shift towards Calvinism facilitated by the arrival of men such as Peter Martyr Vermigli in Zurich led to in creased debate about the extent to which the created order provides the categories of thought necessary for the interpretation of Scripture and the world.

One man more than any other among the Swiss shared Melanch thon's attitudes towards God, creation, the Church and humanity. This was the noted Zurich scholar Conrad Gesner, who taught natural sci ences and ethics in the Lectorium, receiving the first chair in the subject in 1558.[67] As Joachim Staedtke has written, "In Conrad Gesner a Chris tian and natural scientific view of the world are not separated, but are shown to be congruent. Nature is the marvelous creation of God; Gesner had learnt this from the Bible and pursued it in his scientific discover-

---

65. Mark Taplin, "Bernardino Ochino and the Zurich Polygamy Controversy of 1563," (M. Litt dissertation, University of St Andrews, 1995).

66. See M. Geiger, *Basel im Zeitalter der Orthodoxie* (Basel, 1958).

67. It was through Bullinger's influence that Gesner was able to teach natural sci ence in Zurich, though the subordinate nature of the subject was emphasized by the lower salary paid to Gesner for his work. He had to supplement his income by working as a medical doctor. Karin Maag, *Seminary or University*, 134.

ies."[68] Although there is no evidence of correspondence between Gesner and Melanchthon, Gesner wrote extensively about the Wittenberger in his *Bibliotheca Universalis*.[69] Gesner found much in Melanchthon to praise, but several aspects stand out, most notably Melanchthon's antischolastic writings and his irenicism. Melanchthon was particularly praised for his work *Über des Herrenmahl,* in which he attempted to reconcile Lutheran and Zwinglian views. Gesner shared with Melanchthon a conciliatory spirit which derived little pleasure from theological dispute, and for both the *studia humanitatis* held the key to overcoming polemical confrontations.

Gesner's view of Melanchthon differed from that of the church leaders, for whom issues such as predestination and the vexed relationship with Luther were paramount. Gesner was primarily interested in the relationship of theology to natural science, and for him Melanchthon's most important contribution to the Reformation cause was his work on Aristotle. Aristotle, for Gesner, was the great teacher of nature and cosmology, and he made extensive use of Melanchthon's 1554 translation of Ptolemaios' *Tetrabiblos*.[70] An example of the influence on the Swiss of Melanchthon's work on Aristotle is Gesner's *Pandects,* which formed the second and third parts of his *Bibliotheca Universalis,* and was printed in 1548.[71] Here Gesner divided his scientific system into twenty-one groups (*Grammatica, Geographica, Historia,* etc.). For these he employs the necessary *Topoi* outlined in Aristotle as essential for the formulation of dialectical and rhetorical syllogisms. In so doing, as Urs Leu has demonstrated, Gesner developed a *loci*-system for the study of nature.[72] In his consideration of both theological and natural questions, Gesner wanted to demonstrate that every *locus* could be further divided in order to be better understood. His work, as an encyclopedia, was essentially a collection of *loci* based on the model provided by Melanchthon.

<hr />

68. J. Staedtke, "Konrad Gesner als Theologe," *Gesnerus* 23 (1965), 142.

69. Conrad Gesner, *Bibliotheca universalis, sive catalogus omnium scriptorum locupletissimus, in tribus languis, Latina, Graeca, et Hebraica; extantium et non extantium, veterum et recentiorum in hunc usque diem . . . publicatorum et in Bibliothecis latentium . . .* Froschauer, Zurich 1545. fol. 556v–559r.

70. Urs Leu, *Conrad Gesner als Theologe. Ein Beitrag zur Zürcher Geistesgeschichte des 16. jahrhunderts* (New York: P. Lang, 1990), 94. This portion of the essay on Gesner draws heavily from Leu's important book.

71. Pandects were collections of passages in support of various propositions.

72. For Gesner's method, see Leu, *Conrad Gesner,* 191–218.

Melanchthon's use of the *loci* system proved immensely influential on the Swiss in a variety of ways.[73] Fritz Büsser has drawn attention to Zwingli's adoption of Erasmus' method of *loci* in his theological works.[74] But clearly Melanchthon's development of this art had profound implications for the Swiss. The work of Wolfgang Musculus in Bern and Peter Martyr Vermigli in Zurich must be mentioned. Martyr's *Loci Communes* of 1571 were organized posthumously by Robert Masson, minister of the French church in London. Masson's intention was to organize Martyr's ideas in *topoi* according to Calvin's *Institutes*. Despite this, clear parallels with Melanchthon's method appear. Martyr's intention, as outlined in the first edition, echo Melanchthon's belief that the *loci* was the simplest way of teaching, the main tool for analysis and the most profitable manner to answer difficult questions. It was a way of thinking—an art and a science. The intention was to place things in their natural sequence. The structure of Martyr's work is familiar to readers of Melanchthon: God the Creator, God the Redeemer, Predestination and the Church.

It would be too much to suggest that Melanchthon alone was responsible for the development of the *loci* system among the Swiss. The Swiss reformation was shaped by the confluence of several currents: Martyr, for example, was educated in the Thomist tradition of Padua, and although he arrived at many of the same conclusions as Melanchthon and Calvin, it was by a different route. As Richard Muller has argued, Martyr maintained the *sola gratia* of the Reformation, but with a sophisticated treatment of the relationship of faith to rational argument.[75] What separated Martyr from Calvin was the more positive relationship between philosophy and theology, between revelation and a natural knowledge of God. Herman Selderhuis has recently argued that Wolfgang Musculus' *Loci communes* of 1560, printed in Basel, and written during his first ten years in Bern, reveals the influence of both Melanchthon's *Loci* and

---

73. On the importance of Melanchthon's method, see Wilhelm Maurer, "Melanchthon's Loci communes von 1521 als wissenschaftliche Programmschrift," *Luther-Jahrbuch* (1960), 1–50.

74. Fritz Büsser, "Zwingli als Exegete: A contribution to the 450th anniversary of the death of Erasmus," in B. Armstrong and Elsie Mckee (eds), *Probing the Reformed Tradition: Historical Studies in honor of Edward A. Dowey, Jr.*, (Louisville, KY: Westminster/John Knox Press, 1989) 175–96. Büsser argues that Zwingli's method of using *loci* was closer to Erasmus' understanding of scriptural exegesis than was Melanchthon's. His argument is that Zwingli, therefore, is the rightful theological heir to Erasmus.

75. Richard A. Muller, *Post-Reformation Dogmatics*, vol. 1 (Grand Rapids: Baker Book House, 1987), 69.

Bullinger's *Decades*.[76] Melanchthon was important to Rudolf Gwalther and Ludwig Lavater, both of whom wished to stress the continuity between Zwingli and Melanchthon in the search for theological method.

The centrality of the *loci* method among the Swiss churches in the second half of the sixteenth century found expression in Rudolf Gwalther's preface to the 1580 edition of Martyr's *Loci communes*. In an address entitled, *de usu et utilitate Locorum Communium*, Gwalther developed the historical lineage of the *loci* method as the best possible means for instruction.[77] The preface was originally delivered to the theological students in Zurich on 22 August, 1580. From 1556 Peter Martyr had lectured in the Lectorium in Zurich, where students had been trained in the humanist skills of rhetoric and dialectic, and he had been instrumental in integrating the *loci* method into the evolving reformed educational system. Gwalther's address was in praise of this intellectual development, and his encomium took the form of an explication of how *loci* serve to elucidate passages of Scripture. In tracing the genealogy of the *loci* method Gwalther heaped praise upon Melanchthon:

> Philip Melanchthon, who has departed this life and now rests in the Lord, is treated today no less cruelly by his ungrateful disciples, who, if he had not taught them to speak, would not be able to speak. Had the Lord granted him a longer life, he would today adorn Zurich.[78]

This was now the familiar image of Melanchthon in Zwinglian historical writing of the sixteenth century; a man of sorrows beset by ungrateful students who would have joined the Swiss had circumstances permitted. Apart from this mythology, however, there was a clear intellectual agenda underlining Gwalther's reference to Melanchthon. Whether or not the Wittenberger might have allied himself with the Swiss would remain a moot point, but there was no doubting the enduring pedagogical

---

76. Herman J. Selderhuis, "Die Loci Communes des Wolfgang Musculus: Reformierte Dogmatik anno 1560," in Rudolf Dellsperger, Rudolf Freudenberger and Wolfgang Weber (eds), *Wolfgang Musculus (1497–1563) und die oberdeutsche Reformation* (Berlin: Akademie Verlag, 1997), 315.

77. *Loci Communes D.P.M. Vermilii ex variis ipsius authoris scriptis in unum locum collectio in quator classes distributi*. . . . Londini T. Vantrollious 1583.

78. Ibid., Av.

value of his work. Gwalther refers again to Melanchthon's view of the usefulness of the *loci* method for ministers.[79]

> The minister has two duties: first where he is required to explicate a text he must hold to the true meaning. Secondly, he must accommodate his message to the needs of his listeners, mindful of the place and time. Concerning the first point, it is above all essential to consider the whole book from which the locus has been taken, careful not to neglect anything, to muddle or wander beyond the olive trees (as they say) for we hold that Scripture is not to be venerated by the mind alone.[80]

A final illustration of the differing ways in which Melanchthon was received among the Swiss comes from the year of Melanchthon's death. This was also the year of the great quarrel over predestination in Zurich, which resulted in the dismissal of perhaps the most interesting of all the Swiss theologians. As early as the 1530s Theodor Bibliander began to argue for universalism, the idea that orders of creation and not individuals were saved.[81] In a letter from 1535 to Oswald Myconius, who had been one of his sharpest critics, Bibliander argued that he had not wanted to create a scandal with his teaching; he had simply reviewed Erasmus' debate with Luther and had been persuaded by the force of Erasmus' positions.[82] In the same letter he attributed to Melanchthon the fact that Lutheran teaching on predestination had become more acceptable.[83] The

79. For a highly-instructive treatment of the place of the loci in Melanchthon's pedagogy, see Timothy J. Wengert, "Philip Melanchthon's 1522 Annotations on Romans and the Lutheran Origins of Rhetorical Criticism," in Richard A. Muller and John L. Thompson (eds), *Biblical Interpretation in the Era of the Reformation: Essays presented to David C. Steinmetz in honor of his sixtieth birthday* (Grand Rapids: W.B. Eerdmans, 1996), 118–40.

80. Ibid.

81. The best treatment of Bibliander's theology remains E. Egli, "Biblianders Leben und Schriften" in his *Analecta Reformatoria* (Zurich: Zürcher & Furrer, 1901). On predestination, see 70–79. A lucid outline in English of Bibliander's teachings is to be found in J. Wayne Baker, *Heinrich Bullinger and the Covenant. The Other Reformed Tradition* (Athens, Ohio: Ohio University Press, 1980), 39–41.

82. Egli, "Biblianders Leben," 72–73.

83. In the summer of 1535 there was an epistolary exchange between Bibliander and Myconius on the subject of predestination. Myconius upheld the orthodox position against Bibliander's position that God's mercy is freely offered to all, and that the damned lose their salvation on account of their rejection of that mercy. To say that God predestined some to perdition was for Bibliander unthinkable. Egli, "Biblianders Leben," 74.

dispute in the early 1560s had long roots: Bibliander's inaugural lecture on Isaiah, delivered in 1532 in the wake of Zwingli's death, contained a reference to the position of Zwingli which had so appalled both Luther and later Reformed theologians, the divine illumination of the pagans.[84] In his theological work, Bibliander saw in Melanchthon a fellow opponent of the new teaching on predestination which was being forced on the Reformed churches by Calvin. This clearly made his position within the Zurich church very difficult. In 1560 an open quarrel between Martyr and Bibliander resulted in the latter's dismissal; it was a moment of great sadness for Bullinger who, for almost thirty years, had attended Bibliander's daily lectures on the Scriptures. It is an elegant irony that the same bout of the plague carried away both Bibliander and Martyr to continue their dispute in the next world.

In the last years of this dispute over universalism Melanchthon was very much on Bibliander's mind. He wrote an extensive commentary on Melanchthon's dream *Hyena*. Bibliander had clearly read and absorbed Melanchthon's work on history, though the precise connections require further study. Bibliander's *totius historiae ordine rerum ac temporis naturali digestae*, a world history of the evangelical teaching, shares Melanchthon's views on the centrality of history to the Gospel. The work is organized into *loci*, with Bibliander's universalism providing the key intellectual underpinning. Under the locus *Homo* Bibliander wrote:

> Neither the mercy of God, nor the foreknowledge of God, nor the election and predetermination of God contradicts the free will of men. I do not mean the Pelagians, who boast of fulfilling the divine law and thereby achieve salvation without the mercy of God, but those who find in human nature a true judgement of God, given to them by the wisest and greatest Creator.[85]

Under the rubric Melanchthon and the Swiss it would be straightforward to provide a long list of contacts and associations, and indeed there is room for such a study. This essay, however, has attempted something else: it has sought to provide an impressionistic sense of the ambiguities involved in a relationship which existed on many levels: hospitality, po-

---

84. The most comprehensive study of the row over Bibliander's position on predestination remains Joachim Staedtke, "Der Zürcher Prädestinationsstreit von 1560" *Zwingliana* 9 (1953), 536–46.

85. Cited from Egli, "Biblianders Leben," 128.

lemic, consolation, friendship, betrayal, bonds of intellectual enquiry, myth and symbolism. All of these epithets and many more belong to a study seeking to understand a relationship so coloured by contemporary and subsequent confessional polemic. The story must be examined from different angles and perspectives, only some of which could be afforded a mention here. In the study of late medieval and early modern religious cultures historians have become increasingly sensitive to how religion was received, appropriated, and localized. The recent interest in Melanchthon sparked by the celebrations of 1997 is timely reminder that this applies equally to learned as well as to popular cultures.

3

Melanchthon's Reception in Basel

Amy Nelson Burnett

Melanchthon never visited Basel, and to judge from his correspondence he had very few personal connections with the Swiss city on the Rhine. That does not mean, however, that Melanchthon was not important for Basel. On the contrary, the Wittenberg reformer had significant links with the city's church, its university and, perhaps most importantly, with its printing houses. The ties between Melanchthon and Basel evolved over time, reflecting to various degrees Melanchthon's prominence as theologian, pedagogue and humanist. I will describe the changing nature of Melanchthon's reception in Basel by looking first at his personal contacts with Baslers and then at his relations with Basel's printing industry.

I. Early Personal Contacts

Given Basel's status as a center of humanism and of the early evangelical movement, it is not surprising that the young Melanchthon corresponded with the Basel humanist circle and that his early career was avidly followed by them. Not long after his arrival in Wittenberg in 1519, Melanchthon wrote to Wolfgang Capito, at that time cathedral preacher in Basel. According to Melanchthon's letter, he was encouraged to seek Capito's friendship by Johannes Oecolampadius, an old friend from student days at Tübingen.[1] A few months later Melanchthon attested to his friendship with Oecolampadius, who was at that time the cathedral preacher in Augsburg, by dedicating his account of the Leipzig disputation to him,[2] and the two continued to correspond after Oecolampadius' return to Basel in 1523.[3] Yet another member of the Basel humanist cir-

1. Melanchthon to Capito, May 17, 1519; Heinz Scheible, ed., *Melanchthons Briefwechsel, Kritische und kommentierte Gesamtausgabe* (Stuttgart-Bad Cannstatt: Frommann-holzboog, 1977–; hereafter *MBW*), Texte 1: 129–30, no. 57.

2. Ernst Staehelin, ed., *Briefe und Akten zum Leben Oekolampads, zum vierhundertjährigen Jubiläum der Basler Reformation*, 2 vols., (Leipzig: Heinsius, 1927–34), 1: 97–99, no. 63.

3. Melanchthon to Oecolampadius, May 21, 1523; Staehelin, *Briefe und Akten* 1: 221, no. 154.

cle, the Franciscan Konrad Pellikan, kept Melanchthon informed of the progress of the evangelical movement in Basel,[4] while Europe's most famous humanist, Erasmus of Rotterdam, continued his occasional correspondence with the young Melanchthon after moving from Louvain to Basel in 1521.[5]

Melanchthon also met or renewed his contacts with three men in Wittenberg who would later hold significant posts at the University of Basel. The first of these, Simon Grynaeus, had attended Latin school at Pforzheim with Melanchthon and spent a year in Wittenberg before being called to teach at the University of Heidelberg in 1524. Melanchthon dedicated a published oration to the accomplished Greek scholar, and the two men kept in touch after Grynaeus had moved to Heidelberg.[6] In 1529 Grynaeus moved to Basel, where he first held the chair in Greek and later transferred to the chair in New Testament.[7]

The second, Martin Cellarius, was also a school friend of Melanchthon's, this time from Tübingen. In 1519 Cellarius published an open letter to Melanchthon expressing his disbelief that Melanchthon could have attacked their common friend Johannes Eck, but two years later he moved to Wittenberg and lived with Melanchthon while giving private lectures. Influenced by the Zwickau prophets, Cellarius broke with the Wittenberg Reformers in 1522 and left the city. He returned to Wittenberg briefly in 1526, then lived in Strasbourg for several years. In the mid-1530s he moved to Basel where, now using his family name of Borrhaus, he became the professor of Old Testament theology in 1544.[8]

The final Wittenberg figure who would later move to Basel was, of course, Andreas Bodenstein von Karlstadt, who was Borrhaus' predecessor as professor of Old Testament at Basel from 1535 until his death in

---

4. Pellikan to Melanchthon, Nov. 30, 1521, Texte 1: 385–86, no. 182.

5. Melanchthon's first extant letter to Erasmus is from early 1519, *MBW* Texte 1: 95–97, no. 38. Pellikan also transmitted news of Melanchthon to Erasmus, cf. Erasmus' mention of Melanchthon's letter to Pellikan, May, 1524, *MBW* Texte 1: 130–31, no. 322; Erasmus to Melanchthon, Sept. 6, 1524, *MBW* Texte 1: 167–69, no. 341.

6. Dedication from 1523, *MBW* Texte 1: 67–69, no. 277; Melanchthon's reference to a letter from Grynaeus in his own letter to Joachim Camerarius, Dec. 9, 1524, *MBW* Texte 1: 206–8, no. 359.

7. On Grynaeus, see the chapter by René Teuteberg *in Der Reformation Verpflichtet: Gestalten und Gestalter in Stadt und Landschaft Basel aus fünf Jahrhunderten* (Basel: Christoph Merian Verlag, 1979), 29–32.

8. On Borrhaus' early years, see Lucia Felici, *Tra riforma ed eresia. La Giovinezza di Martin Borrhaus (1499–1528)* (Florence: L.S. Olschki, 1995).

1541. His conflicts with Luther and Melanchthon are so familiar that they need not be described here.

During the early years of the Reformation movement, then, Melanchthon had several friends among Basel humanists and future Basel theologians. The fact that most of these friendships dated back to Melanchthon's school years indicates the importance of a common educational experience for the later formation of humanist networks throughout Germany. In the early 1520s, the shared religious concerns of these humanists and their common opposition to Luther's Catholic critics brought them closer together. With the outbreak of the eucharistic controversy in 1525, however, Melanchthon's friendly correspondence came to an end with all except Erasmus. Given Erasmus' unique position, I will not discuss further his relations with Melanchthon.[9] Melanchthon had no further epistolary contact with either Borrhaus or Karlstadt, although he and Luther sent a letter to the Basel Senate requesting its support for Karlstadt's widow and children in May 1542.[10] By early 1526, both Capito and Pellikan had left Basel, the former for Strasbourg and the latter for Zurich. That left Oecolampadius as the only—but also the oldest and the closest—of Melanchthon's former friends in Basel during the later 1520s.

The Basel reformer's close association with Zwingli and his active participation in the polemical battle over the Lord's Supper proved to be an insurmountable obstacle for his relations with Melanchthon. In several letters written to Melanchthon between 1525 and 1529, Occolampadius cited their long friendship while defending his own theological position.[11] Melanchthon finally responded to Oecolampadius while attending the Reichstag at Speyer in 1529, acknowledging his unchanged esteem for the Basel reformer but defending his own belief in Christ's real presence in the Lord's Supper and his opposition to the Zwinglians.[12] His

---

9. On the relations between the two men, see Karl Heinz Oelrich, *Der spätere Erasmus und die Reformation* (Münster: Aschendorff, 1961), 46–49; Wilhelm Schenk, "Erasmus and Melanchthon," *Heythrop Journal* 8 (1967): 249–59.

10. WABr 10: 71f, no. 3756.

11. Cf. 14 Nov. 1525, Staehelin, *Briefe und Akten* 1: 418–20, no. 304; May 21, 1528, Staehelin, *Briefe und Akten* 2: 189, no. 579; and March 31, 1529, Staehelin, *Briefe und Akten* 2: 292–95, no. 645. In a letter to Konrad Sam of Dec. 21, 1528, Oecolampadius refers to yet another unanswered letter to Melanchthon sent via the Frankfurt book fair, i.e. in the fall of 1528; Staehelin, *Briefe und Akten* 2: 271, no. 624.

12. April, 1529], Staehelin, *Briefe und Akten* 2: 308–10, no. 652. On the political (as opposed to theological) reasons for Melanchthon's opposition to the Zwinglians in the period between the Speyerer Reichstag of 1529 and the Augsburger Reichstag of 1530,

letter was published shortly afterwards and Oecolampadius included it, along with his own response, in his dialogue, *Quid de eucharistia veteres senserint*, published in 1530. It would take us too far afield from the general topic of Melanchthon's relations with Basel to describe further the interaction between Melanchthon and Oecolampadius regarding the eucharistic controversy,[13] and Oecolampadius' death in November 1531 prevented any re-kindling of their friendship that might have occurred in the wake of Bucer's mediating activities.

Over the course of the 1530s and 1540s, Melanchthon corresponded occasionally with Grynaeus and established new contacts with several Baslers. But before examining these contacts, and as a context for discussing their significance, let us first consider another aspect of Melanchthon's relations with Basel: his importance for the city's printing houses.

II. Melanchthon and the Basel Printers

After Wittenberg, Basel produced the largest number of Melanchthon imprints during the reformer's lifetime. I have identified 203 Basel imprints containing Melanchthon's work printed between 1518 and 1560. Of these, approximately three-quarters (150 imprints) were written entirely or in part by Melanchthon (including his commentaries on Biblical or classical texts), while the remainder were either editions, translations or paraphrases or contain a letter, a preface or other introductory material by him.[14]

see Wilhelm H. Neuser, *Die Abendmahlslehre Melanchthons in ihrer geschichtlichen Entwicklung (1519–1530)* (Neukirchen-Vluyn: Neukirchener Verlag, 1968), 291–313.

13. It is discussed, inter alia, in Walther Köhler, *Zwingli und Luther: Ihre Streit über das Abendmahl nach seinen politischen und religiösen Beziehungen, Quellen und Forschungen zur Reformationsgeschichte 6* (Gütersloh: Bertelsmann, 1924), 799–804; Ernst Staehelin, *Das theologische Lebenswerk Johannes Oekolampads, Quellen und Forschungen zur Reformationsgeschichte 21* (Leipzig: Heinsius, 1939), 598–616, and especially Ralph Walter Quere, *Melanchthon's Christum Cognoscere. Christ's Efficacious Presence in the Eucharistic Theology of Melanchthon* (Nieuwkoop: de Graaf, 1977), 310–62.

14. Sources for assembling the bibliographical data base: Ralph Keen, *A Checklist of Melanchthon Imprints Through 1560* (St. Louis: Center for Reformation Research, 1988); both the printed version of VD-16 (*Verzeichnis der im deutschen Sprachbereich erschienenen Drucke des XVI. Jahrhunderts* [Stuttgart: Hiersemann, 1983–]) and the on-line version with search function (www.hab.de/avanti/index.html); *MBW*; CR; WA; and the Buchdrucker und -Verleger Katalog of the Basel Universitätsbibliothek. Guido Kisch identified 155 publications by seventeen different printers through 1560; Guido Kisch, *Melanchthons Rechts- und Soziallehre* (Berlin: Walter de Gruyter, 1967), 53 n.5.

Twenty of the 33 printers active in Basel during this period—thus almost two-thirds of Basel's printers—published at least one Melanchthon imprint. Even this figure understates the attraction of Melanchthon's works for Basel's printers. Of the 26 printers established in Basel between 1518–1545, only eight did not publish any Melanchthon imprints, and all of these were either transitory businesses or produced only a few works during these years.

Like Melanchthon's personal contacts with Baslers, the number of Melanchthon publications was very high in the early years of the Reformation and then fell drastically after the onset of the eucharistic controversy (Graph 1).[15] In the six years between 1518–1523, Basel printers turned out 45 Melanchthon imprints. About one-third of these (sixteen imprints) were reprints of works already published in Basel. By contrast, over the next fourteen years (1524–1537), only 29 Melanchthon imprints were published in Basel, with reprints slightly outnumbering first Basel imprints (sixteen reprint editions and thirteen first Basel imprints). Another turning point came in 1538. Ten imprints were published in that year alone, signaling a renewed interest in Melanchthon's works among Basel's printers. Most of these were first Basel imprints of school texts that would be reprinted in the coming years. For the remaining 22 years of Melanchthon's life, publication of his works was comparatively stable, especially for reprints. From 1540 to 1546 Basel's printers generally produced seven Melanchthon imprints each year, but the political tensions surrounding the outbreak of the Schmalkaldic war led to a precipitous drop in the publication of new Melanchthon imprints between 1547 and 1569.[16] Production during the 1550s never quite returned to the previous level, but it did rise to an average of between five and six Melanchthon imprints per year.

What works by Melanchthon did the Basel printers produce? To answer this question, I have divided the imprints into four general categories: theological works by Melanchthon; humanist or pedagogical works by him (including translations, editions and commentaries on classical authors); Melanchthon's endorsements, by way of a preface, dedicatory epistle or other contribution, of the work of another author or editor,

---

15. I have used two year periods to compensate for the sharp swings in the production of early modern printing houses, due to the length of time it took to print longer works; cf. Miriam Chrisman, *Lay Culture, Learned Culture: Books and Social Change in Strasbourg, 1480–1599* (New Haven: Yale University Press, 1982),

16. There were only two Melanchthon imprints in 1547, four in 1548, and two in 1549.

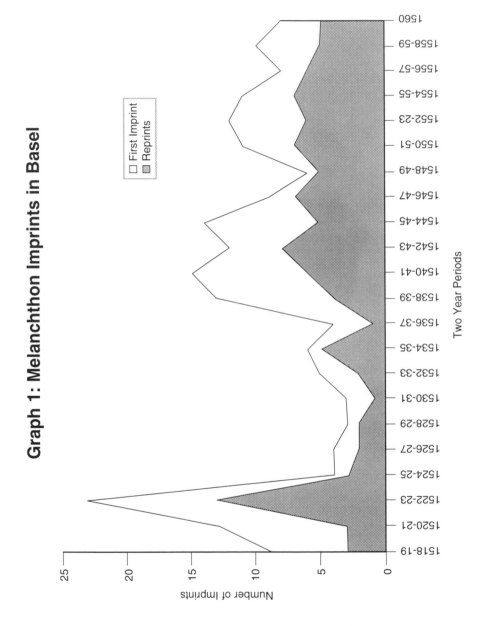

Graph 1: Melanchthon Imprints in Basel

whether theological or humanist in nature; and finally, letter collections and other imprints whose contribution by Melanchthon I have been unable to identify further. These categories are very general, and my distribution of individual works among the four categories could in some cases be disputed.[17] Despite these problems of categorization, however, the groups are sufficient to reveal general trends in the types of works by Melanchthon that were produced in Basel.

Taken as a whole, the largest number of Melanchthon imprints were scholarly or pedagogical texts: slightly less than half (97 out of 203 imprints) fall into this category. Theological texts made up another quarter of the total output (52 imprints). There are 40 imprints with endorsements by Melanchthon. Of the remaining fourteen imprints, six contained letters of Melanchthon to Erasmus and one his letters to Simon Grynaeus.

These total figures do not fully reveal the changing pattern of Melanchthon imprints (Graph 2). By far the largest share of theological imprints were published in the earliest phase of the Reformation: 27 theological works were published between 1518–25, slightly more than half of the 49 total Melanchthon imprints in this period. Thirteen of these theological works were published in 1523 alone. Reflecting the intense printed debate of this period, many of these publications were polemical—defenses of Luther and attacks on the Catholic church—and several were either reprinted by the same printer or published by two or more Basel printers.[18] In 1523 the Basel presses produced Melanchthon's commentary on Romans and I and II Corinthians as well eight editions of his commentaries on the Gospels of Matthew and John either separately or in a combined edition—obviously runaway best sellers! Basel

---

17. For instance, imprints such as Melanchthon's oration, "An Exhortation to the Study of Pauline Doctrine" could easily be assigned to either the theological or humanist/pedagogical category. To provide some consistency, when a work could be classified as belonging to two or more categories, I put the imprint in the category according to the sequence theological, humanist, endorsement or other.

18. Both Andreas Cratander and Johann Froben published Melanchthon's account of the Leipzig disputation; Adam Petri published both Latin and German versions of his apology for Luther against the Paris theologians; Cratander and Petri both published his oration for Luther against Thomas Placentinus.

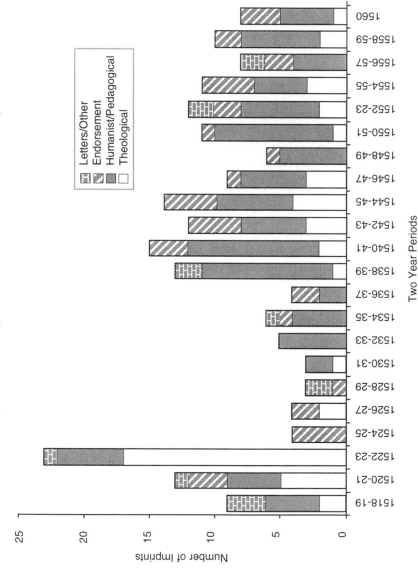

Graph 2: Categories of Melanchthon Imprints

printers also published three editions of Melanchthon's *Loci Communes* during this period. Among the humanist/pedagogical imprints, Melanchthon's textbooks dominated: there were four editions of his *Compendiaria Dialectices Ratio* and three of his rhetoric texts. Only twelve of the Melanchthon imprints during these years were the works of others, seven of these being Melanchthon's endorsement of works by his colleagues in Wittenberg: three imprints of Luther's Galatians commentary and two of his Psalms commentary, as well as two imprints of Bugenhagen's Psalms commentary. Four of the remaining Melanchthon imprints were volumes containing a letter from Melanchthon to Erasmus, and one was an index to Melanchthon's *Loci Communes*.

The eucharistic controversy, and Basel's alignment with the Zwinglians, obviously had an impact on Melanchthon's appeal to the Basel publishing market. The city's printers produced only three of the Wittenberger's theological works over the next twelve years (1526–37): a brief commentary on a passage from Colossians and Melanchthon's German catechism, both published in 1527, and his letter to Johann Oecolampadius included in the latter's *Quid de eucharistia veteres senserint* (1530). The other Melanchthon imprints published during the second half of the decade contained very little that could be directly attributed to the reformer: two editions of Bucer's German translation of Bugenhagen's Psalms commentary (with interpolations supporting a Zwinglian interpretation of the Lord's Supper that Melanchthon did not endorse) that included Melanchthon's original prefatory letter, two more editions of Erasmus' correspondence, and a reference aid to Melanchthon's text book on rhetoric. From 1530, Melanchthon's pedagogical works began to find favor with Basel's printers, appearing at a rate of one or two per year up through 1537. The majority of these were text editions, translations and/or commentaries on classical authors rather than independent works.[19]

At the end of the 1530s, Basel's printers again started producing Melanchthon imprints in quantity. Two significant developments helped revive the interest of Basel printers in Melanchthon as theologian and pedagogue. From the theological side, the signing of the Wittenberg

---

19. In 1531 Heinrich Petri produced a volume that included pedagogical treatises by Agricola, Erasmus and Melanchthon; it was reprinted in 1533 and, in an expanded edition, in 1537. There were four imprints of a Greek-Latin lexicon that contained a brief treatise by Melanchthon on the Greek method of writing dates. The text editions, translations or commentaries by Melanchthon published during this period included works by Plutarch, Terence, Virgil, Cicero, and Euclid.

Concord in 1536 established a fragile truce to the eucharistic controversy. From the scholarly side, the University of Basel, which had reopened in 1532 with only a handful of students, was given new statutes
in 1539 and from that point on attracted an increasing number of students from all parts of Europe. Reflecting especially this latter development, the majority of the Melanchthon imprints in Basel over the next
two decades were humanist text editions or commentaries. After a burst
of twenty humanist imprints between 1538 and 1541, these scholarly
works were produced at the fairly steady rate of two or three imprints
per year over the next two decades. The most popular imprints were
editions of Cicero, Terence, Ovid, and Virgil.[20] Melanchthon's Latin
grammar was published three times and his Greek grammar once after
1539. Basel's printers also produced other linguistic textbooks with prefaces by Melanchthon or incorporating his work.[21]

Melanchthon's theological works also returned to favor with Basel's
printers, although not to the extent that they had enjoyed before 1525.
The market for theological books depended on the prevailing state of
relations between Lutheran and Reformed theologians, and the production of theological texts was therefore more volatile than it was for humanist texts. Beginning in 1538, the number of Melanchthon's theological works gradually increased, only to drop off in 1548–1549, in the wake
of the Schmalkaldic War and the controversies surrounding the
Augsburg Interim. For the next decade his theological works were published at the rate of about one per year.

The Wittenberger's most popular theological work printed in Basel
was unquestionably his *Loci Communes*. The second version of the *Loci* was
published in 1543 (after being included in the five volumes of Melanchthon's *Opera* published in 1541), and seven printings of the third version
appeared in Basel before the author's death in 1560. Other theological
works included the acts of the Council of Trent with a refutation by Melanchthon, the Saxon Confession submitted at Trent in 1551, and a
Greek translation of the Augsburg Confession. Melanchthon's explication
of the Lord's Prayer was also included in Myconius' Latin translation of

20. There were nine imprints of Melanchthon's annotations on various works of
Cicero (with or without the Ciceronian texts commented on), nine imprints of Terence's
commentaries with Melanchthon's annotations, five imprints of Melanchthon's comments on Virgil and four imprints of his comments on Ovid.

21. For instance, Thomas Linacre's *de emendata structura Latini* (four imprints), Michael Neander's *Graecae linguae erotemata* (five imprints) and the Greek-Latin lexicon
(seven imprints after 1540).

Oecolampadius' catechism, which was memorized by all students in the city's Latin schools. As a defender of Protestant doctrine against the Catholics, Melanchthon apparently appealed to the Baslers, and during the polemical lull between the signing of the Wittenberg Concord and the outbreak of the second eucharistic controversy, his other theological works were attractive as well.

Who were the printers who published Melanchthon's works in Basel? During the first decade of the Reformation Adam Petri produced 26 Melanchthon imprints, fifteen of them theological works, four humanist or pedagogical works, and seven others, including commentaries by Luther and Bugenhagen with prefaces by Melanchthon. After Adam Petri's death in 1527, his son Heinrich assumed control of the printing house. Heinrich Petri had studied in Wittenberg in the mid-1520s, but unlike his father he had little interest in publishing Melanchthon's theological works.[22] In 1535 he issued a new edition of Bugenhagen's Psalms commentary with Melanchthon's preface, a work his father had published four times in the 1520s,[23] but Heinrich Petri's other Melanchthon imprints were school texts: three editions of a handbook of pedagogical treatises that included one by Melanchthon, and three editions of Ovid with commentary by Melanchthon. Together with Valentin Curio, he also printed six editions of a Greek-Latin lexicon that included a brief treatise by Melanchthon.

Nicolaus Brylinger made a business of producing Melanchthon's classical editions for teaching purposes. After publishing Melanchthon's Greek grammar in 1538, Brylinger went on to produce several extremely successful editions, with multiple reprints, of texts by Terence, Cicero, and Virgil, as well as other school texts of works provided with prefaces by Melanchthon. In all, Brylinger produced 27 Melanchthon imprints.

By far the largest number of imprints were produced by Johann Oporinus, who published 46 works between 1542 and 1560.[24] Oporinus ran the largest printing house in Basel in the mid-sixteenth century, and

22. On Heinrich Petri, see the biographical note in Alfred Hartmann and Beat Rudolf Jenny, eds., *Die Amerbachkorrespondenz* (Basel: Universitätsbibliothek, 1942–) 7: 177–82.

23. He may have been hoping to capitalize on what had been a financial success for his father, who published two editions of the Latin original in 1524 and two editions of Bucer's German translation in 1526.

24. On Oporinus, see Martin Steinmann, *Johannes Oporinus, ein Basler Buchdrucker um die Mitte des 16. Jahrhunderts* (Basel/Stuttgart: Helbing & Lichtenhahn, 1967).

this is admittedly only a small proportion of the estimated 1000 works produced by him, but he dominated the market in Melanchthon imprints during the 1550s: 70 percent of the imprints with identified printers published after 1551 were published by Oporinus.[25] Of the 46 Oporinus editions, twelve were theological works, twenty were humanist/pedagogical works or editions, ten were works by other authors with a preface by Melanchthon and four were letter collections or other works.

Oporinus' most successful Melanchthon imprints were the Wittenberger's textbooks: the *Loci Communes*, which Oporinus published five times between 1543–1560 (and at least two more editions after 1560) and his Latin grammar, which Oporinus produced three times between 1550–1557. One need not look too far afield to explain the popularity of these works: in 1551, the university of Basel revised its statutes to require that all beginning students use Melanchthon's Latin grammar.[26] Then, as now, publishing texts that all students had to buy was a profitable business! There was no similar statutory requirement that theology students study the *Loci*, but student notes have been preserved in Basel's university library from a course of lectures on the *Loci* given by the Antistes, Simon Sulzer, in (ostensibly Reformed) Basel.[27] Oporinus may have been publishing the *Loci* for a larger audience in Germany, but apparently he also had a profitable market for the work in Basel as well.

Melanchthon met Oporinus in the fall of 1536, while the Wittenberger was visiting the University of Tübingen at the behest of Duke Ulrich; Oporinus carried a letter from Melanchthon to his friend Jakob Milichius in Freiburg.[28] Until 1542 Oporinus taught Greek at Basel's university, but in that year he turned his full energies to the printing business. One of his first publications, a translation of the *Qur'an* with an accompanying collection of letters by prominent theologians justifying its publication, got him into trouble with the Basel Senate; production was halted and Oporinus was jailed briefly. Melanchthon, who had provided a preface for the Qur'an, followed the affair as closely as he was able from distant Wittenberg, passing on information to his friend Johannes Lang in Er-

25. Thirty-two out of 46 imprints.

26. Rudolf Thommen, *Geschichte der Universität Basel, 1532–1632* (Basel: Detloff, 1889), 342.

27. Basel Universitätsbibliothek Handschriftenabteilung A VII 54; the lectures are undated but were probably given in the 1550s or early 1560s. Sulzer came to Basel in 1548; he taught Hebrew from 1552–54, when he was appointed to the chair in New Testament. In 1564 he transferred to the chair in Old Testament.

28. CR 3: 164, no. 1469; *MBW Regesten 2*, no. 1793.

furt. Melanchthon's interest was not purely dispassionate; he had sent Lang's manuscript of the Greek church father Epiphanios to Oporinus to be printed, and he was annoyed that the Basel printer would prefer to print the "delusions of Mohammed" first.[29]

Almost all of Oporinus' Melanchthon imprints were reprints of works that had first been published elsewhere, but Melanchthon did send a few works, like the Epiphanios, to Basel for their first printing. In 1551, for instance, he forwarded a translation of Heliodorus into Latin by Stanislaus Warszewicki to Oporinus for publication.[30] He also provided a preface to Wenceslaus Grodecius' *Tabula Poloniae*, published by Oporinus in 1558.[31]

It is difficult to say more about the professional (let alone the personal) relationship between the theologian and the printer, given the fact that only a few letters remain from their correspondence. Oporinus sent books to Melanchthon, sometimes via the latter's son-in-law Kaspar Peucer, from the Frankfurt book fair.[32] In view of the difficulties of sending letters from Basel to Wittenberg, it is understandable that Oporinus would take advantage of the Frankfurt fair to correspond with Melanchthon.[33] The two men met again in person in 1557, while Melanchthon was attending the colloquy in Worms. Oporinus and his fellow Basler Nicolaus Brylinger had again encountered censorship problems, this time over the publication by Brylinger's son-in-law of a work that

29. CR 4: 909, no. 2586; CR 5:45, no. 2643. On the Qur'an affair, see Steinmann, *Oporinus*, 20–31. The work by Epiphanios did not appear until 1544; cf. *MBW* Regesten 5, no. 3639 (CR 4: 852f, no. 2532)

30. *MBW* Regesten 6, no. 6056 (CR 7: 765, no. 4879). The work appeared the following year.

31. *MBW* Regesten 7, no. 8478.

32. Cf. *MBW* Regesten 6, no. 6056 (CR 7: 765, no. 4879), where Melanchthon thanks Oporinus for books sent; in a letter to Peucer dated Sept. 1556, Oporinus responds to Peucer's requests for books, tells him what works he is considering publishing, and asks Peucer to tell his father-in-law that if Melanchthon would provide a copy of Bernard von Breidenbach's account of his pilgrimage to the Holy Land, along with a preface, Oporinus would publish it. Melanchthon did not take Oporinus up on his offer. Otto Clemen, "Vier Briefe des Buchdruckers Johann Oporin an Kaspar Peucer," in idem, *Kleine Schriften zur Reformationsgeschichte (1897–1944)*, ed. Ernst Koch (Repr. Leipzig: Zentralantiquariat der DDR, 1987), 184–187.

33. Cf. the complaints to Melanchthon about lost letters made by another Basler, Celio Secundo Curione, letters of Mar. 1, 1551, and Dec. 1, 1552; Otto Clemen, "Briefe aus Basel an Melanchthon," in idem, *Kleine Schriften*, 257–73. In the 1520s Oecolampadius had also relied on the book fairs as the most reliable means of sending a letter to Wittenberg; cf. above.

gave an unflattering (although accurate) account of Maurice of Saxony's motives during the Schmalkaldic wars. Oporinus appealed for Melanchthon's intervention with the Elector's secretary, who had had Brylinger jailed and who threatened to do the same to Oporinus.[34]

Melanchthon maintained contact with yet another individual involved with the Basel printing industry: the Bohemian humanist Sigismund Gelenius. Gelenius had stayed with Melanchthon for a few months in 1524 before moving to Basel, where he became a corrector for the Frobens.[35] Melanchthon had tried to recruit Gelenius for a teaching position in Nuremberg in 1526, but Gelenius had rejected the offer and remained in Basel for the rest of his life.[36] Gelenius dedicated an edition of Aristophanes' comedies to Melanchthon in 1547,[37] and in a sense Melanchthon returned the favor after Gelenius' death in a eulogy published in 1554.[38]

This discussion of both Oporinus and Gelenius brings us back to a consideration of Melanchthon's personal contacts with Basel and Baslers during the later decades of his life. Similar to the pattern of Melanchthon imprints in Basel, there was a gradual increase of contacts between Melanchthon and Basel following the signing of the Wittenberg Concord, but Basel remained on the periphery of Melanchthon's concerns. Basel's Senate and its church leaders took a new interest in Wittenberg as Bucer and Melanchthon were working out the Wittenberg Concord, but most of their contact with and news from Wittenberg came via Strasbourg and Bucer, not from Wittenberg or from Melanchthon himself.[39]

With few exceptions the letters that did pass directly between Wittenberg and Basel were polite but superficial, generally recommendations for the letter's bearer. Many of these were students going from Basel to Wittenberg, or vice versa.[40] Others were religious refugees, such as the

---

34. *MBW* Regesten 7, no. 8381; cf. Steinmann, *Oporinus,* 92–93.

35. Staehelin, Briefe und Akten 1: 283–84, no. 199. On Gelenius, see *Amerbachkorrespondenz* 9/1: 335–53.

36. CR 1: 720, no. 316 and 1: 806, no. 393.

37. *MBW* Regesten 4, no. 4494.

38. The eulogy was contained in a preface to Wenceslaus Nicolaides, *Cantiones evangelicae . . . quae in ecclesiis Boemicis . . . canuntur*, Wittenberg: Rhau, 1554; cf. *Amerbachkorrespondenz* 9/1: 336.

39. An example of this type of transmission is the portion of Melanchthon's letter to Bucer that was copied by the Basel pastor Johann Gast in his letter to Bullinger, Oct. 25, 1548; *MBW* Regesten 5, no. 5310 (CR 7: 157, no. 4372).

40. Cf. Myconius' recommendation for several Basel students returning to Wittenberg, May 1551 (*MBW* Regesten 6, no. 6090), Amerbach's recommendation of three

Spaniard Franciscus Dryander, who moved from Wittenberg to south
Germany and ended up working as a corrector for Oporinus in the fall
of 1546, or the Italian Lelio Sozzini, who arrived in Wittenberg in 1550
provided with a recommendation from Oswald Myconius, the head of
Basel's church.[41] Sozzini's countryman and fellow refugee Celio Secundo
Curione, who taught on the arts faculty of Basel's university, tried several
times to establish more regular correspondence with Melanchthon, but
the Wittenberger's responses contained little more than rhetorical plati-
tudes.[42]

III. Melanchthon and Basel: Some Conclusions

It is clear, in looking at both Melanchthon's personal relations with
Baslers and his professional contacts with Basel's printing houses, that
after the opening years of the Reformation, Melanchthon was much
more important for Basel than Basel was for Melanchthon. The break-up
of Basel's first humanist sodality in the early 1520s, combined with the
theological breach between Wittenberg and Switzerland over the Lord's
Supper, ended Melanchthon's direct contacts with the city. Oecolampadius' persistent efforts to win Melanchthon's acceptance, if not his approval, of Zwinglian doctrine were fruitless. Even after the end of the
first eucharistic controversy, Basel remained on the periphery for Melanchthon. His contacts with the city were infrequent and almost exclusively professional.

Melanchthon's neglect of Basel after 1525 was at first reciprocated.
Basel's printers were extremely important in spreading Melanchthon's
works through south Germany and Switzerland in the early 1520s, but
they followed the change in theological climate, and for more than a
decade after 1525 they showed little interest in Melanchthon's works.
After a fragile truce was worked out with the Wittenberg Concord, however, Melanchthon's reputation as a world-renowned humanist scholar
and pedagogue again drew the attention of Basel's printers. They saw a
profitable market for his school texts, both in Germany and for their own
university students, and they were quick to provide those texts. Mel-

French students in 1558 (*Amerbachkorrespondenz* 10/2: 747–50, no. 4331); and Melanchthon's recommendation of students to Amerbach in 1545 (*Amerbachkorrespondenz* 6: 140,
no. 2717), and again in 1551 (*Amerbachkorrespondenz* 8: 9–10, no. 3391).

41. *MBW* Regesten 6, no. 5826.

42. On Curione's correspondence with Melanchthon, see Markus Kutter, *Celio
Secundo Curione. Sein Leben und sein Werk (1503–1569)* (Basel: Helbing & Lichtenhahn,
1955), 147–48, and the correspondence contained in Clemen, "Briefe aus Basel."

anchthon's mediating position in the eucharistic controversy also made his theological works attractive to Basel's church leaders, who increasingly fell under suspicion of having Lutheran leanings over the course of the 1550s. Scholarship (and the desire for profit!) ultimately triumphed over theological politics in Basel's relationship with Melanchthon, but Melanchthon's own irenic theological position helped make that triumph possible.

Melanchthon's evolving relationship with Basel is perhaps best exemplified in the life of Bonifacius Amerbach, one of the city's most famous "native sons" during the middle third of the sixteenth century. Born in 1495, Amerbach was a young law student at the time that the Reformation began. His correspondence reflects the intellectual and religious excitement of the early 1520s, and in particular the esteem he and his friends had for Philip Melanchthon, who seemed to incorporate the best of both the humanist and the evangelical movements. To his former teacher Ulrich Zasius, Amerbach wrote that "Philip, though young, [is] nevertheless most learned not only in the knowledge of humane letters but also of theology and philosophy." A friend studying in Wittenberg reported on the unpleasant conditions in the city, concluding that "if Melanchthon were not teaching the arts and Christ with such a fervent spirit, I swear I wouldn't remain here another day or night." From Basel Amerbach was able to answer requests for copies of Melanchthon's works from friends in Italy and France.[43]

Amerbach's early enthusiasm for the evangelical movement gradually faded, particularly after the open break between Luther and Erasmus.[44]

---

43. Amerbach to Ulrich Zasius, Aug. 22, 1519, *Amerbachkorrespondenz* 2, no. 675; Albert Burer to Basilius Amerbach (Bonifacius' brother), Aug. 31, 1521, no. 809. Request for and receipt of Melanchthon's works from Alciati and Parmentier, 2: 318–20, no. 300; 2: 383, no. 876; 2: 440, no. 929; 2: 448, no. 938. Cf. Guido Kisch's description of Amerbach's early correspondence and of the works by Melanchthon owned by Amerbach now in the Basel Universitätsbibliothek, *Melanchthons Rechts- und Soziallehre* (Berlin: Walter de Gruyter, 1967), 54–59. Kisch does not describe Amerbach's later correspondence with Melanchthon, because the later volumes of the *Amerbachkorrespondenz* had not been published when he wrote his book.

44. Amerbach was a devoted disciple of Erasmus and the administrator of the foundation created with Erasmus' legacy. After the official introduction of the Reformation in Basel in 1529, Amerbach ran afoul of the authorities by refusing to receive the Lord's Supper in its new Zwinglian form. In 1532, as his troubles with the authorities became more acute, he wrote a letter to Luther describing his difficult situation and stating that he would accept Luther's and Melanchthon's judgment in the affair; *Amerbachkorrespondenz* 4: 48–49; the letter apparently was never sent. Amerbach was eventually reconciled to the eucharistic doctrine of the Basel church, primarily through Bucer's mediation.

As his own reputation as a jurist grew, Amerbach's attitude towards Melanchthon became more detached. He continued to purchase and to study Melanchthon's works, including his later theological writings published in Wittenberg.[45] Unlike Curione, however, Amerbach did not seek out contact with Melanchthon, and when he received letters in 1545 and again in 1551 from the Wittenberger commending students to him, he did not use them as an opportunity to establish a regular correspondence. Professional respect and personal distance are a far cry from the excited enthusiasm of the early 1520s, but they are also signs of greater maturity and self-confidence. What is true of Bonifacius Amerbach on an individual level can also be applied to the intellectual, religious and printing community in Basel as a whole in its attitude towards Melanchthon by the last years of the Wittenberger's life.

45. Kisch, *Soziallehre*, 56–57 and n. 18, includes Melanchthon's *Examen . . . qua commendatur ministerium Evangelii* (Wittenberg, 1556) and his *ad impios articulos bavariae Inquisitionis* (Wittenberg, 1559) among Amerbach's library.

4

Melanchthon As a Humanist and a Reformer

Deszo Buzogany

Melanchthon is usually considered as both a humanist and a reformer. Many of the books and studies written about him present him as a theologian. It is also worthwhile studying the humanist intellectual components of his personality, since, after all, a great proportion of his works are ones which present him as a deep thinking, thorough intellectual, writing with sublime eloquence.

Both theological debates and the newly-organized church profited a great deal from his humanism; and one should mention in this regard the service he rendered in composing and compiling the confessions. Thus, everything that shapes Melanchthon's theological work with class, its intellectual nature and proper sublimation to the salvation doctrines, was taken from the so-called "pagan arts." He brought into the domain of the church and the faith the useful and usable parts of the enormous amount of classical knowledge and put them in the service of God's Word, while at the same time subordinating them to the Word.

Melanchthon the theologian is also always present in his works written on the topic of the seven liberal arts. To those who know him only through his theological works, his humanism seems exaggerated, and we are almost shocked by the fact that he often refers to these classical authors, expounding these disciplines, or writing eulogies about them. This was self-evident in that age, when scientific work meant quoting the traditions of the classics. The age was that of late humanism. But Melanchthon went further than praising and quoting the classics. He always checked carefully and explored the possibility of building these originally pagan disciplines into the values and education of the Protestant church. In Melanchthon's view they provide a useful service in the better understanding and clearer transmission of God's Word.

"Ut rosa adflorem, flos fructum, fructus odorem, sic schola dat morem, mos sensum, sensus honorem." (As the rose produces flowers, the flowers bear fruits, and the fruits give off a pleasant smell, this is how the school produces virtue, virtue leads to reason, and reason produces appreciation.) This handwritten note dated from the beginning of the 17th century, found on one of the pages of Melanchthon's Grammar brought by some traveling student to Transylvania, fits perfectly with his personality, because after all, he was a thorough educator and served education with his whole life, both within and outside the school. His textbooks played a crucial role in the development of Transylvanian Protestantism, and later, Reformed education in the 16th century. Hundreds of these textbooks are still found in several libraries in Transylvania.

The humanist Melanchthon knew that the disciplines of the trivium, the first section of the seven liberal arts, could only help the reviving Church, if they were used in the service of God's Word. As a result of this rule, the three disciplines of the trivium were integrated in the following way: Grammar gives us the meaning of the original text of Holy Scripture, Dialectic serves the understanding of the text and the consistency of the sermon's content, while Rhetoric gives us God's Word in a way that makes it vivid and effective.

But for the moment let us take a look at Dialectic alone as clear evidence of the humanist and reformer Melanchthon's sublime knowledge. But before we begin a detailed analysis, let us describe briefly the seven liberal arts, to which this discipline belongs.

I always ask my students at the Reformed Theological Seminary in Kolozsvár this trick question: Can you tell me what are the seven liberal arts? My students usually enumerate several art-type activities, like poetry, painting, film etc., which have something to do with the arts of today. So, what are the seven liberal arts?

In higher education in the middle ages, a student yearning for knowledge had to learn quickly this small verse, which would introduce him to the world of the arts (we call them disciplines today): "Gram[matica] loquitur, Dia[lectica] vera docet, Rhet/orica] verba colorat, Mus[ica] canit, Ar[itmetica] numerat, Ge[ographia] ponderat, Ast[rologia] colit astra." (Grammar speaks, dialectics teaches facts, rhetoric colors speech, music sings, arithmetic counts, geography measures, and astrology studies the stars). In the early middle ages the sciences were separated into two groups. Depending on the number and character of the disciplines, they called them "verbal arts" (trivium: grammar, dialectics, rhetoric), and mathematical sciences (quadrivium: arithmetic, music, geometry and astronomy). Obviously the Latin names of these sciences refer to the number of the disciplines in each group. But let us now examine the dialectics of Melanchthon which belongs to the first group, the trivium.

I. The Praise of Dialectics

Melanchthon wrote two essays about dialectics. We do not know when the first, *De Dialectica*, was written. He probably composed it in the earlier period of his life. After a general introduction, he emphasizes the significance of this discipline:

> Among all the arts of humanism, dialectics is the most important, not only because of its usefulness for studying other arts, but also for making judgments in court-trials and in many other matters we deal with in life. Nothing can be taught systematically or learned perfectly without dialectics, which creates methods for every case, shows the origin, development and the outcome of things. It reveals and searches out confused and ambiguous things, it enumerates and arranges sections, and if something is to be proved, it indicates the sources of the arguments.[1]

Dialectics helps us to define the correct relationship between things and helps us to separate disparate elements. Complicated contradictions cannot be solved even by the most intelligent person without this science. "That is why Plato says the following: the only way to teach and learn is transferred by Dialectic, which was given to mankind by the immortal gods, for the useful purpose of teaching each other, and learning from one another everything which is necessary during life."[2] Religion, justice, law and many other useful things must be taught to the people. These subjects, however, remain confusing and incomprehensible, unless they are correctly lined up (put in a correct relationship to each other), arranged and united by dialectics. Therefore, this science provides light to every other discipline because it clarifies obscure and unfamiliar things, with that "godly flame, which was brought to the people by Prometheus,

---

1. "... omnium artium humanarum Dialecticam maxime necessariam esse, non solum ad artes alias tractandas, sed etiam ad controversias forenses, et pleraque alia negotia in vita iudicanda. Nihil enim; ordine doceri, nihil perfecte disci potest, nisi adhibita Dialectica, quae in unaquaque causa methodum informat, ostendit initia, progressiones, et exitus rerum ... Confusa et ambigua retexit et partitur, membra enumerat ac disponit, indicat argumentorum fontes, si quid est probandum." CR 10. 908–9.

2. "Itaque Plato gravissime dixit, unam hanc docendi ac discendi viam, quae in Dialectica traditur, a Deis immortalibus donatam esse generi humano, propter hanc summam utilitatem, ut docere homines inter se ac discere possent, quod in omni vita maxime necessarium est." CR 10. 909.

as Plato said."[3] "Thus, the art of dialectics is like the *Hermes Trismegistos*,[4] which is the interpreter of the people and gods in the temples, public affairs, schools, the public forum, and the Senate."[5] Plato, in his works, always took the opportunity to encourage the sophists of his age to study this discipline, because, if they ignored it, the youth of future generations would learn only useless things.

Melanchthon did not like those who approached the higher sciences without systematic dialectical examination, and "stray as though they were wandering in the night on *terra incognita*."[6] Theologians and jurists were those who brought dialectics from the background to the forefront *(ex umbra in aciem)*, because they could not have defended themselves without this tool *(suas personas sine hoc instrumentum tueri possunt)*.

> Paul taught the handling of the Word of God correctly. How can some-body do this, who does not know the correct method of distinguishing and systematizing things? What can be more monstrous for the doc-trines of the Church than mixing and muddling heterogeneous things such as the doctrine of Law and Gospel, the spiritual and the civil duties, the sacraments and the sacrifices? Without a frequent and well timed practice of dialectics no one can study these things with sufficient safety.[7]

Melanchthon was concerned about the Church and theological science because of the frequent lack of system and regularity. Without method only empty stories can be told, not the clear and perfect doctrine *(perfecta*

---

3. ". . . omnibus artibus lumen adfert [scil. dialectica – BD], sicut Plato inquit, a Prometheo aliquo divinitus ad homines perlatam esse, ἅμα φανοτάτῳ τινὶ πυρὶ." CR 10. 909.

4. The expression: κοινὸς ἑρμῆς used by Melanchthon was taken from Aristotle and Menandros, who use it with the following everyday meaning: the revealed thing must be shared with those present. Obviously Melanchthon wants to refer here to the sharing of spiritual things.

5. "Est igitur Dialectica veluti κοινὸς ἑρμῆς interpres Deorum atque hominum, in templis, in foro, in scholis, in iudiciis, in Senatu." CR 10. 909.

6. "Quo magis reprehendi sunt hoc tempore, qui sine Dialectica properant ad superiores artes, in quibus quoniam sine Dialectica methodum reperire nullam possunt, ita errabunt, ut si in ignotissimis regionibus nocte iter facerent." CR 10. 909.

7. "Paulus praecepit verbum Dei ὀρθοτομεῖν. Id quomodo faciet, qui nullam sciet apte distinguendi et partiendi racionem? Quid erit monstrosius, doctrina religionis, si diversi loci miscebuntur, et confundentur, quales sunt, doctrina legis et Evangelii, vitae spiritualis officia, et vitae civilis officia, sacramenta et sacrificia? Neque quisquam satis cautus erit in talibus locis, nisi multum ac diu exercitatus in Dialectica." CR 10. 909–10. Melanchthon refers here to the second letter of Paul to Timothy (2 Tim 2:15).

doctrina). At the end of his speech he again encouraged the youth to study dialectics actively and with persistence, approaching it as the instrument of every other higher science.

The date of his second study is known: he wrote it in 1528 for the graduation of Iacobus Milichius, who obtained the degree of Master of Arts in that year. "Since the customs of this school are quite familiar to you, I think, it is no longer necessary for me to prove with large explanations why I step up here to speak," he began. Later he stated that he was not led by his own purposes in making this speech, but by the instructions of previous wise men who introduced this custom. He felt that he was bound to explain the correct way and methods of studying, correcting at the same time an earlier dangerous mistake which made the studying process impossible because of its harmful method. "While granting Masters' degrees to these young men whose studies we know, we warn most of the students not to practice science without method and order."[8] In the end he followed a similar path to his first speech, only with new ideas and from new standpoints. "How can anyone judge complicated contradictions, who doesn't study deeply the useful sciences, but only tastes them briefly and hastily, like dogs drinking from the banks of the Nile?"[9] Order and method in study are what help all of us to get complete knowledge from our favorite science. Melanchthon emphasized frequently that the correct method of studying provides an important role in this information-gathering process, supported with a maxim taken from the work *Oeconomicus* by Xenophon: If something lacks order, it is not worthy of respect, and is useless.

Melanchthon concentrated his attention on pseudo-thinkers, who studied theology and justice without first mastering dialectics. They were like the man mentioned by Cicero, who tried to lift himself up by his own hair. "Plato," says Melanchthon, "in his work, *The Republic*, calls those who imagine that they get satisfaction from the other arts without dialectics illegitimate philosophers; and since illegitimate children have no right to inheritance, so much more should all who first break into the

8. "Cum scholae consuetudo vobis nota sit, non arbitrabar mihi opus esse longa defensione, cur huc ad dicendum accesserim. . . . Nos itaque dum hoc tempore horum adolescentium, quibus Magisterii titulum concedemus, studia cognoscimus, animadvertimus magnam iuventutis partem, sine ratione atque ordine in literis versari." CR 11. 159–60.

9. "Quid autem iudicabit de obscurissimis controversiis is, qui non penitus introspexit bonas artes, sed obiter degustavit eas fugiens, velut canes e Nilo bibunt?" CR 11. 160.

field of other disciplines without mastering this art, be forbidden, by some kind of praetorian decree, from studying all other sciences."[10] Continuing his analysis he also said that dialectics was useless if studied briefly by simply learning some of this art's rules. We need to master it precisely, and achieve some practice in it. And this practice is as important as the knowledge of a science's principles. "As nobody can be either a painter just by watching Dürer paint, or a musician just by seeing Adolph play on the strings, so nobody should believe that he is going to be a master in dialectics without composing something, or disputing, in a word who has no practice in this art."[11] Melanchthon gathered an endless scientific supply of classical writings which praise everything from the fables of Aesop through the wisdom of philosophers, jurists, or the brave and outstanding medical practitioners.

Finally Melanchthon reached the point where dialectics, as a science, could be used in the Church, expounding that, although the essence and content of the holy science was not rooted in philosophy, nevertheless the church sermon, as the external instrument of handling the Word, took its form and frame from dialectics and other arts, so that preaching could only be structured with their help. And because, from his point of view, the theologian needed to be the most informed and skilled in everything, and had to know everything in the best possible way, it was not proper for him to neglect studying these arts. For instance, when he was to speak clearly and intelligibly about the nature of man, comparing it to the parts of the human body, he needed to have knowledge of dissertations written on this subject.

> How much light can be shed on the holy sciences by somebody who puts the philosophical doctrine about the virtues next to the holy sciences, and does not show what does and does not link the two? I think personally that it is essential to define accurately the character of both sciences [theology and philosophy], to delimit their differences clearly, and to indicate precisely their bounds, in order to stop philosophy from trespassing onto the territory of Christian doctrines, as the jurists would say.

10. "Plato in Repub. spurios Philosophos adpellat eos, qui sine Dialectica, satisfacere se aliis artibus existimabant, quare sicut spuriis non licet haereditatem petere, ita procul ab omnium literarum tractatione praetorio aliquo edicto submoveri debebant illi, qui ante irrumpunt in alias disciplinas, quam hanc artem perceperint." CR 11. 161.

11. "Sicut non statim pictor est qui Durerum pingentem vidit, nec cytharoedus, qui vidit Adolphum eruditissime tangentem fides: ita non putet se Dialecticam callere is, qui nihil scripsit, non disputavit, denique qui artem non exercuit." CR 11. 161.

If our ancestors had done this, the infection of Church doctrines would not have lasted until now.[12]

A theologian also needs to know history, and the movement of stars and celestial bodies, said Melanchthon, without further explanation. A speech should end with stimulation, illustrating how important the first step of the trivium is to progressing in the fields of the other sciences: "Starting well is to be already half-done, therefore you can also make progress in the higher sciences [the *quadrivium*, e.g. theology] if you start studying it correctly, namely, if you take along with you for the mastering of the other arts the knowledge of the sciences I am speaking about [the *trivium*]. This warning is emphasized at least as well by me as by your other teachers."[13]

II. A Textbook about Dialectics

Given our limitations of space and time we cannot afford to present the *Dialectics* of Melanchthon in its entirety, so we will give you only a description of some specific parts of it.

Following the first edition of his *Rhetoric* Melanchthon immediately started to write his *Dialectics*. Analyzing the text of various editions, one can separate it into three stages, that of 1520, 1528 and 1547.

The first edition was published in 1520 in Leipzig under the title *Compendiaria dialectices ratio*. Melanchthon's name is not on the title page, but it appears at the end of the dedication letter addressed to Johannes Schwertfegerus, who taught law in Wittenberg, and died on May 10, 1524. Luther recommended Iustus Ionas to replace him. In the dedication Melanchthon referred to his *Rhetoric* published a year earlier, emphasizing the fact that it could not be treated exhaustively without knowing the dialectics. If dialectics were absent, the speakers could say

12. "Quantum lucis adferet sacris literis, qui Philosophorum doctrinam de moribus cum illis conferet et ostendet, quae consentiant, quae non consentiant? Ego vero etiam necessarium esse iudico, ostendere utrunque doctrinae genus et intervalla certa regione describere, et fines eorum regere, ut jureconsulti loquuntur, ne possit iterum in Christianae doctrinae possessionem Philosophia irrumpere. Quod si fecissent veteres, non usque adeo contaminata esset ante haec tempora doctrina ecclesiastica." CR 11. 162.

13. "Quod si dimidium facti qui bene coepit habet, profecto et vos in superioribus disciplinis plus promovebitis, si recte coeperitis, hoc est, si earum literarum, de quibus dico, scientiam ad eas attuleritis. Haec quamquam sedulo praeceptores vestri monent, tamen et ego . . ." CR 11. 163.

nothing certain or acceptable. As for the reason for writing the *Dialectics,* he said that the students' persistent demand forced him to write it, because, as he stated, most teachers of the time neglected this science. "Therefore, taking time away from my other studies, I wrote out the method of discussing in the shortest way I could."[14] This version appeared in 1521 in three places (Basle, Leipzig, The Hague), in 1522 in two places (Basle, Paris), and also in 1523 in three places (Strasbourg, Basle, Augsburg). But other editions are known as well.[15] On June 26, 1529, Melanchthon wrote about his second version to Camerarius, stating that he had emended his *Dialectics* shortly before, rewriting and completing the last two chapters.[16] It seems that he started correcting the first version already in 1527, since Brettschneider seems to have known in a letter dated July 2, 1527 that Melanchthon had written that he had edited it and made it more complete. But there is no point in looking for that letter in that year because of some typographical mistake which caused a 6 to turn into a 7. Thus Melanchthon actually wrote the letter to Ioachim Camerarius in 1526 and mentioned correcting the *Dialectics* and giving the corrected version to his students, having decided to take them through the whole encyclopedia.[17] It seems that he had already finished correcting the book by June 1529, since in his letter dated June 10 he informed Fridericus Myconius that it was a serious test of strength revising the *Dialectics,* which now, in his words, would appear in a much better form.[18] The work thus enriched in content was published that very

14. "Neque enim rhetorica citra dialecticorum usum commode tractari absolvique possunt [. . .] Haec ut copiose tractarem, studiosi quidam a me contenderunt, quod eo sint loco nostris temporibus, ut et magna professorum pars artis usum ignoret. Suffuratus igitur horas aliquot studiis mei, disserendi rationem descripsi, idque quam potui brevissime." CR 1. 153–54. Nr. 67. It is worth comparing it with the letter addressed to Bernardus Maurus, in which he gives a fuller account of the relation between rhetoric and dialectics. CR 1. 62–66. Nr. 32.

15. CR 1. 509.

16. "Dialectica mitto Michaeli, quae nuper recognovi, et posteriores duos libellos retexui, et ita tractavi, ut totam artem complexum me esse putem." CR 1. 1084. Nr. 624. Preceding this, dated on July 15 we read that he restarted his lectures on dialectics at the request of new students, and that he wanted to complete it with Aristotle's *Organon.* CR 1. 1081. Nr. 622.

17. "Ego meam διαλεκτικὴ perpolio. Nunc enim pueris meis trado, quos per universam ἐγκυκλοπαίδεαν χειραγωγεῖν statui." CR 1. 803. For Brettschneider's reference see CR 13. 507–8.

18. In this period he worked at a feverish pace, and according to one of Luther's letters addressed to Iustus Ionas, even his health was at stake because of his exhausting

year *(Dialectices Phil[ippi] Mel[anchthonis] libri quatuor ab auctore ipse de integro in lucem conscripti ac editi. Item rhetorices praeceptiunculae doctissimae),* and later was published seven more times.[19] This version was the one which Paulus Eberus, one of Melanchthon's disciples, added to and published in 1544 in Wittenberg entitled: *Dialecticae praeceptiones collectae a Philippo Melanthone,* indicating in its introduction that it could hardly please the author, who would surely have rewritten it himself if he had had the time.

Melanchthon's *Dialectics* gained its final form in 1547, printed in the middle of the year under the title of *Erotemata dialectices, continentia fere integram artem, ita scripta, ut juventuti utiliter proponi possint. Edita a Philippo Melanthone. Viteb[ergae], 1547.* The book was highly successful, inasmuch as on October 18, 1547 Melanchthon wrote to his pastor, "The dialectics have been sold in 3000 copies. Now they are reprinting it, and it needs some correction."[20] As for pastor Casparus Aquila,[21] he wrote on November 10 of the same year that he could not send the *Dialectics* because he was out of town during its printing, and when he came back every single copy had been sold. "Therefore, there will soon be another edition, containing many corrections, since some parts of the material need more careful consideration. But I think, if God helps us, I can send you a copy of this edition within one month."[22]

We can find out about some of Melanchthon's rewriting from the letter he sent to Joannes Aurifaber.[23] He made essential and structural

public work. ("Philippus sese macerat cura rei ecclesiasticae et rei publicae usque ad periculum valetudinis." CR 1. 1074.)

19. Wittenberg, 1531; Paris, 1532; Wittenberg, 1533, in the same year in the same location again; Wittenberg 1536; Leipzig, 1536 and Strasbourg 1542. CR 13. 509.

20. "Vendita sunt tria millia exemplorum Dialectices. Nunc recuditur, et emendatione indiget." CR 6. 705.

21. Aquila was born August 7, 1488 in Augsburg, studied in Italy and Switzerland, in 1510 was elected pastor of Gengen, and from there he went to Wittenberg in 1520. His posts were: 1522 Sickingen, 1523 Eisenach, 1527 Saalfeld where he was elected bishop in 1528. He appears in 1548 in Schmalkalden as an exile and from there returned to Saalfeld in 1552. He died in 1560. CR 10. 334.

22. "Dialecticos libellos ideo non misi, quia cum ederentur, ego aberam in iugis Herciniis, et me reverso exemplaria omnia vendita erant. Mox igitur instituta est secunda editio, in qua multa erunt emendatiora; habui enim de quibusdam materiis δευτέρας φροντίδας. Mittam igitur eius editionis exempla intra mensem Deo volente." CR 6. 722.

23. Aurifaber was born in 1517 in Bratislava. His original name was Goldschmid. He was Melanchthon's disciple, and later his friend. He began teaching as a lector in the University of Wittenberg. On June 16, 1550 he was awarded a doctorate and later

changes only in the chapter "De loco causarum," although he was not totally satisfied with the corrections. He was about to go to Leipzig, where he intended to discuss the question with Aurbachius. The small stylistic corrections did not affect the content of the other part of the book.[24] The corrected version was rapidly printed, because he wrote at the beginning of December to Hieronimus Baumgartner: "I send you a copy of the *Dialectics,* not as if I wanted you to read some trifles like this, but only because momentarily I have no other lecture to send you."[25] He also sent a copy of the newly-published book to Vitus Theodor's son in the middle of December.[26] This edition was very successful, since it was totally sold out in only two months. This is proved by Melanchthon's letter written to Mattheus Collinus at the academy of Prague, where he already spoke about the third edition of the book.[27] The *Dialectics* were finally published in more than ten editions.

III. Dedication

Melanchthon dedicated the *Dialectics* to Joachim Camerarius's son John, out of respect for his father. He told the young man that this science helped people to distinguish clearly the reasons and logical process of a text used for persuasion, steering audiences away from falseness by revealing the lies. Following the general introduction he explored more

was invited to teach theology at the Rostock Academy, thanks to the recommendation of Melanchthon. Aurifaber was in Regensburg already in 1554, where he also taught theology and led the Consistorium. In 1567 he returned to Bratislava, as the pastor of St. Elisabeth church and the inspector in charge of the supervision of church and schools. He also died there in 1568. CR 10. 336.

24. "In dialecticis περὶ συνεκτικοῦ, in loco causarum a me erratum est. Mutavi eum locum etsi ne nunc quidem mihi aut tibi satisfactum est. Sed iam eo Lipsiam, cum Aurbachio ea de re disputaturus. In alliis partibus libelli, etsi quaedam emendavi, tamen res non sunt mutatae." CR 6. 725–26.

25. Baumgartner was a senator of Nürnberg, born there on March 9 to a wealthy noble family. He studied in his native town of Eittenberg, where he became acquainted with both Luther and Melanchthon. He continued as senator until his death in 1565. CR 10. 337. The fragment of the letter to him states: "Mitto tibi exemplum Dialectices, non quod has nugas a te legi velim, sed quia nunc alia iucundiora, quae mitterem, non habebam." CR 6. 749.

26. Vitus Theodor (formerly Dietrich) was a beloved disciple and friend of both Luther and Melanchthon. This is evidenced by the fact that Melanchthon wrote him 235 letters between 1530 and 1549. He became a pastor in Nüremberg, where he died on March 26, 1549. CR 10. 415. For the letter referring to the sending of the dialectics look at CR 6. 750.

27. "Dialecticam mitto, qualis nunc tertio edita est." CR 6. 816.

practical domains, pointing to the character of the dialectics to be used in the Church. First of all he wished to convince his colleagues and students not to speak against this use of the science of dialectics, "I encourage them, but also ask them for the sake of God's glory and the Church's salvation not to neglect Dialectics, and not to acclaim the silly speeches of people who revile this science and declare it useless for the Church."[28] He was convinced that this science became abominable and detested in the age when it was not taught as an art, but as an obscure shadow, or an incomprehensible and unexplainable labyrinth of rules, unfamiliar even to scholars. "But I," said Melanchthon, "teach the real, not the compromised, but the original Dialectics as taken partly from Aristotle, and partly from some of his very clever interpreters, like Alexander Aphrodiensis or Boetius. And I think it is very useful not only in the public forum and the court of justice, or in philosophy, but also in the Church."[29] He referred to the use of this discipline in the Church when he said that even if God's will, law, sin, the gospel and many other important things were evident from the holy books given by God, without dialectics one could hardly speak about them coherently and with structure. Besides, he saw the use of the science not only in clarifying a doctrine's meaning, but in providing understanding for the Church.[30] Therefore a discipline like this ought not to be used in the service of arguing, chattering or vanity, but had to be used for a high standard, clarity, science, and the love of truth. He was convinced that this way of intelligent speaking and teaching of the truth was given by God as a gift, and was extremely necessary in the explanation of the holy doctrines, and in the search for truth in other domains.[31] Again he defended Aristotle against those who attacked his work and thought it useless, recommending to his students to read Aristotle's works in Greek. He thought it useful for the students to reinforce the teachings of this great Greek thinker with the handbooks

28. "Hos et adhortor, et propter gloriam Dei ac propter Ecclesiae salutem obtestor, ne Dialecticam negligant, nec applaudant insulsis sermonibus eorum, qui vituperant eam, et Ecclesiae inutilem esse clamitant" CR 6. 655.

29. "Ego veram, incorruptam, nativam Dialecticam, qualem et ab Aristotele, et aliquot eius non insulsis interpretibus, ut ab Alexandro Aphrodisiensi et Boetio accepimus, praedico. Hanc affirmo non modo in foro et in iudiciis, aut in philosophia, sed etiam in Ecclesia valde utilem esse." CR 6. 655.

30. "Imo Dialectica opus est, non solum ut doctrina lucem habeat, sed etiam ut sit concordiae vinculum." CR 6. 655.

31. . . . veram docendi et ratiocinandi viam sciamus Dei donum esse, et in exponenda doctrina coelesti et inquisitione veritatis in aliis rebus necessariam." CR 6. 656.

of Joannes Caesarius and Iodocius Willicchus, saying, "I also made every effort in this edition to include the whole art, therefore I think this discipline very useful for the youth to study. I also attached a bibliography to indicate the sources of my teachings."[32]

The texts of the following sections can be found in the book published in 1580, in Leipzig. It starts with a short δεφινιτιον of dialectics, "Dialectics is the art or the way of correct, exact and clear teaching, correct definition and division, the rebinding of wrong connections or disproving of errors.[33]

The word *dialectics* comes from the Greek word *dialegomai,* which means to speak with somebody while exchanging opinions. As a definition this is obviously a collage of the meanings of the Latin expressions *(disputo, dissero).* This definition is expanded upon in the subtitle, as though in answer to the question, what does dialectics deal with? Melanchthon's answer is "with every topic and question which can be taught to people, like arithmetic, which deals with things concerning counting."[34] Man as a rational being was endowed by God with the notion of numbers, to be able to differentiate things without mixing them and without everything becoming a chaotic mixture *(in unum chaos miscenda).* Therefore it is necessary to know that God is one, and the creature is one, substance is one and essence is one, while God and his enemy Satan are two different things. "Therefore dialectics does not create new things, it only teaches us the method and form of teaching" *("non nasci res in Dialectica, sed modum et formam docendi tradi in Dialectica").* Melanchthon finished his work by praising the disciple with the maxim of Petrus Hispanus, a definition which Melanchthon fully supported,

> Dialectics is the art of arts, the science of sciences, which gives the way to the origin of every method. This is foolish praise, but you need to un-

---

32. "Ego quoque in hac editione propemodum integram artem complexus sum, et hanc rationem tradendae artis utilem fore studiis iuventutis exsistimo. Et τεχνολογικά quaedam inserui, quae fontes praeceptorum ostendunt." CR 6. 657.

33. *Erotemata Dialectices, continentiae fere integram artes, ita scripta, ut iuventuti utiliter proponi possint, Edita a Philippo Melanch[tone].* Lipsiae. (In fine: Lipsiae, imprimebat Ioannes Steinmann Anno M.D.LXXX.) "Dialectica est ars seu via, recte, ordine, et perspicue docendi, quod fit recte definiendo, dividendo, argumenta vera connectendo, et male cohaerentia seu falsa retexendo et refutando." CR 13. 513.

34. "Circa omnes materias seu quaestiones, de quibus docendi sunt homines, sicut Arithmetica versatur circa omnes res numerandas." CR 13. 514. In some of the following explanatory sentences he makes a detailed presentation of the relationship between the two disciplines.

derstand, dialectics is the art of arts, which is better not in its dignity, but in its usefulness to serve every art and discipline. . . . Finally says [Petrus Hispanus] it shows the way to the origin of every method, which means that it creates method, or teaches every discipline. . . . If some orator wants to speak about repentance, than he has to provide the definitions, the parts, the reasons, the effects.[35]

Melanchthon saw the difference between rhetoric and dialectics in the fact that dialectics presents the summary of things but rhetoric expounds them widely, and decorates them with new ideas. He tried to emphasize the importance of studying this discipline partly by means of two quotations taken from Plato and partly with the words of Paul concerning the selection of a bishop. Paul says concerning the selection of a bishop that he must be suitable as a teacher (idoneum ad docendum), "and he similarly warns the doctors to handle correctly the word of God, or as he says *orthotomein*, which surely means dialectics because it is the correct way of teaching and dividing."[36] Firstly, Melanchthon thought it necessary to be careful and not let different things get mixed. We must make a difference between the Law and the Gospel, the commandments and the promises, the outside order, or the common truth, and the inside order or the truth of the heart. "These show clearly enough that creating correct differentiations and definitions is very necessary, and this is done by dialectics. But this discipline must be taught with restraint, and the youth must get used to the simple explanation of truth, not through the rules of arguing or using finger-pointing and intrigue."[37]

---

35. "Dialectica est ars artium, scientia scientiarum, ad omnium methodorum principia viam habens. Laudatio videtur ridicula, sed sic intelligatur: Dialectica est ars artium, id est non dignitate antecedens, sed usu serviens omnibus artibus et scientiis. . . . Deinde inquit, ad omnium methodorum principia viam habens, id est, in omnibus materiis methodos, hoc est, viam docendi instituens . . . Si concionatori dicendum erit de poenitentia, exponet et ipse definitiones, partes, causas, effectus." CR 13. 515.

36. CR 13. 517. Melanchthon combines here several quotations from the Bible. One is 1 Tim 3: 2, "oportet ergo episcopum . . . doctorem [esse]," the other Tit 1:9, "potens sit [scil. episcopus] et exhortari in doctrina sana et eos qui contradicunt arguere," and 2 Tim 2:15, "-recte tractandum [according to Melanchthon: secare] verbum veritatis [according to Melanchthon: verbum Dei]." The last one is worth quoting in Greek too, because it contains the expression used by Melanchthon:, "*orthomounta [orthotomein] ton logon* τοζ αλτηειασζ."

37. "Hic satis apparet, valde necessariam esse diligentiam recte dividendi et definiendi, quae sunt opera Dialectices. Sed sobrie tradatur ars, et assuefiat adolescentia ad simplicem veritatis explicationem, non ad studium cavillandi, aut ad sycophanticam.

We have examined how dialectics helps us to organize questions, and how it illuminates the world of notions. The following is a perfect example of how Melanchthon harmonized the two disciplines. God, says Melanchthon's definition, is a formless substance, intelligent, almighty, wise and good, true, gracious, holy, fully independent, the final cause of all nature, order, and the good of nature. He demands that humanity behave according to his will, and punishes those who work against him. It is a definition which can also be made by people outside the church;[38] but in the church the following addition is necessary because we need to speak about God as He revealed himself in evident testimonies. Therefore we need to complete the definition with the methodical description of God's person, as follows: the eternal Father, whose son is his own image, and Son, who carries the image of his father, and Holy Spirit in whom God reveals himself, created the heaven and earth and everything in them, and gathers the eternal Church from the human race, and revealed his will in evident testimonies, as through the resurrection of the dead.[39]

From the point of view of the will another category comes to light, faith as knowledge.

> Faith is knowledge, Melanchthon again formulated, and through it we accept every teaching given by God to the Church with solid conviction including the promise of forgiveness, which if we accept it, gives us absolution for our sins. This promise also gives us trust in the Son of God, in whom, if we rest, we will reach high up to God, being sure that he will accept us and hear us; and we pray to him.[40]

Hactenus προλεγόμενα εψδίε΄α recitata sunt. Nunc, Deo iuvante, artem ipsam inchoabimus." CR 13. 517.

38. "Hanc descriptionem mentes humanae, etiam extra Ecclesiam, et sine singulari revolutione, discunt ex demonstrationibus, et membra praecipua sunt in hac tabella." CR 13. 530.

39. "Ideo in Ecclesia ad priora membra diserte adduntur personarum nomina: . . . et pater aeternus, qui genuit filium imaginem suam, et filius, qui est imago patris, et Spiritus Sanctus sicut patefecit se divinitas, qui condidit coelum et terram, et caetereas naturas in eis, et in genere humano sibi colligit aeternam Ecclesiam, et suam voluntatem illustribus testimoniis, ut resuscitatione mortuorum, declaravit." CR 13 530–31.

40. "Fides est noticia, qua firmo assensu amplectimur totam doctrinam a Deo traditam Ecclesiae, et is hac etiam promissionem reconciliationis, quam apprehendentes accipimus remissionem peccatorum fiducia filii Dei, et hac fiducia acquiescentes in filio Dei, accedimus ad Deum, et nos recipi et exaudiri statuimus, et eum invocamus." CR 13 538–39.

On this level Melanchthon's systematic argumentation received an unusual impulse regarding Reformed doctrines. "Hope," he continued, "is the sure expectation of eternal life given by the Son of God, and awaiting the divine help and assistance during misfortunes. Faith and hope differ, because faith means also knowledge and above all also trust. . . . But hope is the expectation of the future salvation."[41] Love means obedience to God's commandments through true faith and joy. The apostle John defines love in his first epistle: love for God means submitting to his orders, "We understand this definition better when our heart is set on fire with a fervent love for God."[42] Fear of God, called servile fear, is the protector of order and skill, which leads us to fear God's anger, but when combined with faith it becomes a virtue like fear of parents. Patience is a virtue which shows up in obedience to God in hard times and teaches us to become perfect, and not to act against God's will when crushed by pain.[43] That was the way in which Melanchthon created a step by step science in God's service and for Reformation's goals.

I would like to end this contribution with a footnote which I think is appropriate at this point. On August 26, 1636 an unknown admirer of Melanchthon noted in one of his books in Debrecen, *"Frustra doctores sine me colluere sorores"* that is, "without this discipline no other science can really be practiced."

41. "Spes est expectatio vitae aeternae propter filium Dei certa, et expectatio auxilii et mitigationis calamitatum in hac vita, iuxta consilium Dei. Differunt fides et spes, quia fides et noticiam significat, et deinde fiduciam . . . Spes autem est expectatio futurae liberationis." CR 13 539.

42. "Sed si arderent corda nostra magno incendio amoris erga Deum, haec definitio magis intelligi posset." CR 13 539.

43. Timor Dei, qui vocatur servilis, et est custos disciplinae, est habitus, qui inclinat ut revera expavescamus agnitione irae Dei et poenarum. [. . .] Tolerantia est virtus obediens Deo in aerumnis, quas docet perferendas esse, ita, ne fracti dolore faciamus contra mandata Dei. . . ." CR 13 539.

5

What Hath Wittenberg to Do with Heidelberg?
Philip Melanchthon and the Heidelberg Catechism

Lyle D. Bierma

What hath Wittenberg to do with Heidelberg? Or more specifically, what does Philip Melanchthon of Wittenberg have to do with the catechism of Heidelberg? At first glance, it may appear to be very little. Wittenberg and Heidelberg not only were located in different regions of the German empire, several hundred miles apart, but in the early 1560s the former was Lutheran and the latter in the process of becoming Reformed. What is more, Melanchthon died in April 1560, and the Heidelberg Catechism (HC) was not composed until 1562 or adopted until January 1563—two to three years after Melanchthon's death. The distance between Melanchthon and the HC was as much temporal as geographical or ecclesiastical.

Nevertheless, many scholars have claimed to find evidence in the HC of Melanchthon's influence. Some have traced particular features of the catechism back to Melanchthon: e.g., the threefold division of the material (Misery, Deliverance, and Gratitude);[1] the central theme of comfort;[2] the definition of faith;[3] the references to knowing Christ and his

---

1. Maurits Gooszen, "Inleiding," *De Heidelbergsche Catechismus: Textus Receptus met Toelichtende Teksten* (Leiden: Brill, 1890), 97; Bard Thompson, "The Palatinate Church Order of 1563," *Church History* 23 (December 1954): 347; Jan Rohls, *Theologie reformierter Bekenntnisschriften* (Göttingen: Vandenhoeck & Ruprecht, 1987), 24; Erdmann Sturm, *Der junge Zacharias Ursinus: Sein Weg vom Philippismus zum Calvinismus* (Neukirchen: Neukirchener Verlag, 1972), 250. Cf. August Lang, *Der Heidelberger Katechismus und vier verwandte Katechismen* (Leipzig: Deichert, 1907), LXXX: "So entstand aus der Verbindung jenes lutherischen Gedankens mit der Idee der Dankbarkeit die bekannte Dreiteilung: Elend, Erlösung, Dankbarkeit. Hierdurch erledigt sich auch, was man öfters über die Ähnlichkeit der Disposition des Heid. mit der Anlage der ersten Ausgabe der Loci Melanchthons, resp. des Römerbriefs ausgeführt hat."

2. E. F. Karl Müller, *Die Bekenntnisschriften der reformierten Kirche* (Leipzig: Deichert, 1903), LII; Sturm, *Zacharias Ursinus*, 249. Sturm notes (ibid., n. 16) that the notion of "comfort" (*consolatio*) is found in Melanchthon's German *Examen ordinandorum* more

benefits;[4] the doctrine of the real presence of Christ in the Lord's Supper;[5] the concept of "Bekehrung" (conversion);[6] the interpretation of the Fifth Commandment;[7] the wording of HC 114;[8] and the paucity of references to predestination in the catechism.[9]

Others have described this legacy in far broader terms. Heinrich Heppe, in an attempt to establish a historical basis for the union of Lutheran and Reformed churches in Hesse in the mid-nineteenth century, insisted that the HC was thoroughly Melanchthonian and but a later catechetical form of Melanchthon's 1558 Frankfurt Recess.[10] Bard Thompson, following the lead of Philip Schaff,[11] saw the theology of both the HC and the Palatinate liturgy as a synthesis of Melanchthonian and Calvinist doctrine.[12] Ursinus's most recent biographer in English, Derk Visser, claims (without elaborating) that "much of the *Heidelberg Catechism* can be found in the writings of Melanchthon."[13] Nothing, however, surpasses the nineteenth-century rhapsodic description by John W. Nevin of the spirit or tone of the document:

than forty times.

3. Lang, *Heidelberger Katechismus*, CI; Wilhelm Neuser, "Die Väter des Heidelberger Katechismus," *Theologische Zeitschrift* 35, no. 3 (1979): 182–83.

4. Neuser, "Väter," 183–84.

5. See, among others, Philip Schaff, *History of the Christian Church*, 4th ed., 7 vols. (New York: Scribner's, 1903), 7:669.

6. Lang, *Heidelberger Katechismus*, CI.

7. Ibid.

8. Ibid.

9. Johannes H. A. Ebrard, *Das Dogma vom heiligen Abendmahl und seine Geschichte*, 2 vols. (Frankfurt: Zimmer, 1846), 2:603–4; Neuser, "Väter," 191.

10. Heinrich Heppe, "Der Charakter der deutsch-reformirten Kirche und das Verhältniss derselben zum Lutherthum und zum Calvinismus," *Theologische Studien und Kritiken* 23, no. 3 (1850): 681, 685, 687–88; idem, *Geschichte des deutschen Protestantismus in den Jahren 1555–1581*, 4 vols. (Marburg: Elwert, 1852–59), 1:446, n. 2. Cf. Lowell H. Zuck, "Heinrich Heppe: A Melanchthonian Liberal in the Nineteenth-Century German Reformed Church," *Church History* 51 (December 1982): 430.

11. Philip Schaff, "Geschicht . . . des Heidelberger Katechismus," *Zeitschrift für die historische Theologie* 3 (1864): 328.

12. Bard Thompson, "Reformed Liturgies: An Historical and Doctrinal Interpretation of the Palatinate Liturgy of 1563, Mercersburg Provisional Liturgy of 1858, Evangelical and Reformed Order of 1944, and Their Sources" (B.D. thesis, Union Theological Seminary, New York, 1949), 1, n. 2; 6, n. 27; 7–8.

13. Derk Visser, *Zacharias Ursinus: The Reluctant Reformer—His Life and Times* (New York: United Church, 1983), 142.

The Catechism is no cold workmanship merely of the rationalizing intellect. It is full of feeling and faith. . . . A rich vein of mysticism runs everywhere through its doctrinal statements. A strain of heavenly music seems to flow around us at all times, while we listen to its voice. It is moderate, gentle, soft, in one word, *Melanchthonian*, in its whole cadence.[14]

What are we to make of these claims? In what follows I shall argue that one may be able to build a circumstantial case for Melanchthon's influence on the HC but that identifying precisely where that influence is in the text is next to impossible. Certainly the evidence adduced in the past for Melanchthon's distinctive stamp on the catechism is not convincing.

The gulf between Melanchthon and the HC was bridged in part by his longstanding ties to the Palatinate territory where Heidelberg was situated, to the Palatinate Reformation during the decade before his death, and to Zacharias Ursinus, very likely the primary author of the HC. Melanchthon was actually a native of the lower Palatinate, born in the little town of Bretten on February 16, 1497.[15] He received his education in Bretten, Pforzheim, Heidelberg, and Tübingen—all in the lower Palatinate and the nearby duchy of Württemberg—and he was awarded the B.A. degree from Heidelberg University at the age of fourteen before transferring in 1512 to the University of Tübingen. When he returned to Heidelberg on a visit twelve years later, the now-famous reformer was honored by the university faculty, who presented him with a silver goblet in recognition of his many achievements. A year later (1525) both the elector and the peasants of the Palatinate asked him to serve as an arbitrator in the peasant uprisings in the area, a service he performed willingly but with little success.

The Palatine electors had been soliciting advice from Melanchthon as early as the 1540s, but during the Palatinate reformation under Otto Henry (1556–59) and Frederick III (1559–76), Melanchthon became something of a long-distance chief advisor. It was he, for example, who convinced Otto Henry to appoint Tilemann Hesshus as head of the diverse theological faculty in Heidelberg in 1557 and who assisted with

---

14. John W. Nevin, *The Commentary of Dr. Zacharias Ursinus on the Heidelberg Catechism*, trans. G. W. Williard (Grand Rapids: Eerdmans, 1954), xvi.

15. For the details of Melanchthon's life, see Clyde L. Manschreck, *Melanchthon: The Quiet Reformer* (New York: Abingdon, 1958), and Robert Stupperich, *Melanchthon*, trans. Robert H. Fischer (London: Lutterworth, 1965).

the reorganization of the University of Heidelberg a year later.[16] Already before becoming elector in 1559, Frederick had found himself moving away from Gnesio-Lutheranism to positions represented by Philip Melanchthon. He had come to prefer Melanchthon's "altered" version of the Augsburg Confession and had been a signatory to the Frankfurt Recess, a confessional consensus statement drawn up by Melanchthon in 1558.[17] When Frederick wrote to Melanchthon for guidance during the acrimonious Lord's Supper debates in Heidelberg in 1559, he considered Melanchthon's response significant enough to have it published a year later in both the original Latin and German translation.[18] Melanchthon declined several invitations to join the faculty of the University of Heidelberg, but even from Wittenberg his influence on Otto Henry and Frederick III was of such strength that they and the beginnings of the reformation they supervised have often been characterized by historians as "Melanchthonian" or "Philippist."[19]

Melanchthon also left his mark on Zacharias Ursinus, one of his students in Wittenberg and later the major contributor to the Heidelberg Catechism.[20] Ursinus left his boyhood home of Breslau in 1550, at the age of fifteen, and matriculated at the University of Wittenberg. For the next seven years he became not only Melanchthon's pupil but a boarder at his home and a close and loyal friend. He accompanied his teacher to

16. Fred H. Klooster, *The Heidelberg Catechism: Origin and History* (Grand Rapids: Calvin Theological Seminary, 1982), 60–61.

17. Ibid., 104, 78.

18. Walter Henss, *Der Heidelberger Katechismus im konfessionspolitischen Kräftespiel seiner Frühzeit* (Zurich: Theologischer Verlag, 1983), 8–11. Cf. also Visser, *Zacharias Ursinus*, 107–8.

19. E.g., James I. Good, *The Origin of the Reformed Church in Germany* (Reading, PA: Daniel Miller, 1887), 128, 134; idem, *The Heidelberg Catechism in Its Newest Light* (Philadelphia: Publication and Sunday School Board of the Reformed Church in the United States, 1914), 133; Klooster, *Heidelberg Catechism*, 83, 104; Henss, *Heidelberger Katechismus*, 1; Christopher J. Burchill, "On the Consolation of a Christian Scholar: Zacharias Ursinus (1534–83) and the Reformation in Heidelberg," *Journal of Ecclesiastical History* 37, no. 4 (1986): 569.

20. For an overview of Ursinus's life and writings, see Karl Sudhoff, *C. Olevianus und Z. Ursinus: Leben und ausgewählte Schriften* (Elberfeld: Friderichs, 1857); G. Bouwmeester, *Zacharias Ursinus en de Heidelbergse Catechismus* (The Hague: Willem de Zwijgerstichting, 1954); and Visser, *Zacharias Ursinus*. On Ursinus's contribution to the Heidelberg Catechism, see Fred Klooster, "The Priority of Ursinus in the Composition of the Heidelberg Catechism," in *Controversy and Conciliation: The Reformation and the Palatinate, 1559–1583*, 73–100, ed. Dikran Y. Hadidian (Allison Park, PA: Pickwick, 1986).

Torgau when the plague descended upon Wittenberg in 1552, to the religious colloquy in Worms in 1557, and on a visit to Heidelberg later that same year. When Ursinus took up his first teaching post at the St. Elizabeth Gymnasium in Breslau, he used Melanchthon's catechetical *Examen ordinandorum* as a textbook and was soon compelled to defend Melanchthon's view of the Lord's Supper that it contained. These *Theses on the Doctrine of the Sacraments*, published in 1559, prompted Melanchthon to respond that he had "never seen anything so brilliant as this work."[21] Upon Melanchthon's death in April 1560 and Ursinus's departure from Breslau a couple of months later, Ursinus gradually moved into the Reformed orbit. Nevertheless, Melanchthon's stamp on Ursinus's theology, pedagogy, and approach to reform was never eradicated by later Zwinglian and Calvinist influences.[22]

In light of Melanchthon's connections to the Palatinate region and reformation, of his lifelong impact on Frederick III and Ursinus, and of the presence of Philippists on the HC drafting committee itself,[23] it would be strange indeed if Melanchthon did not exert some influence, however indirect, on the tone and content of the catechism. Identifying that influence in the text, however, is no simple task. For one thing, most of the records of the preparation of the HC have been destroyed or lost, and thus we know little about the sources and procedures used in the construction of the document or the discussions that took place within the committee. Moreover, one of Frederick III's purposes in commissioning the HC was to bring about confessional unity among the Philippists, Calvinists, and Zwinglians in his realm without moving outside the bounds of the Augsburg Confession or violating the terms of the Peace of Augsburg.[24] The catechism, therefore, was something of a consensus document, which emphasized common ground and mediating positions, not the distinctives of a particular theological tradition. Thus it

---

21. Cited in Good, *Heidelberg Catechism*, 250.

22. George W. Richards, *The Heidelberg Catechism: Historical and Doctrinal Studies* (Philadelphia: Publication and Sunday School Board of the Reformed Church in the United States, 1913), 28, 133; Good, *Heidelberg Catechism*, 45; Sturm, *Zacharias Ursinus*, passim (esp. 1–3); Richard A. Muller, *Christ and the Decree: Christology and Predestination in Reformed Theology from Calvin to Perkins* (Durham, NC: Labyrinth, 1986), 124. Burchill ("Zacharias Ursinus," 580) goes so far as to say that Melanchthon remained a dominant influence throughout [Ursinus's] career. See also ibid., 580–83.

23. Klooster, "Priority of Ursinus," 78–80; idem, *Heidelberg Catechism*, 110–13.

24. Klooster, *Heidelberg Catechism*, 154–55.

should not surprise us if distinctive Melanchthonian emphases in the catechism are difficult to identify.

That is precisely what we find when we examine past claims for Melanchthon's influence on the theology of the HC. We begin with a look at the threefold division of the catechism, outlined in HC 2:

Q. What must you know to live and die in the joy of this comfort?

A. Three things: first, how great my sin and misery are; second, how I am set free from all my sins and misery; third, how I am to thank God for such deliverance.[25]

The wording here and tripartite structure of the HC follow closely the so-called *Catechesis minor* (CMi), composed in 1562 by Ursinus as a preparatory document for the HC, and the basis for some ninety of the catechism's 129 questions and answers. CMi 3 reads as follows:

Q. What does God's word teach?

A. First, it shows us our misery; second, how we are set free from it; and third, what thanks must be given to God for this deliverance.[26]

What are the roots of this threefold structure? Gooszen and others have maintained that it reflects the influence of Melanchthon's 1521 edition of the *Loci communes theologici*,[27] which itself grew out of his early exegetical work on Paul's Epistle to the Romans.[28] This is certainly a possibility. Like the book of Romans, the *Loci communes* moves, generally speaking, from a treatment of sin and law, to the gospel, grace, and justification, and finally to love and the life of the redeemed Christian.[29]

---

25. For the German text of the HC, see Lang, *Heidelberger Katechismus*, 2–52. I am using the English translation in *Ecumenical Creeds and Reformed Confessions* (Grand Rapids: CRC Publications, 1987), 13–77.

26. For the Latin text of the CMi, see Lang, *Heidelberger Katechismus*, 200–218. I am using an unpublished English translation by John Medendorp and Fred H. Klooster.

27. See n. 1 above.

28. Gooszen, "Inleiding," *Heidelbergsche Catechismus*, 97. See also Timothy J. Wengert, "Philip Melanchthon's 1522 Annotations on Romans and the Lutheran Origins of Rhetorical Criticism," in *Biblical Interpretation in the Era of the Reformation: Essays Presented to David C. Steinmetz in Honor of His Sixtieth Birthday*, ed. Richard A. Muller and John L. Thompson (Grand Rapids: Eerdmans, 1996), 131.

29. For the Latin text of the 1521 *Loci communes theologici*, see *Corpus Reformatorum: Philippi Melanchthonis Opera Quae Supersunt Omnia* [CR], 28 vols., ed. C. G. Bretschneider

But a Melanchthonian basis for this threefold structure is not the only possibility. In 1961 Walter Hollweg published an essay on the sources of the HC in which he argued that two confessions composed by Theodore Beza in 1559 ought to be reckoned as major influences on the structure, theological content, and even some of the wording of the HC.[30] These two confessions, the *Confessio christianae fidei* and *Altera brevis fidei confessio*, were well known in Heidelberg, and the latter was translated into German in 1562, probably by Caspar Olevianus.[31] Hollweg points to the striking structural parallel between the threefold division of the HC and the threefold work of the Holy Spirit outlined in Articles 17–21 of the *Altera confessio*: first, the Spirit makes us aware of our sinfulness through the law; second, he comforts us with the message of salvation revealed in the gospel; and third, he sanctifies us through the mortification of the old nature and the creation of a new nature.[32] Hollweg acknowledges the dissimilarity between the third element here and the third part of the HC, but he maintains that the structure of the HC required that sanctification be treated in Part I in the third section of the exposition of the Apostles' Creed ("God the Holy Spirit and our Sanctification"), an exposition that the *Altera confessio* does not include. However, by substituting "gratitude" for "sanctification," says Hollweg, Ursinus was still indebted to Beza. The content and even some of the language of HC 86 and 116, which introduce the section on Gratitude and the subsection on Prayer, respectively, can be traced to particular articles in both of Beza's confessions.[33]

One does not need to range beyond the Lutheran sphere of influence, however, to find other possible sources of the HC's threefold structure. As Lang pointed out, the focus of the first two sections of the HC on human misery and deliverance had a Reformation catechetical pedigree going all the way back to Luther's own *Eyn kurcz form der zeehen*

(Halle, 1834–60), 21:81–227. An English translation is found in Wilhelm Pauck, ed., *Melanchthon and Bucer*, Library of Christian Classics [LCC], vol. 19 (Philadelphia: Westminster, 1969), 18–152.

30. Walter Hollweg, "Die beiden Konfessionen Theodor von Bezas: Zwei unbeachtete Quellen zum Heidelberger Katechismus," in *Neue Untersuchungen zur Geschichte des Heidelberger Katechismus* (Neukirchen: Neukirchener Verlag, 1961): 86–123. For a critique of Hollweg's thesis, see Sturm, *Zacharias Ursinus*, 251–53.

31. Ibid., 92–94.

32. The 1562 German translation text of the *Altera confessio* is appended to Hollweg, "Beiden Konfessionen," 111–23 (Arts. 17–21: 116–18).

33. Hollweg, "Beiden Konfessionen," 100–110.

gepott . . . of 1520.[34] Furthermore, the connection between good works and *gratitude* in the life of the redeemed, which is mentioned in Melanchthon's 1521 *Loci communes* and later in his *Apology of the Augsburg Confession*,[35] was not limited to Melanchthon. It also appeared in Leo Jud's Shorter Catechism (1541) and in Johannes Brenz's Small Catechism (1535), the latter of which was incorporated into the Palatinate Church Order under Otto Henry and used for many years in Heidelberg.[36]

A more likely Lutheran source for the three-part structure of the HC, however, is a summary of doctrine by Nikolaus Gallus of Regensburg, a former student of Melanchthon's who later became a strident Gnesio-Lutheran. This work, composed in 1554 and reprinted in Heidelberg in 1558, is divided into three sections: (1) law, sin, and repentance; (2) gospel and faith; and (3) good works.[37] According to Gallus, it is through the law that we come to know our misery, through the message of the gospel that we are delivered from such misery, and through good works that we display our thankfulness to God for what he has done for us.[38]

34. Lang, *Heidelberger Katechismus*, LXXX: ". . . die in zahlreichen Katechismen der Reformation . . . beliebt gewordene Einteilung . . . welche Luther in seiner 'kurzen Form der Gebote, des Glaubens, und des Vaterunsers' (Weimarer Ausg. 7:204 . . .) dargeboten hatte. . . . Luther sagt dort: 'Allso leren die gepott den menschen seyn kranckheit erkennen . . . Darnach helt yhm der glaub vor . . . , wo er die ertzney, die gnaden, finden sol.' Ursin schrieb in [C]Mi für 'kranckheit' miseria . . . , für 'ertzney' liberatio. . . ."

35. *Loci communes* (1521), in CR 21:181: "Iam hoc quoque spectandum est, quod opera, ut fructus, ita indicia, testimonia, signa spiritus sunt . . . Nam ubi fide degustavimus misericordiam dei . . . non potest animus non redamare deum, ac gestire et velut gratitudinam suam mutuo aliquo officio, pro tanta misericordia testari;" *Apology of the Augsburg Confession* 4.189, in *Die Bekenntnisschriften der evangelisch-lutherischen Kirche*, 4th ed. (Göttingen: Vandenhoeck & Ruprecht, 1959), 197.

36. Leo Jud, *Ein kürtze Christenliche underweysung* . . . , in Lang, *Heidelberger Katechismus*, 79: "Güte werck . . . als ein dancksagung die wir Gott thünd. . . ." (Q/A 86); Johannes Brenz, *Fragstücke des christlichen Glaubens* (1535), in Christoph Weismann, *Eine Kleine Biblia: Die Katechismen von Luther und Brenz* (Stuttgart: Calver, 1985), 114: "Frag: Warum sollen wir gute Werk tun? Antwort: . . . dass wir den Glauben mit guten Werken bezeugen und unserm HERRN Gott für seine Guttaten dankbar sein sollen." Cf. Klooster, *Heidelberg Catechism*, 92, 173.

37. Nikolaus Gallus, *Ein Kurtze Ordenliche summa der rechten Waren Lehre unsers heyligen Christlichen Glaubens*, in Johann M. Reu, ed., *Quellen zur Geschichte des kirchlichen Unterrichts in der evangelischen Kirche Deutschlands zwischen 1530 und 1600*, vol. 1/1 (1904; reprint, Hildesheim: Georg Olms, 1976), 720–34.

38. Ibid., 724, 731.

This phraseology appears to adumbrate not only the structure of the HC but some of the doctrinal substance as well.[39]

In sum, although there *may* be a direct link between Melanchthon's 1521 *Loci communes* and the structure of the HC, this is not the only, and perhaps not the most likely, explanation. Ursinus could have been inspired by a number of earlier sources, both Lutheran and Reformed, that had employed part or all of this structure. It is possible, of course, that those sources were themselves dependent to some degree on Melanchthon, but then Melanchthon's influence on the division of the HC was at best very indirect.

The same is true of Melanchthon's alleged influence on the HC's doctrine of the Lord's Supper. Ebrard, Nevin, Heppe, and Schaff all spoke of a "Melanchthonian-Calvinist" view of the Eucharist in the HC—seen particularly, according to Schaff, in the HC's "theory of the spiritual real presence" of Christ.[40] In point of fact, however, the HC has very little to say about the *nature* of Christ's presence in the Supper or even about Christ's presence there at all. Certainly there is no trace in the catechism of the technical theological vocabulary that both Melanchthon and Calvin had used to describe the real presence of Christ. For example, as far back as the *Apology of the Augsburg Confession* in 1531, Melanchthon had declared that Christ is "truly and substantially [*substantialiter*] present" in the Lord's Supper, and Calvin had asserted in the Genevan Catechism (1545) that believers are made partakers of the "substance" (*substantia*) of Christ as they partake of the elements.[41] Both of these notions appeared again in Ursinus. In his 1559 *Theses on the Doctrine of the Sacraments*, Ursinus states that Christ is "truly and substantially present" to believers in the Lord's Supper, and in his so-called *Catechesis maior* (CMa), another *Vorlage* for the HC, we read that the "eating of Christ" is not just a sharing in his merits and the gifts of the Holy Spirit but also a communication of the person and *substantia* of

39. Neuser ("Väter," 188) thinks that Gallus's work "liegt zweifellos eine Vorlage für die Heidelberger Dreiteilung vor."

40. Ebrard, *Dogma*, 2:604, 606; John W. Nevin, "Doctrine of the Reformed Church on the Lord's Supper," *Mercersburg Review* 2, no. 5 (1850), in idem, *The Mystical Presence and Other Writings on the Eucharist*, ed. Bard Thompson and George H. Bricker (Philadelphia: United Church, 1966), 314–15, 376; Heppe, "Charakter," 681; Schaff, *History*, 7:669.

41. For Melanchthon see *Apology* 10.1, in *Bekenntnisschriften*, 247–48. For Calvin, see the Genevan Catechism [GC] Q/A 353, in *Calvin: Theological Treatises*, ed. J. K. S. Reid (Philadelphia: Westminster, 1954), 137. The Latin text is found in *Joannis Calvini Opera Selecta* [OS], vol. 2, ed. Peter Barth and Wilhelm Niesel (Munich: Kaiser, 1952), 140.

Christ himself.[42] All such "substance" language, however, is missing in both the CMi and the HC. So also is any explanation of how precisely the material signs of the sacrament are related to the spiritual blessings they signify.[43] If anything, it may be this silence that reflects the influence of Melanchthon, who in his *Responsio* to Frederick III during the Lord's Supper controversy in the Palatinate advised that all formulae for the presence of Christ in the Eucharist be set aside and that one rely only on the Pauline statement in 1 Cor. 10:16 that the bread of the Lord's Supper is "the communion of the body of Christ."[44]

When Schaff referred to the HC's doctrine of the *spiritual* real presence of Christ as Melanchthonian-Calvinist, he may have had in mind the catechism's emphasis on the Holy Spirit as the bond of union between Christ and the believer in the Lord's Supper. To eat the crucified body of Christ and to drink his poured-out blood means, according to HC 76, that "through the Holy Spirit, who lives both in Christ and in us, we are united more and more to Christ's blessed body." By the visible signs of bread and cup "he wants to assure us . . . that we, through the Holy Spirit's work, share in his body and blood . . ." (HC 79). This, of course, was a key theme in Calvin's thought, as many have recognized.[45] In Melanchthon, however, the focus is more on the Son than on the Spirit in the Lord's Supper—not because Melanchthon regarded the Holy Spirit's role as insignificant but because he felt that discussion of the Spirit's efficacy could too easily be misconstrued in the Zwinglian sense of *limiting* Christ's presence in the Supper to his Spirit.[46]

42. Ursinus, *Theses complectentes breviter & perspicue summam verae doctrinae de Sacramentis* . . . , in idem, *Tractationum theologicarum*, vol. 1 (Neudstadt: Harnisch, 1584), 359. For the Latin text of the CMa, see Lang, *Heidelberger Katechismus*, 152–99 (CMa 300: 195). I am using an unpublished English translation by John Medendorp and Fred H. Klooster.

43. For more on this, see Lyle D. Bierma, *The Doctrine of the Sacraments in the Heidelberg Catechism*, Studies in Reformed Theology and History, New Series (Princeton: Princeton Theological Seminary, forthcoming).

44. CR 9:960–62. Cf. HC 77, where 1 Cor. 10:16 is quoted in the answer to a question about Christ's promise to nourish and refresh believers with his body and blood.

45. E.g., Sudhoff, *Olevianus und Ursinus*, 116–17; Richards, *Heidelberg Catechism*, 90; Brian A. Gerrish, "Sign and Reality: The Lord's Supper in the Reformed Confessions," in *The Old Protestantism and the New: Essays on the Reformation Heritage* (Chicago: University of Chicago, 1982), 125; Sturm, *Zacharias Ursinus*, 302, 304, 305.

46. Ralph W. Quere, "Christ's Efficacious Presence in the Lord's Supper: Directions in the Development of Melanchthon's Theology after Augsburg," *The Lutheran Quarterly* 29 (1977): 22–23, 25.

Furthermore, references to the Spirit's binding of believers to Christ in the Lord's Supper appear in the *Consensus Tigurinus* (Zurich Consensus) between Calvin and Bullinger in 1549 and in Bullinger's own subsequent writings. In the *Consensus Tigurinus*, the two reformers profess that since Christ's finite body is contained in heaven, one's spiritual communion with him at the Lord's Supper is achieved solely through the Holy Spirit.[47] Bullinger makes much the same point in the Second Helvetic Confession. Believers receive the body and blood of Christ "not in a corporeal but in a spiritual mode, through the Holy Spirit." These benefits are "communicated to us spiritually by the Spirit of God."[48] When the HC states, therefore, that in the Lord's Supper we share in the body and blood of Christ through the work of the Holy Spirit, it picks up an emphasis better described as Bullingerian-Calvinist than Melanchthonian-Calvinist.

What we have discovered about an alleged Melanchthonian structure and doctrine of the Lord's Supper in the HC holds true for most of the other claims of Melanchthon's influence as well: the catechism contains themes that are indeed found in Melanchthon but are not unique to him. For example, as Lang has observed, the central motif of comfort in the HC is common not only in Melanchthon but also in Luther and in the earlier Reformed catechetical tradition, most strikingly in one of John a Lasco's catechisms in 1553.[49] The definition of faith in HC 21 as both knowledge (*erkandtnusz*) and trust or assurance (*vertrawen*) may also go back through Ursinus's catechisms to Melanchthon, as both Lang and Neuser maintained, but these fundamental elements of faith appear together also in Leo Jud's Larger Catechism of 1534 and in Calvin's Genevan Catechism of 1545.[50] Neuser suggested that the HC's references

47. *Consensus Tigurinus* III, VI, VIII, XII, XIV, XXI, XXIII, XXV. The Latin text of the Zurich Consensus can be found in *Ioannis Calvini Opera Quae Supersunt Omnia* [CO], 59 vols (= CR, vols. 29–88), ed. G. Baum, E. Cunitz, and E. Reuss (Halle, 1834–60), 7:733–48. An English translation by Ian Bunting was published in the *Journal of Presbyterian History* 44 (1966): 45–61.

48. *Confessio Helvetica posterior* 21.5, 6, in *Creeds of Christendom*, ed. Philip Schaff, 3 vols. (1919; reprint, Grand Rapids: Baker, 1990), 3:292, 293.

49. Lang, *Heidelberger Katechismus*, LXVII. Lang quotes the phrase "Atroost int leven ende sterven" from Q/A 125 of a Lasco's *De Catechismus, oft Kinderleere* . . . (1553), found in Abraham Kuyper, ed. *Lasci Opera*, 2:341–475. Cf. also Sturm, *Zacharias Ursinus*, 249.

50. Leo Jud, *Catechismus. Christliche klare vnd einfalte ynleitung* . . . (1534), in Gooszen, "Catechismus," *Heidelbergsche Catechismus*, 34: "Der Glaube begreift zwey Dinge: Erstlich, Erkenntnisz Gottes. . . . Zum andern, anhangen dem erkannten Gut und steif

to a believer's sharing in Christ and all his benefits (HC 20, 53, 55, 65) have their roots in Melanchthon's famous dictum, "To know Christ is to know his benefits," but this is also a well-known emphasis in Calvin.[51] Finally, Lang's assertion that the linkage between repentance and conversion in HC 88–90 is one of the few places in the catechism where a Melanchthonian influence can be still be detected is weakened by Lang's own admission that Calvin treats the two concepts in a similar fashion in the *Institutes*.[52]

Lang also found Melanchthonian traces in the HC's interpretation of the Fifth Commandment and in HC 114 on the keeping of the law. This is again a possibility,[53] but I should like to explore the larger question whether the HC's whole perspective on the law owes something to Melanchthon. For, Melanchthonian or not, there are some significant non-Reformed emphases in this area where the catechism is usually considered to be its most Reformed.[54] The six questions and answers that introduce the section on gratitude and lead into an exposition of the Ten Commandments begin with HC 86 on good works:

Q. We have been delivered from our misery by God's grace alone through Christ and not because we have earned it: why then must we still do good?

A. To be sure, Christ has redeemed us by his blood. But we do good because Christ by his Spirit is also renewing us to be like himself, so that in all our living we may show that we are thankful to God for all he has done for us, and so that he may be praised through us. And we do good so that we may be assured of our faith by its fruits, and

---

darauf vertrauen . . ." (Q/A 21). For Calvin, see GC 111, 113, 119, in *Theological Treatises*, 105, 106 (OS 2:92, 93).

51. See, e.g., *Institutes* 3.1.1, 3.3.1.

52. Lang, *Heidelberger Katechismus*, LXXI. Lang includes here a quotation from *Institutes* 3.3.5.

53. Like HC 114, Ursinus speaks of an "[initium] illius obedientiae, quam lex Dei requirit. . . ." (CMa 211, in Lang, *Heidelberger Katechismus*, 182) and Melanchthon of an "inchoatam obedientiam iuxta praecepta Dei" (*Examen ordinandorum*, CR 23:34). Sources for the HC's treatment of the Fifth Commandment are almost certainly Ursinus's CMi 90 and CMa 192, possibly Melanchthon's *Loci* (CR 21:703ff.), but also possibly Calvin's GC 185–95 (*Theological Treatises*, 113–14 [OS 2:104–6]).

54. Klooster, *A Mighty Comfort: The Christian Faith According to the Heidelberg Catechism* (Grand Rapids: CRC Publications, 1990), 37, 93; *Evangelical Dictionary of Theology*, s.v. "Heidelberg Catechism."

so that by our godly living our neighbors may be won over to Christ.[55]

What is striking about HC 86 is that the answer is not what one might expect from the way the question is formulated. The question is literally, "Why are we supposed to do good works?" (*Warumb sollen wir gute werck thun?*). According to the answer, we are supposed to do good works because Christ who has redeemed us by his blood also renews us in his image by the Holy Spirit. We must do good works, therefore, not because of any external compulsion of the law but because of the internal renewal of the Holy Spirit. And Christ is renewing us by his Spirit so that by that renewal, i.e., by the "fruits of faith" and "godly living" that the Spirit produces in us, God may be thanked and praised, we may be assured of our salvation, and our neighbors may be won to Christ.[56]

As we move from the question to the answer, then, what we see is a subtle shift in the meaning of the verb *sollen*. The question implies that we are supposed do good works according to a necessity of obligation: why must we, why ought we, why should we do good works? The answer suggests, however, that we are supposed to do good works according to a necessity of consequence: we cannot but do good works. In those in whom the Spirit of Christ is at work producing faith and renewal, good works are the inevitable result, the necessary consequence or after-effect of that renewal.[57] As the catechism puts it elsewhere, Christ by his Holy Spirit "makes me wholeheartedly willing and ready from now on to live for him" (HC 1). The same God who created us "in his own image, that is, in true righteousness and holiness" (HC 6) is now recreating us in that same image (HC 86). Those in whom the Spirit produces faith (HC 65)

---

55. *Ecumenical Creeds,* 53 (Lang, *Heidelberger Katechismus,* 35–36).

56. Over against Klooster (*Mighty Comfort,* 95–96), I, John Hesselink ("The Law of God," in *Guilt, Grace, and Gratitude: A Commentary on the Heidelberg Catechism,* ed. Donald J. Bruggink [New York: Half Moon, 1963], 172), and Fritz Büsser ("Die Bedeutung des Gesetzes," in *Handbuch zum Heidelberger Katechismus,* ed. Lothar Coenen [Neukirchen-Vluyn: Neukirchener Verlag, 1963], 163–64), I would maintain that assurance and witness in HC 86 are not motivations for our good works but the effects or benefits of the good works that Christ produces in us by the Holy Spirit. The English translation of HC 86 in *Ecumenical Creeds* (53) is incorrect, therefore, when it adds the line "And we do good" just before "so that we may be assured . . . and so that . . . our neighbors may be won. . . ." Not only do the words "and we do good" not appear in the German text, but they suggest that assurance and witness are motives for doing good.

57. Cf. Hesselink, "Law of God," 170–71.

and who are grafted into Christ by that faith find it "impossible . . . not to produce fruits of gratitude" (HC 64).

It is from this perspective, then, that the HC goes on to treat the law in detail. According to HC 86, we do good works because we have to, not because the law says we must but because they are the inevitable fruits of renewal by the Spirit within. HC 88 and 90 go on to describe this renewal as a coming-to-life, literally a resurrection (*aufferstehung*) of the new self that involves a desire and a love to live according to God's will in all good works. What then are good works? Those done out of true faith and in conformity to God's law (HC 91) as found in the Decalogue (HC 92). Then follows the exposition of the Ten Commandments in HC 93–113. Finally, when all the commandments have been explained, the catechism addresses the questions of the extent of this renewal and conformity to the law in this life and of the function of the law in the sanctification of believers. Even though the catechism claims that it is impossible for those grafted into Christ not to produce fruits of conformity to the law, it also acknowledges at the end of the exposition of the law that we are not yet fully renewed and that the law still has a role to play in the life of the believer. Those converted to God cannot obey these commandments perfectly because even the holiest have only a small beginning of this obedience in this life (HC 114). God wants the commandments pointedly preached, therefore, so that we may come to a greater knowledge of our sin and more eagerly look to Christ and so that we never stop striving to be renewed (HC 115).

This is not the same approach to the law, however, taken in Reformed catechisms that are often suggested as major sources of the HC. Why must we do good works? According to the Shorter Catechism of Leo Jud of Zurich (1541), good works are indeed given by the Spirit of Christ (Q/A 85),[58] but they are also a duty of service that we owe to God. Since we are members of God's covenant, it is only just and proper that we keep that part of the covenant that applies to us, namely, that we walk holy and blameless before his face (Q/A 86).[59] According to Calvin's Genevan Catechism, too, good works are directed by the Holy Spirit and proceed from the Holy Spirit, but since they are prescribed in God's law,

---

58. Leo Jud, *Ein kürtze Christenliche underweysung* . . ., in Lang, *Heidelberger Katechismus*, 78.

59. "Zum anderen sind die güten werck ein schuldige pflicht vnn dienst die wir Gott schuldig sind. . . . so gebürt sich vnnd ist billich dasz wir den artickel im pundt, der vns zügehört, haltind, namlich dasz wir frommklich vnn vnschuldigklich vor sinem angsicht wandlind . . ." (ibid., 79).

they also represent conformity to a rule of life and worship that we are "obliged" to keep, that "demands . . . strict perfection from us," toward which we "ought to aim" and "must strive."[60] According to Ursinus's CMa, finally, the Spirit renews us in the image of God (Q/A 1) and restores us in the righteousness that the law requires (Q/A 36). It is impossible that there be true faith in us without its fruits (Q/A 141). Nevertheless, because God's covenant is valid only for those who keep it, we are "obligated" (*obligavimus*) to live in holiness (Q/A 141); the fruit of faith is something to which God's covenant of grace "obliges" (*obligat*) us (Q/A 142). We are still "bound" (*astringimur*) to the Ten Commandments after Christ abolishes the law, and we "owe" (*debemus*) an even greater obedience to him now that God's grace in Christ has been clearly revealed (Q/A 151).[61] Virtually none of this language of obligation to the law, so prevalent in these earlier Reformed catechisms, can be found in the HC.[62]

The same is true of HC 115's summary of the role of the law in the life of the redeemed, often called the "third" or "didactic" use of the law. HC 115 reads as follows:

> Q. No one in this life can obey the Ten Commandments perfectly: why then does God want them preached so pointedly?

> A. First, so that the longer we live the more we may come to know our sinfulness and the more eagerly look to Christ for forgiveness of sins and righteousness. Second, so that, while praying to God for the grace of the Holy Spirit, we may never stop striving to be renewed more and more after God's image, until after this life we reach our goal: perfection.

The second reason why God wants the commandments preached, namely, so that we persevere in our striving to be renewed, has its roots in the Reformed tradition. Similar statements can be found in the Genevan Catechism and the CMa, major *Vorlagen* for the HC, and in

---

60. GC 121, 122, 128–32, 225, 229, in *Theological Treatises*, 106, 107, 118 (OS 2:94, 95–96, 111, 112).

61. CMa, in Lang, *Heidelberger Katechismus*, 152, 156, 173, 172, 174.

62. A possible exception might be the language of HC 94, where the question reads, "What does the Lord require [*erfordert*] in the first commandment?"

Calvin's *Institutes*.[63] As Calvin puts it, the law exhorts the residual flesh in the believer "like a whip to an idle and balky ass, to arouse it to work."[64]

The first reason given above, however, is foreign to these Reformed sources—at least as a *third* use of the law. The notion of the law as uncovering our sin so as to lead us to Christ does appear in Calvin and Ursinus as what is usually called the "second" or "theological" use of the law, but only in reference to unbelievers or to believers prior to conversion, not, as in the HC, to believers after conversion.[65]

Are these non-Reformed elements in the catechism's treatment of the law perhaps Melanchthonian? This is an attractive possibility because there indeed are parallels to these ideas in Melanchthon. With respect to the spontaneous good works of the believer, for example, Melanchthon had stated in the 1521 *Loci* that

> those who have been renewed by the Spirit of Christ now conform voluntarily even without the law to what the law used to command. . . . Therefore, . . . we will and desire spontaneously and from the heart what the law demands . . . The Spirit of God cannot be in the human heart without fulfilling the Decalogue. The Decalogue is therefore observed by necessity.[66]

However, in the late 1520s and 1530s, as a result of his further exegetical work, the antinomian challenge of John Agricola, interactions with Roman Catholics, and the ecclesiastical exigencies of the day, Melanchthon began to place a greater emphasis on the importance of the law in the life of the converted.[67] In fact, he was the first Protestant ever to talk about a third use of the law when he increased the number of uses from two to three in the 1534 edition of his commentary on Colossians.[68]

---

63. GC 229, in *Theological Treatises*, 118 (OS 2:112); CMa 150, in Lang, *Heidelberger Katechismus*, 174; *Institutes* 2.7.12.

64. *Institutes* 2.7.12 (LCC 20:361).

65. Calvin, GC 228, in *Theological Treatises*, 118 (OS 2:111–12); *Institutes* 2.7.6–9. Ursinus, CMa 149, in Lang, *Heidelberger Katechismus*, 173. Cf. Hesselink, *Calvin's Concept of the Law* (Allison Park, PA: Pickwick, 1992), 241.

66. LCC 19:123, 127.

67. See Melanchthon, "Instruction for the Visitors of Parish Pastors in Electoral Saxony" (1528), in *Luther's Works* [LW], vol. 40, ed. Conrad Bergendoff (Philadelphia: Muhlenberg, 1958), 275–78 (*Weimar Ausgabe* [WA] 26:202–4); *Apology* 4.122–400, in *Bekenntnisschriften*, 185–233. Cf. Timothy J. Wengert, "The Origins of the Third Use of the Law: Philip Melanchthon's Commentary on Colossians (1534)" (paper presented at the annual Sixteenth Century Studies Conference, San Francisco, CA, October, 1995).

68. Wengert, "Origins," 1.

This third use made its way into the 1535 edition of the *Loci communes*, and in even more detail in the 1543 *Loci*. In the latter edition, Melanchthon identifies two dimensions to this third function of the law. First, it exposes the remnants of sin in the believer's life so that one may grow in knowledge of sin and in repentance. Second, it teaches the particular works in which God wants us to exercise obedience.[69] This second, or didactic, dimension to the third use of the law is found also in Calvin and Ursinus;[70] the first, or pedagogical, dimension does not appear in Reformed theological literature until twenty years later in the HC.

As in the cases we examined earlier, however, these Melanchthonian parallels cannot be identified exclusively with Melanchthon. So far as the necessity of good works is concerned, Luther had argued already before Melanchthon that one who is justified does good works "out of spontaneous love in obedience to God."[71] Saying that a Christian must do good, he once claimed at the table, is like saying that God must do good or that the sun must shine; good works are a necessary consequence of faith.[72] This concept would continue to be discussed and refined in Lutheran circles in the various antinomian controversies, and at the end of these debates, the Formula of Concord would still state that insofar as a person is born anew by the Spirit of God, "he does everything from a free and merry spirit," not by compulsion of the law.[73]

The same is true of the pedagogical dimension to the third use of the law in HC 115. An earlier parallel to this can certainly be found in Melanchthon and, so far as I have been able to tell, only in Melanchthon.

---

69. CR 21:719.

70. Calvin, *Institutes* 2.7.12; Ursinus, CMa 150, in Lang, *Heidelberger Katechismus*, 174.

71. "The Freedom of the Christian" (1520), in LW 31, ed. Harold J. Grimm (Philadelphia: Muhlenberg, 1957), 359 (WA 7:60).

72. *Table Talk* cited (without reference) in E. Doumergue, *Jean Calvin. Les hommes et les choses de son temps*, 7 vols. (Lausanne: Bridel, 1910), 4:195. The Formula of Concord, Solid Declaration 4.10–12 quotes a long excerpt from Luther's preface to the Epistle to the Romans, where he says, "It is impossible for [faith] not to be constantly doing what is good" (*The Book of Concord*, trans. and ed. Theodore G. Tappert [Philadelphia: Muhlenberg, 1959], 553 [*Bekenntnisschriften*, 941]). Cf. also Paul Althaus, *The Ethics of Martin Luther* (Philadelphia: Fortress, 1972), 30–42.

73. Formula of Concord, Solid Declaration 6.17–18, in *Book of Concord*, 566–67 [*Bekenntnisschriften*, 967]). For the various antinomian controversies in sixteenth-century Lutheranism, see Robert Kolb, "Historical Background of the Formula of Concord," in *A Contemporary Look at the Formula of Concord*, ed. Robert Preus and Wilbert Rosin (St. Louis: Concordia, 1978), 13–16, 26–29, and 33–36.

But we must remember that the HC never describes the preaching of the law here as a "third use" of the law. In fact, nowhere does the catechism number the uses of the law at all. Without assigned numbers, Answer 115a could be understood not as a dimension of the third use of the law, such as we find it in Melanchthon, but as an application of the second use of the law to believers, such as we find it in Luther, who did not think it necessary to create a separate use for believers.[74] In that case, Answer 115 is a remarkable splice of the Lutheran second use (115a) and the Reformed third use (115b) of the law.

What, then, does Melanchthon of Wittenberg have to do with the catechism of Heidelberg? As we have seen, this is not an easy question to answer. It depends in part on what is meant when one describes the catechism as Melanchthonian. If this means only that there are certain similarities in tone or doctrine between the HC and Melanchthon's writings, then the term may be appropriate. If, however, it means that these similarities are unique to Melanchthon and/or represent the *influence* of Melanchthon, then this label should be used sparingly, tentatively, and perhaps not at all. The most anyone has been able to show is certain parallels in tone, structure, and theology, and parallels do not necessarily reflect influence.

Corroborating circumstantial evidence may be found, of course, in the fact that Melanchthon had such close ties to the leaders and reformation of the Palatinate and to the primary author of the HC. But the difficulty in demonstrating influence is aggravated by the fact that we know so little about the actual preparation of the catechism and that Frederick III was seeking a confessional consensus among the Protestant parties of Heidelberg. That search for consensus may explain why so much of what scholars in the past have identified as distinctively Melanchthonian in the HC can also be found in other Reformation traditions. It may also explain the phenomenon we encountered in HC 115, where it appears that emphases from the Lutheran and Calvinist traditions are combined in a single answer.

Because of its multiple sources, the HC can be described as a cloth of many colors. But since, as Klooster has aptly put it, this cloth is not "a patchwork quilt" of these sources but "an original tapestry marvelously woven,"[75] the Melanchthonian threads that this tapestry almost certainly contains are very hard to pick out. They are simply too indistinct in color

74. Wengert, "Origins," 3.
75. Klooster, *Heidelberg Catechism*, 177.

and too finely woven into the fabric to be identified clearly, and the task of unraveling them is next to impossible. Frederick III would be most pleased.

6

Ordo docendi: Melanchthon and the Organization of Calvin's *Institutes*, 1536–1543

Richard A. Muller

I. Calvin's "Second Edition": The Importance of 1539

The name and reputation of John Calvin are inseparably joined to the *Institutes of the Christian Religion*, first published in 1536 and given its final form in the edition of 1559. Comparison of the two editions, moreover, evidences a massive development from catechetical manual to theological system.[1] The movement from the first form of the *Institutes* to its final form was accomplished by the addition of new topics, new materials, expanded discussions of the original materials, and some reordering of the topics themselves. There was also, equally importantly, a change in the literary genre of the document itself. The first form of the *Institutes* was clearly modeled on catechesis, probably on Luther's two catechisms[2]—the

---

1. On the text-history and development of Calvin's *Institutes*, see: Julius Köstlin, "Calvin's Institutio nach Form und Inhalt, in ihrer geschlichtlichen Entwicklung," *Theologische Studien und Kritiken* 41 (1868): 7–62, 410–86; Emile Doumergue, *Jean Calvin, les hommes et les choses de son temps*, 7 vols. (Lausanne, 1899–1917), IV: 1–17; Benjamin B. Warfield, "On the Literary History of Calvin's Institutes," in John Calvin, *Institutes of the Christian Religion*, trans. John Allen, 7th ed. (Philadelphia: Presbyterian Board of Christian Education, 1936), xxx–xxxi; Wilhelm Niesel, *The Theology of Calvin*, trans. Harold Knight (London: Lutterworth, 1956; repr. Grand Rapids: Baker, 1980), 9–21, 246–54; François Wendel, *Calvin: The Origins and Development of His Religious Thought*, trans. Philip Mairet (N. Y.: Harper & Row, 1963), 111–49; Jean-Daniel Benoit, "The History and Development of the *Institutio*: How Calvin Worked," in *John Calvin*, ed. G. E. Duffield (Appleford: Sutton Courtney Press, 1966), 102–17.

2. Thus, Lefranc, "Introduction," in *Institution de la religion chrestienne de Calvin* (1541), 11–12; Albert Autin, *L'Institution Chrétienne de Calvin* (Paris: Société Française d'Éditions littéraires et techniques, 1929), 77; Wilhelm Neuser, "The Development of the *Institutes* 1536 to 1559," in *John Calvin's Institutes: His Opus Magnum*, ed. B.J. van der Walt (Potchefstrom: Institute for Reformational Studies, 1986), 33, 38–39; Alister E. McGrath, *A Life of John Calvin: A Study in the Shaping of Western Culture* (Cambridge, MA: Basil Blackwell, 1990), 137. But note the very careful evaluation of the extent of Luther's theological influence in Willem van't Spijker, "The Influence of Luther on Calvin

two subsequent forms (1539ff. and 1559) were, as indicated by Calvin's letter to the reader, a series of theological disputations and commonplaces (*loci communes*) or "topics" in theology.[3]

The entire literary history of the *Institutes* would occupy a far longer study than this one—here I will examine only the point of transition between the first edition (1536) and the second major pattern of organization (1539–50).[4] The *Institutes* of these intermediate editions is certainly the least frequently examined, despite the fact that it was the *Institutes* in that version that framed Calvin's theology for twenty years at the peak and center of his career. The 1539 *Institutes* has not only been neglected by scholars, it had also been criticized as ill-organized. I propose to reverse that judgment and to describe the 1539 *Institutes* as a well-ordered and finely argued essay in theology and, beyond that, a work which (taken together with Calvin's 1540 *Commentary on Romans* and his catechetical writings of 1537–38) marks perhaps the most crucial theological development in his career. The 1539 edition also provides insight into Calvin's conception of his theological task and into his ongoing theological conversation with other reformers, most notably, in this case, Philip Melanchthon.

Specifically, the prefatory letters to the 1539 *Institutes* and the *Commentary on Romans*, taken in the context of Calvin's catechetical works of 1537–38 and of a consideration of Melanchthon's theological method, provide evidence that Calvin drew himself away from the form and intention of the 1536 *Institutes* and entirely reframed his conception of the theological task between the publication of the first edition of his *Institutes*

According to the *Institutes*," in *John Calvin's Institutes: his opus magnum. Proceedings of the second South African Congress for Calvin Research July 31-August 3, 1984*, ed. B. J. van der Walt (Potchefstroom: Potchefstroom University for Christian Higher Education, 1986), 83–105.

3. On this point, see T. H. L. Parker, *Calvin's New Testament Commentaries*, 2d ed. (Louisville: Westminster/John Knox Press, 1993), 89–90.

4. In the following essay, I have used Joannes Calvinus, *Christianae religionis institutio, totam fere pietatis summam, et quicquid est in doctrina salutis cognitu necessarium, complectens: omnibus pietatis studiosis lectu dignissimum opus, ac recens editum* (Basel: Platter & Lasius, 1536); Ioannes Calvinus, *Institutio christianae religionis nunc vere demum suo titulo respondens* (Strasbourg: Wendelin Rihel, 1539); Ioannes Calvinus, *Institutio christianae religionis nunc vere demum suo titulo respondens* (Strasbourg: Wendelin Rihel, 1543). I have also consulted John Calvin, *Institutes of the Christian Religion* (1536), trans. and annotated Ford Lewis Battles, rev. ed. (Grand Rapids: Eerdmans, 1986). The 1536 *Institutes* is also available in *Ioannis Calvini opera quae supersunt omnia*, ed. Guilielmus Baum, Eduardus Cunitz, and Eduardus Reuss, 59 vols. (Brunswick: Schwetschke, 1863–1900), I; there is no modern edition of the 1539 text.

and the appearance of the second edition. What is more, the shift in literary genre and the outward evidence of that shift, namely, the reorganization of the *Institutes*, bear the unmistakable marks of a Melanchthonian influence. This is not to discount relationships between the *Institutes* and the thought of Zwingli, Bucer, and Bullinger. It is our purpose here to chart the shift in Calvin's thought and to identify its relationship to Melanchthon's theological method.

II. Order and Method in Calvin's Writings, 1537–39

Calvin's prefaces to the 1539 *Institutes* and the 1540 *Commentaries on the Epistle to the Romans* were not only written in close temporal proximity to each other—they also reflect similar concerns. Indeed, Calvin's prefaces to the two major editions of the *Institutes* (Latin, 1539; French, 1541) and to the *Commentary on Romans* (1540) should be regarded as an interrelated set of statements concerning not only the method he chose to follow in his work but also concerning the program of writing that he began with the 1539 *Institutes* and the Romans commentary—the program that he followed, with little alteration, for the remainder of his life. The relationship between Calvin's letter to the reader from the 1539 *Institutes* and the preface to his 1540 Romans commentary is particularly significant. Indeed, in the latter Calvin argued forcefully for the rectitude of his adoption of the form of a running commentary on the text of the Bible without recourse to the logical and methodological device of identifying the *loci* or *topoi* addressed by the biblical authors in the course of their argument. In the former, Calvin noted that his *Institutes*, as recast in 1539, was to be constructed in such a way as to relieve him of the necessity of developing either *loci communes* or *disputationes* as part of his approach to the text in his commentaries.[5]

Once the division of labor and Calvin's positive assessment of the *locus* method is rightly understood, then the full significance of his differences with Bucer and Melanchthon becomes clear as well. On the one hand, Calvin countered Bucer's rather burdensome style with his emphasis on

---

5. Calvin, *Institutio* (1539), "Epistola ad Lectorem," fol. *1v (*CO* 2: 3–4); Calvin, *Commentarii ad Romanos* (1540), "Calvinus . . . Grynaeo," fol. A4r–v, A5v: in *CO* 10: 403–5 (*CTS Romans*, xxv–xxvi); cf. I. John Hesselink, "Development and Purpose of Calvin's Institutes," *Reformed Theological Review* 24 (1965): 69–70. On the humanistic stress on the identification and ordering of *topoi* or *loci communes*, see Manfred Hoffmann, *Rhetoric and Theology: The Hermeneutic of Erasmus* (Toronto: University of Toronto Press, 1994), 6, 8, 25, 37–38, 145–48. Also note Jerry H. Bentley, *Humanists and Holy Writ: New Testament Scholarship in the Renaissance* (Princeton: Princeton University Press, 1983).

brevitas and *facilitas*: Calvin's method would hold to the text but would do so expeditiously.[6] On the other hand, as implied by his prefatory letter to the *Institutes*, Calvin presupposed the necessity of gathering *loci* or topics in the course of his exegetical labors—his intention, however, was to place them in his *Institutes*, not in his commentaries.[7]

The *argumentum* placed by Calvin at the beginning of his exposition of the Epistle to the Romans evidences another dimension of Calvin's approach both to the text of Scripture and to theological formulation. His humanistic training pressed him to understand that the preliminary identification of the *argumentum, dispositio, scopus,* or *methodus* of a text was integral to the work of interpretation. In the case of the *argumentum* of the Epistle to the Romans, Calvin offers his readers the initial insight, which he held in profound agreement with Melanchthon, that "the entire Epistle is so methodically arranged" that it is a model of the art of rhetoric and dialectic.[8] The understanding of this Epistle, given its excellence in substance and arrangement, provides the proper "entrance . . . to all the most hidden treasures of Scripture."[9]

We have, here, in a nutshell, Calvin's theological method: the running exposition of the biblical text in commentary and sermon, coupled with the elicitation of theological *loci* from the text and the gathering of those *loci* together with the important dogmatic *disputationes* of Calvin's time into the form of a basic instruction or *institutio* in theology. All that needs to be added is to establish the right order of expression or teaching, the *ordo recte dicendi* and the *methodus* or *via*,[10] according to which the *loci* would be organized—and that emphasis also appears in the 1539 *Institutes*, as does Calvin's development of a new series of topics in conjunc-

---

6. See Richard Gamble, "*Brevitas et facilitas*: Toward an Understanding of Calvin's Hermeneutic," *Westminster Theological Journal* 47 (1985): 1–17.

7. Calvin, *Institutio* (1539), "Epistola ad lectorem," fol. *1v; and cf. Parker, *Calvin's New Testament Commentaries*, 89.

8. Calvin, *Commentarii ad Romanos* in *CO* 49: 1 (*CTS Romans*, xxix); cf. Melanchthon, *Elementa rhetorices*, in *CR* 13: 431–32.

9. Calvin, *Commentarii ad Romanos* in *CO* 49: 1 (*CTS Romans*, xxix).

10. Calvin, *Institutio* (1539), fol. 2: note that Calvin's phrase in 1539 is *ordo recte dicendi*, "right order of expression or speech." This form is retained in the 1543 edition, but altered to *ordo recte docendi*, "right order of teaching" in Calvin, *Institutio* (1550), I.3, ad fin. The change occurred earlier in the French: Calvin, *Institution* (1541), fol. 3 reads simply "ce que l'ordre requiert" but the very next edition, Calvin, *Institutio* (1545), fol. 3 offers, "ce que l'ordre d'enseigner requiert."

tion with the original catechetical order.[11] So too, in 1539, could Calvin state that "the arrangement of divine wisdom" was so "ordered and disposed" that it evidenced a most "beautiful agreement among all its parts."[12] The identification and exposition of that order and disposition can be identified as the "systematic" aspect of Calvin's method in the *Institutes*,[13] but it is clearly an aspect of his larger method, in which the topical and organizational drive cannot be separated from the exegetical effort.

Indeed, Melanchthon had indicated in his analysis of the rhetorical flow of Romans that "since the best mode of interpretation is to reveal the disposition of the speech, we have discussed the order of all the topics, propositions, and arguments. ..."[14] Melanchthon also had made an explicit connection in his 1532 Romans commentary between his discussion of topics in the commentary and his development of the doctrinal topics in the *Loci communes theologici*.[15] The point in fact adumbrates Calvin's comment in the 1539 *Institutes* to the effect that one ought not to look in his commentaries for *loci communes*—albeit, in critique of Melanchthon, Calvin drew the line of distinction between *commentarius* and *loci communes* far more sharply. Yet, it is precisely at the point of their methodological disagreement that the positive relationship between Calvin and Melanchthon bears fruit, namely, in the question of the identification of the theological *topoi* and of the proper location of developed *topoi* or *loci* in a particular genre of theological work.[16] The thesis can be

11. Calvin, *Institutio* (1539), fol. 2; cf. Calvin, *Institutio* (1559), I.i.3; cf. James I. Packer, "Calvin the Theologian," in *John Calvin: A Collection of Essays*, ed. Gervase Duffield (Grand Rapids/Appleford: Eerdmans/Sutton Courtney Press, 1966.), 157–59 with Abel Lefranc, *Calvin et l'eloquence française* (Paris: Fischbacher, 1934), 29.

12. Calvin, *Institutio* (1539), fol. 12; cf. Calvin, *Institutio* (1559), I.viii.1.

13. Cf. Ronald S. Wallace, "Calvin's Approach to Theology," in *The Challenge of Evangelical Theology: Essays in Approach and Method*, ed. Nigel Cameron (Edinburgh: Rutherford House, 1987), 137–41; with John H. Leith, "Calvin's Theological Method and the Ambiguity in his Theology," in *Reformation Studies: Essays in Honor of Roland H. Bainton*, ed. Franklin H. Littell (Richmond: John Knox, 1962), 111–13.

14. Melanchthon, *Dispositio orationis in epistola Pauli as Romanos* (1529), in *CR* 15: 445; on Melanchthon's understanding of *loci* see Manfred Hoffmann, "Rhetoric and Dialectic in Erasmus' and Melanchthon's Interpretation of John's Gospel," in *Philip Melanchthon (1497–1560) and the Commentary*, ed. Timothy J. Wengert and M. Patrick Graham (Sheffield: Sheffield Academic Press, 1997), 65–72.

15. Melanchthon, *Commentarii in Epistolam Pauli ad Romanos*, in *CR* 15: 499.

16. Cf. Parker, *Calvin's New Testament Commentaries*, 89; with Robert Kolb, "Teaching the Text: The Commonplace Method in Sixteenth Century Lutheran Biblical Commentary," *Bibliothèque d'Humanisme et Renaissance* 49 (1987): 571–85.

stated quite simply: the years 1537–1539 marked perhaps the most significant new point of departure in Calvin's theological career—and what occurred in these years can be discerned in the program enunciated in the two prefaces, the Romans preface and the *Institutes* preface. One should also consider the concrete manifestation of the program, first in the preliminary topical expansion found in the catechisms of 1537–38 and then in the Romans commentary itself and the organization of the radically revised *Institutes* of 1539. At the foundation of this development was the theological conversation with Melanchthon.

III. From Catechesis to *Lo ci communes*: the *Institutes*, 1536–1539

Three documents from Calvin's early years in Geneva offer crucial evidence of the first issues addressed by Calvin as he identified the patterns or forms that his theology would take and as he considered issues of its organizational development: first, the famous *Christianae religionis institutio* (1536) and then the two catechisms—less known, but highly significant indices of Calvin's early thought: the *Instruction & confession de Foy dont on use en l'Eglise de Genève* (1537) and the *Catechismus, sive christianae religionis institutio* (1538).[17] Specifically, these three documents offer evidence of the issues and motives leading to the reorganization of the *Institutio christianae religionis* in 1539, during Calvin's exile in Strasbourg. The three works, the first *Institutio* and the two catechisms, are all catechetical in their design and intention. Nonetheless, there is a difference: the longer *Institutio* of 1536 follows the precise order of a catechism, the latter two essays, albeit brief, add topics beyond the usual catechetical order and, therefore, indicate a transition toward another theological form.[18]

Calvin's 1536 *Institutes*, as already noted, was patterned as a catechetical manual, in six chapters: i. *De Lege, quod Decalogi explicationem continet*; ii. *De Fide, ubi et Symbolum (quod Apostolicum vocant) explicatur*; iii. *De Oratione, ubi & oratio dominica enarratur*; iv. *De Sacramentis*; v. *Sacramenta non*

---

17. *Le Catéchisme français de Calvin, publié en 1537, réimprimé pour la première fois*, avec deux notices par Albert Rilliet & Théophile Dufour (Geneva: H. Georg, 1878); *Catechismus, sive christianae religionis institutio* (Basel: 1538). Note the facsimile edition and translation, *Catechismus, sive christianae religionis institutio . . . Catechism or Institution of the Christian Religion*, trans. Ford Lewis Battles, 4th ed. (Pittsburgh: Pittsburgh Theological Seminary, 1976).

18. See the discussion in I. John Hesselink, *Calvin's First Catechism: A Commentary*, with F.L. Battles' translation of the 1538 Catechism (Louisville: Westminster/John Knox Press, 1997), 39–43.

esse quinque reliqua quem pro sacramentis hactenus vulgo habita sunt, declaratur: tum qualia sint, ostenditur; vi. *De libertate christiana, potestate ecclesiastica, & politica administratione.*[19] The first five chapters reflect the standard catechetical topics and, indeed, follow the order of Luther's catechisms. The final chapter, on Christian freedom, church powers and political administration, also reflects Luther's model: it contains the same topics as the "table of household duties" (*tabula oeconomica*) at the conclusion of the *Small Catechism.*[20]

Calvin altered this basic catechetical model in the new *Institutes* of 1539 by the addition of a series of new chapters. His decision, moreover, as noted specifically in the new preface or "letter to the reader" of his 1539 *Institutes*, was to move away from his initial catechetical approach and to refashion the work into an instruction of candidates for the ministry. This decision is also apparent in his reflection in a letter to Farel that he was viewed by the Strasbourgers "not so much as a pastor" as an "instructor,"[21] and in his decision to recast not only the *Institutes* but also the subsequent catechisms.

The trajectory of development here is important: the new *Institutes* retained the chapters of the first edition, but also drew on the topics developed in Calvin's intervening catechetical exercises.[22] Specifically, eight topics appear in the catechisms of 1537–38 that are not found in the first edition of the *Institutes*: the universal fact of religion, the distinction between true and false religion, free choice, election and predestination, church offices, human traditions, excommunication, and the civil magistracy. Of these eight chapters, those on free choice, election and predestination, church offices, human traditions, excommunication, and the civil magistracy transfer directly to the 1539 *Institutes*. The initial chapters on religion of the 1537/38 catechisms are not as broad in design as the initial chapters of the 1539 *Institutes*, namely the chapters on the *cognitio*

19. Calvin, *Institutio* (1536), fol. 42, 102, 157, 200, 285, 400, respectively. Still the most detailed comparative synopsis of the various editions of the *Institutes* is that offered by the editors of the *Calvini Opera: CO* 1: li–lviii.

20. See Martin Luther, *Catechesis minor,* in *Concordia Triglotta: Libri symbolici Ecclesiae Lutheranae, Germanice-Latine-Anglice* (St. Louis: Concordia Publishing House, 1921), 560–61. Edward F. Meylan, "The Stoic Doctrine of Indifferent Things and the Conception of Christian Liberty in Calvin's *Institutio Religionis Christianae,*" *Romanic Review* 28 (1937): 138–39, identified the discussion of Christian freedom of the 1536 *Institutes* and the separate chapter on the subject in the 1539 edition as an adaptation of the chapter of the same name found in Melanchthon's *Loci communes.*

21. Calvin to Farel, 27 October 1540, in *CO* 11: 90–93 (*Letters,* I, 212).

22. Cf. Battles, "Preface," in *Catechismus* (1538), iv–v.

Dei and *cognitio hominibus*—yet even here we find a clear continuity: the new catechetical topics are found as subtopics in the chapter on the knowledge of God.[23] At the same time, moreover, as these topics were added to the *Institutes*, Calvin omitted them from his catechisms.[24]

The 1539 expansion of the *Institutes* was accomplished not only by the addition of eight entirely new chapters but also by the division of the fourth and sixth chapter of the 1536 edition into three chapters each (10–12 and 14–16)—resulting in an expansion of the *Institutes* from six to seventeen chapters. This expansion was accomplished, however, without major alteration of the order of the original topics: at the heart of the 1539 *Institutes*, Calvin retained the original catechetical structure, conflated with the eight new chapters.[25] Apart from the rearrangement of the order of discussion of the false sacraments, there was in fact no reordering of the original six chapters. Parker's statement that the 1539 edition repesented a movement from a catechetical to a systematic order is, thus, not entirely correct: within the 1539 edition, the original catechetical order continued to function as an ordering principle.[26]

As Parker certainly recognized, the 1539 *Institutes* was marked by a major alteration of genre and purpose, so significant for the development of the text that the full form and purpose of the 1539 edition cannot be inferred from the 1536 edition or from the expanded catechetical model of 1537–38. It is also pointless to attempt to explain the entire structural development of the *Institutes* on the basis of Calvin's early ex-

---

23. N.B., "human traditions" is subsumed under CaXIV, *De potestate ecclesiastica* in Calvin, *Institutio* (1539), fol. 371–78 and only becomes a separate, new chapter in 1543: Calvin, *Institutio* (1543), caXIII (fol. 337–50).

24. Cf. John Calvin, *L'Institution puérile de la doctrine chrestienne faicte par manière de dyalogue* (1541) in *Opera Selecta*, 2: 152–56; idem, *Le Catéchisme de l'église de Genève, c'est a dire le formulaire d'instruire les enfants en la chrestienté* (1541–42; Geneva: Jean Girard, 1545) and *Catechismus ecclesiae genevensis, hoc est formula erudiendi pueros in doctrina Christi* (Strasbourg: Wendelin Rihel, 1545), in *CO* 6: 1–146; translation in *Tracts* 2: 33–94. Note that the Jean Girard, 1545 edition of the *Catéchisme* is the earliest known exemplar.

25. Thus: 1. *De cognitione Dei*; 2. *De cognitione hominis & libero arbitrio*; 3. *De lege; Explicatio Decalogi* (i); 4. *De fide; Expositio symboli Apostolici* (ii); 5. *De poenitentia*; 6. *De iustificatione fidei, & meritis operum*; 7. *De similitudine ac differentia veteris ac novi testamenti*; 8. *De praedestinatione & providentia Dei*; 9. *De oratione* (iii); 10. *De sacramentis* (iv.a); 11. *De baptismo* (iv.b); 12. *De coena Domini* (iv.c); 13. *De libertate Christiana* (vi.a); 14. *De potestate Ecclesiastica* (vi.b); 15. *De politica administratione* (vi.c); 16. *De quinque falso nominatis sacramentis* (v); 17. *De vita hominis Christiani*: see Calvin, *Institutio* (Strasburg: 1539), fol. 1, 17, 58, 97, 157, 186, 225, 244, 272, 296, 305, 327, 353, 360, 378, 393, 414, respectively.

26. T.H.L. Parker. *Calvin: An Introduction to His Thought*, 1st American ed. (Louisville, KY: Westminster/John Knox Press, 1995), 5.

perience, or to assume that Calvin's conversion can be elicited as the guiding principle of the 1536 text that carries over into his later work. Nor is it convincing to argue that Calvin's initial identification of sacred doctrine as "knowledge of God and knowledge of ourselves" explains either the role of the *duplex cognitio Dei* or of the creed in establishing the order of topics in the final edition of the *Institutes*.[27]

Rather than develop such speculative theories about the structure and order of the *Institutes*, the text itself ought to be used to resolve the question. Comparison of the 1536 edition with the catechisms of 1537–38 and with the 1539 text of the *Institutes* reveals that some chapters, notably those on the two testaments and predestination, have no antecedent in the 1536 text, but do relate to the catechisms. Nor does the 1536 text, in and of itself, offer reasons why some of its topics were greatly elaborated in the next edition and others not. And then there are the chapters on the "knowledge of God" and the "knowledge of man" that have only the briefest topical precedent in either the 1536 text or the text of the catechisms.

There are at least four identifiable grounds for the development of new chapters and topics and for the recasting of the work in a new genre. Some of the development does rest on the 1536 text and represents an elaboration of extant materials. Other development of the text relates directly to Calvin's personal theological growth as he was called on to preach sermons, deliver lectures, and write his catechisms, tracts, and treatises. Nor ought we to discount the changes in Calvin's reformatory work as he moved from Geneva to Strasbourg and engaged in the life of worship and liturgy. And, finally, Calvin both learned from and increasingly drew on the works of predecessors and contemporaries.

We note these four possible grounds of the development in sequence: first, Calvin did build on themes present in the 1536 edition.[28] Thus, the

---

27. Ford Lewis Battles, "Calculus Fidei," in *Interpreting John Calvin*, ed. Robert Benedetto (Grand Rapids, MI: Baker Books, 1996), 147–50; and idem, "Introduction" in *Institutes: 1536 Edition*, xxxiv–xxxvi. Note also that the phrase *duplex cognitio Dei* or *duplex cognitio Domini*, although implied in the McNeill/Battles translation of *Institutes*, I.ii.1, "Of the resulting twofold knowledge of God we shall now discuss the first aspect; the second will be dealt with in its proper place," is not actually found in Calvin's Latin, which reads, ". . . hinc duplex emergit eius cognitio: quarum nunc prior tractanda est, altera deinde suo ordine sequitur." The phrase can, of course, be inferred from the chapter—as, indeed, from the titles of Books I and II of the *Institutes*, "De cognitione Dei Creatoris" and "De cognitione Dei Redemptoris"—and it remains a useful way of characterizing the relationship between the arguments of Books I and II.

28. T. H. L. Parker, *John Calvin* (Tring: Lion, 1977), 73–74.

discussion of repentance found in the 1536 edition was developed into a separate chapter in 1539.[29] The single chapter on Christian freedom, ecclesiastical and civil powers has become three separate chapters, and the implication of these issues for Christian life, present in the original discussion, has developed into a new final chapter.[30] In addition, the first sentence of the 1536 edition, in which "sacred doctrine" is said to consist in "two parts, the knowledge of God an the knowledge of ourselves,"[31] has become, perhaps, the basis for two new introductory chapters, "On the Knowledge of God" and "On the Knowledge of Man."[32] (But one can hardly claim that the single 1536 sentence grew into two chapters apart from theological interests not immediately evident in the 1536 text.)

Many of the additions and changes made in 1539 and in the emendations and additions of 1543 and 1550 have no clear relationship to the 1536 text. One might argue that the new chapter on justification by faith was the logical elaboration of the original definition of faith, but this sort of argument does not reveal the reason for creating a separate chapter or topic of justification. Beyond this, the new chapters, *De similitudine ac differentia veteris ac novi testamenti* and *De praedestinatione & providentia Dei*, are totally without precedent in the 1536 edition,[33] and the many shorter additions to the text that Calvin made in the second (1539), third (1543), and fourth (1550) editions of the *Institutes* are similarly incapable of easy explanation as mere elaborations of the initial text. The chapters on the two testaments, predestination, and providence actually mark out major differences between the 1536 and the 1539 *Institutes*, differences adumbrated in the catechetical writings of 1537–38.

Above all, the internal logic of the 1536 text in no way accounts for the total alteration of literary genre that took place in the 1539 edition:

29. Cf. Calvin, *Institutio* (1536), fol. 299–358 with Calvin, *Institutio* (1539), V, fol. 157–86.

30. Calvin, *Institutio* (1536), i.e., caVI (fol. 400–514); cf. Calvin, *Institutio* (1539), i.e., caXIII–XV (fol. 353–93) and caXVII (fol. 414–34). On this new final chapter see Jacques Pannier, "Notes historiques et critiques sur un chapitre de l'*Institution* écrit à Strasbourg (1539)," *Revue d'Histoire et de Philosophie Religieuses* (1934): 206–29.

31. Calvin, *Institutio* (1536), fol. 40: "Summa fere sacrae doctrinae duabus his partibus constat, Cognitione Dei, ac nostri."

32. Cf. Calvin, *Institutio* (1536), fol. 40 with Calvin, *Institutio* (1539), I, ad init. (fol. 1): "Tota fere sapientiae nostrae, quae vera demum ac solida sapientia censeri debeat, duabus partibus constat: cognitione Dei, & nostri"; II, ad init. (fol. 17): "Non sine causa, veteri proverbio, tantopere homini commendata semper fuit cognitio ipsius"; and note Calvin, *Institutio* (1559), I.i.1, ad init; II.i.1, ad init.

33. Calvin, *Institutio* (1539), caVII, VIII.

Calvin's carefully phrased letter to the reader of 1539, the related "argument" prefaced to the 1541 French translation of the *Institutes*, and the rather pointed editing of the title of the work, all indicate that Calvin understood the transition from 1536 to 1539 as a major shift in the genre of the document. This shift in genre was clearly marked by Calvin's alteration of the title: the title of the 1536 edition, rendered literally, reads "Of the Christian Religion, an Institution, embracing nearly an entire summary of piety and what is necessary to know of the doctrine of salvation: a work most worthy to be read by all those zealous for piety."[34] The title of the 1539 edition offers a significant contrast: "An Institution of the Christian Religion, now at last truly corresponding to its title."[35] Nowhere, however, does Calvin explain the nature of the change or why this edition is truly an *institutio* and, presumably, no longer a catechetical summary of piety and doctrine. He could assume the intelligibility of the catechetical series (which remained unchanged)—but he offered no explicit *argumentum* or *methodus* to explain either the new shape of the whole work or the presence of the new chapters at beginning, middle, and end which, by their mere presence, now redefined the nature of the work as no longer simply catechetical.

In an attempt to unlock this puzzle of the order and arrangement of the 1539 *Institutes*, Fritz Büsser has hypothesized that Calvin relied on Zwingli's *De vera et falsa religione commentarius*.[36] The order and substance of Zwingli's *Commentarius*, however, can at best offer only a partial explanation of the arrangement of the 1539 *Institutes*. The initial order of topics in the *Institutes*—God (or knowledge of God), human nature, sin and free choice—is common enough in theology that Calvin did not need to model his work on Zwingli's *Commentarius* to develop this series of topics

---

34. Joannes Calvinus, *Christianae religionis institutio, totam fere pietatis summam, et quicquid est in doctrina salutis cognitu necessarium, complectens: omnibus pietatis studiosis lectu dignissimum opus, ac recens editum* (Basel: Platter & Lasius, 1536); cf. the description of this edition in Rodolphe Peter and Jean-François Gilmont, *Bibliotheca Calviniana. Les oeuvres de Jean Calvin publiées au xvie siècle: Écrits théologiques, littéraires et juridiques*, 2 vols., 1532–1564 (Geneva: Droz, 1991–94), I: 35–39.

35. John Calvin, *Institutio christianae religionis nunc vere demum suo titulo respondens* (Strasbourg: Rihel, 1539); cf. Gilmont, *Bibliotheca Calviniana*, I: 58–64.

36. Fritz Büsser, "Elements of Zwingli's Thought in Calvin's *Institutes*," in *In Honor of John Calvin, 1509–64*. Papers from the 1986 International Calvin Symposium McGill University, ed. Edward J. Furcha (Montreal: McGill University, 1987), 3–9; cf. August Lang, "The Sources of Calvin's *Institutes* of 1536," *Evangelical Quarterly* 8 (1936): 132, 137; Reinhold Seeberg, *Text-book of the History of Doctrines*, trans. Charles E. Hay (Grand Rapids: Baker Book House, 1977), II: 393–94.

in his *ordo recte docendi*. So also, if Zwingli's discussion in the *Commentarius* of the "cognitio Dei ac nostri" actually did inspire Calvin's initial sentence in the 1536 edition and, by way of that sentence, the two opening chapters of the 1539 edition,[37] Zwingli's *Commentarius* did not juxtapose a discussion of the Old and New Testaments with a chapter on predestination, nor did it set the sacraments and Christian freedom together, as Calvin's 1539 *Institutes* does. One might contend, of course, these elements of Calvin's arrangement of topics might simply be original to his own work—but there is one other major antecedent yet to be examined, Melanchthon's *Loci communes theologici* of 1535.

IV. The Melanchthonian Moment

From the perspective of the "method and disposition" (*modus et dispositio*) of the topics or *loci* in theology, an examination of Melanchthon's prefaces to his *Loci communes theologici* and of his exegetical and rhetorical analyses of the Epistle to the Romans provides several significant insights into Calvin's ordering and arrangement of chapters in the 1539 *Institutes*. Melanchthon wrote a series of prefaces to his *Loci communes*, each time altering the argument to address different issues, but nonetheless always noting the importance of the correct identification *loci* or identification of a suitable *methodus* or *ordo* for his work. This interest in *methodus*, moreover, echoes the basic definitions found in Melanchthon's celebrated *Elementa rhetorices*.[38] By way of contrast, Zwingli does not raise the issue of order and organization in the prefatory sections of his *De vera et falsa religione*.[39] At one point in the development of his *Loci communes* Melanchthon argued that the order for the topics of theology ought to mirror the creed—yet in the cases of theologically significant but non-credal topics, such as sin, the promises of God, law and gospel, should be set forth in their "historical series" as the Prophets and Apostles had done.[40] In complete disjunction with Zwingli's arrangement of topics, moreover, Melanchthon assumed the historical priority of Law over Gospel prior to

---

37. Zwingli, *De vera et falsa religione commentarius*, in *Opera* III: 155–72, the *loci de Deo* and *De homine*, Zwingli's third and fourth topics, respectively.

38. Cf. Melanchthon, *Loci communes* (1521), col. 81; (1535–36), col. 253–54; (1543) col. 603–4 with idem, *Elementa rhetorices*, in *CO* 13: 573.

39. Zwingli, *De vera et falsa religione commentarius*, in *Opera* 3, 147–54 (*Commentary*, 54–55).

40. Melanchthon, *Loci communes theologici*, *CR* 21: 254 (1533); and 349 (1535).

Law, a view reflected in all editions of Calvin's *Institutes*.[41] Melanchthon also consistently argued for the interpretive centrality of Romans to the New Testament and, by extension, the fundamental place of the interpretation of Romans in the development of Christian theology, a point echoed early on by Calvin in his *Épitre a tous amateurs de Jésus Christ* (1535).[42]

These points of relationship between Melanchthon's and Calvin's method, their understandings of Law and Gospel, the relationship of the two Testaments, and other *loci* belonging to the exegesis of Romans in the sixteenth century raise the possibility of a Melanchthonian influence on Calvin, particularly in the reorganization of the *Institutes* in 1539. Of course, Calvin is known for his theological differences with Melanchthon over free choice and predestination and for his methodological problems with Melanchthon's approach to the commentary.[43] If, however, Calvin rejected Melanchthon's use of the *locus* method in his commentary, an examination of the *Argumentum* to Calvin's own commentary, of his actual exegesis of texts, and of his identification of theological topics indicates a positive use of the arguments found in Melanchthon's *Dispositio orationis in Epist. Pauli ad Romanos* (1529/30).[44] This particular work of

41. Cf. Zwingli, *De vera et falsa religione commentarius*, in *Opera* III: 191, 199, 203, *Evangelium*, *De poenitentia*, and *De lege*, respectively.

42. See Melanchthon, *Declamatio de studio doctrinae Pauli*, in *CR* 11: 43–41; idem, *Theologiae studiosis Philippus Melanchthon S.* [viz., Melanchthon's preface to the *Operationes in Psalmos*], in *WA* 5: 24–25; cf. Jean Calvin, *Épitre a tous amateurs de Jésus-Christ: Préface à la traduction française du Nouveau Testament par Robert Olivetan (1535)* . . . *avec Introduction sur une édition française de l'Institution dès 1537?* ed. Jacques Pannier (Paris: Fischbacher, 1929), 38–40. Also note Luther, *Vorrede auff die Epistel S. Pauli an die Roemer*, *WADB* 5: 1, "diese Epistel ist das rechte Heubtstueck des newen Testaments"; also note the *Oratio de Paulo Apostolo, habita a Christophoro Iona*, in *CR* 11: 626: "Dixi de genere doctrinae, quod Paulus maxime illustravit, ac de aliis quibusdam doctrinae locis"; and cf. the discussion in John Schneider, *Philip Melanchthon's Rhetorical Construal of Biblical Authority: Oratorio Sacra*, Texts and Studies in Religion 51 (Lewiston: E. Mellen Press, 1990), 100–101, 167–81.

43. See Wendel, *Calvin*, 134–35, 264; Parker, *Calvin's New Testament Commentaries*, 87–90. The older scholarship has obscured the issue of Melanchthon's formal or structural influence by its emphasis on the substantive differences between Melanchthon's and Calvin's doctrines of free choice and predestination: cf. Köstlin, "Calvins Institutio nach Form und Inhalt," 39–41.

44. *CR* 15, cols. 441–92. Cf. Richard A. Muller, "*Scimus enim quod lex spiritualis est*: Melanchthon and Calvin on the Interpretation of Romans 7:14–23," in *Philip Melanchthon (1497–1560) and the Commentary*, 216–37; with Joel Edward Kok, "The Influence of Martin Bucer on Calvin's Interpretation of Romans: A Comparative Case Study" (Ph.D Dissertation: Duke University, 1993), 168, 171–73, which balances the influence of

Melanchthon, moreover, stands in the trajectory of a series of works in which Melanchthon sought to ground the theology of the Reformation on the Epistle to the Romans: the early *Theologica institutio in Epistolam Pauli ad Romanos* (1519),[45] the *Loci communes theologici* of 1521,[46] and the series of editions of Melanchthon's lectures and commentary on Romans—the *Annotationes in Epistolas Pauli ad Romanos et ad Corinthios* (1522), and the commentary itself (1532 and 1540). Likewise, the interpretation of Romans stood at the beginning and remained at the theological center of Calvin's theological program. Given, moreover, Calvin's comments concerning Melanchthon's *locus* method in the preface to his commentary and his decision, at the same time to place all of the theological *loci* and *disputationes* that arose in his work as a commentator into the newly re-cast *Institutes*, we may hypothesize an even deeper relationship between Calvin and Melanchthon on the basic issue of order and method than has usually been noted.

In Melanchthon's rhetorical analysis of the Epistle to the Romans, the Apostle's introductory *narratio* (1:18–3:31) served to establish the fundamental proposition that "we are justified by faith." The design of the *narratio* was to move from the negative or counter-proposition that "all people are under sin (*sub peccato*),"[47] toward the establishment of the proposition that justification must occur by faith. Following this *narratio*, the Apostle concludes the first major section of the epistle with a full statement of the argument on faith and justification (chapter 4) and an epilogue (5:1–11).[48] The second section of the epistle, as analyzed by Melanchthon, has an entirely different structure: instead of a discursive flow, the epistle presents a series of related theological *loci*: the topics of sin (*peccatum*), Romans 5:11–19; law (*lex*), 5:20–7:25; and grace (*gratia*), 8:1–8. Within the extended *locus* on the law Melanchthon identified a subtopic or excursus on good works (6:1–7:6). Melanchthon identified the third section of the epistle (chapters 9–11), as an extended topical discus-

Bucer against that of Melanchthon, concluding that in "significant instances, Calvin's interpretation of Romans is closer to Melanchthon's than to Bucer's."

    45. *CR* 21: 49–60.

    46. *CR* 21: 81–228.

    47. On Melanchthon's rhetorical analysis of Romans, see Rolf Schäfer, "Melanchthon's Hermeneutik im Römerbrief-Kommentar von 1532," *Zeitschrift für Theologie und Kirche* 60 (1963): 216–35.

    48. See Timothy J. Wengert, "Philip Melanchthon's 1522 Annotations on Romans and the Lutheran Origins of Rhetorical Criticism," in *Biblical Interpretation in the Era of the Reformation: Essays Presented to David C. Steinmetz in Honor of his Sixtieth Birthday*, ed. Richard A. Muller and John L. Thompson (Grand Rapids: Eerdmans, 1996), 131–35.

sion of the "people of God," in which the relationship of Israel to "the calling of the Gentiles" and predestination were the basic formal *loci*. A fourth section of the epistle (chapters 12–15) presented ethical and moral issues: good works (12), the civil authorities (13), Christian liberty and offense (14).

This Melanchthonian analysis of the structure and order of topics in the Epistle to the Romans offers a solution, more suitable than either the claim of an internal logic or of Zwinglian influence, to several of the questions concerning Calvin's work on the second edition of the *Institutes*. Specifically, it explains the topics of the chapters added by Calvin to the 1539 text, the order of those new chapters, and the new structure given to the *Institutes* as a whole. In addition to sharing with Melanchthon the assumption that Romans provided theology with its central exegetical focus, Calvin also appears to have drawn on Melanchthon's very specific sense of the topical arrangement of Romans as the ideal point of departure for theology.[49] Thus, the chapters added by Calvin to the *Institutes* in his reconstitution of the work in 1539 are precisely the topics identified by Melanchthon as the Pauline *loci*—and they are placed into the *Institutes* in the Pauline order, as defined by Melanchthon. The two new introductory chapters of the *Institutes*, the knowledge of God and the knowledge of man, including the problem of free choice and sin, model the initial *narratio* and first *locus* of Romans. Then follow, interspersed with the older materials, law, grace and faith, justification, the two testaments, predestination, the church and the magistrate. Calvin's chapter on the "similarity and distinction of the Old and New Testaments" not only reflects the exegesis of Romans, but specifically Melanchthon's identification of the relationship of the testaments as the *topos* of Romans 9–11, namely, the people of God throughout history. In his 1536 *Loci communes*, Melanchthon specifically identifies the topic of the two testaments as the Pauline *locus* of the people of God.[50] Melanchthon's 1536 *Loci communes* are also the place where he first identified predestination as a separate *locus* in his theology and placed it, in the Pauline order, following the *locus* on the Old and New Testaments and prior to the discussion of the church and the civil order.[51] It was certainly this Pauline pattern of argument, as identified in Melanchthon's *Dispositio orationis* and *Loci communes* of 1521 and 1536, that accounts for the additions to

---

49. Cf. Wengert, "Philip Melanchthon's 1522 Annotations" 135–36.
50. Melanchthon, *Loci theologici* (1535), in *CR* 21: 453–54.
51. Melanchthon, *Loci communes* (1535), in *CR* 21: 450–53.

Calvin's 1539 *Institutes* and that explains the placement of predestination after the discussion of the Old and New Testaments. This particular point of order and organization is reflected in Beza's explanation of his *Tabula praedestinationis*: "unless there is some significant reason to do otherwise," Beza wrote, a teacher ought to follow "Paul in the Epistle to the Romans," inasmuch as "this is the proper path (*methodus*) through all of theology: he proceeds from the Law to the remission of sins and then, gradually, to the highest degree."[52]

Beyond this, Calvin's discussion of the law and its threefold use in both the 1536 and the 1539 *Institutes* reflects a Melanchthonian model[53] Distinction between the *usus pedagogicus* and the *usus normativus* of the law was not found either in Luther's writings or in Melanchthon's 1521 *Loci communes*. It arose out of Melanchthon's debates with Agricola in the early 1530s,[54] and appeared as a distinct theological model for the first time in Melanchthon's 1535/36 *Loci communes*. Calvin's 1536 *Institutes* already followed a pattern similar to Melanchthon's 1535/36 *Loci communes*, identifying three uses of the law and setting them after the exposition of the Decalogue. The normative use of the law then stands just prior to the doctrine of justification. In his 1539 *Institutes* Calvin developed his discussion of the three uses of the law as the conclusion to his analysis of the Decalogue. The *tertius usus*, however, no longer could serve as the transition to his doctrine of justification,[55] inasmuch as in 1539, the law is separated by the chapters on faith, creed, and repentance from the discussion of justification.[56] Yet even here in this arrangement of materials, Calvin reflects Melanchthon's reading of the Pauline order of law, gospel, grace

52. Theodore Beza, *Tabula praedestinationis*, VII, par. v, in *Tractationes theologicae*, 3 vols. (Geneva, 1570–82), I: 197.

53. Calvin, *Institutio*(1559), II.vii.6–12; cf. Calvin, *Institutio* (1536), in *CO* 1: 49–51; *Institutio* (1539), III, fol. 91–94; and Calvin, *Institution* (1541), with Melanchthon, *Loci communes* (1536), in *CR* 21: 405–7. There is no clear distinction of uses of the law to be found either in Zwingli's *Commentarius* or in Bullinger's *De testamento*: at most the reader could infer two uses, a civil and a theological. Bullinger did eventually posit a threefold use of the law: see *Decades*, III.viii (Cambridge: Cambridge University Press, 1849–52), II: 242–44 — a development that may reflect the influence of Calvin.

54. See Timothy J. Wengert, *Law and Gospel: Philip Melanchthon's Debate with John Agricola of Eisleben over* Poenitentia (Grand Rapids: Baker Book House, 1997), 177–210.

55. Cf. Melanchthon, *Loci communes* (1535/6), in *CR* 21: 405–6: following the order civil, pedagogical, normative with Calvin, *Institutio* (1536), in *CR* 1: 49–51 arguing for the order pedagogical, civil, and normative use.

56. Calvin moved the discussion of the three uses of the law to the beginning of his exposition of the law only in the 1559 edition of the *Institutes* (II.vii.6–12): see the *Synopsis Editionum Institutionis Calvinianae* in *CO* 1: lii.

(justification and faith), and the distinction of the Old and New Testaments, by moving from law to faith and creed, repentance, justification, and the distinction of Old and New Testaments (The difference between Calvin's and Melanchthon's models is caused in large part by Calvin's discussion of the gospel in the form of chapters on faith and creed: in short, the catechetical model of 1536 remains, now merged into the series of Pauline *loci*.)

Further evidence of the Melanchthonian model can be seen in revisions of the 1539 text that took place in 1543. Whereas the work as a whole has expanded from seventeen chapters to twenty one, Calvin added only one entirely new *locus*: the chapter on vows (*De votis*). Significantly, Calvin did not place his discussion of vows with the other ecclesiological topics, namely, among the concluding chapers of the *Institutes*. Instead the new chapter appears between the chapters on the law and the chapter on faith. There is no precedent for this placement of vows in Zwingli's *Commentarius*, in fact there is a major difference in order and arrangement in Zwingli's work, which places vows after the sacraments and marriage, before the invocation of saints and merit.[57] Here too, Melanchthon's 1535/36 *Loci communes* offers much clearer precedent: Melanchthon's discussion *de monachorum votis* is one of the latter sub-topics of the *locus* on the law, prior to the *loci* on the Gospel and faith.[58]

By way of conclusion, we should set firmly aside various claims made concerning the order and method of the early editions of the *Institutes*, whether McGrath's unsubstantiated assertion that the 1539 edition was "poorly organized" or Bouwsma's comment that Calvin's "*Institutes* is not logically ordered."[59] Calvin chose to follow the order of *loci* identified by Melanchthon as that of the Epistle to the Romans. Contrary to what has been claimed, the organization of the 1539 *Institutes* is remarkably refined, combining as it does the law-gospel model of the original catechism with the new topics drawn from Romans, without altering either— indeed, preserving and interpreting the catechetical model by way of the Pauline structure.

Given the profound methodological relationship between Calvin's 1539 *Institutes* and Melanchthon's *Loci communes theologici* of 1521 and

---

57. Cf. Zwingli, *Commentarius* (*Commentary*, 260–67).

58. Melanchthon, *Loci communes* (1535–36), in *CR* 21: 128 and following.

59. McGrath, *Life of John Calvin*, 138; William J. Bouwsma, "Calvinism as *Theologia Rhetorica*," in *Calvinism As Theologia Rhetorica*, ed. Wilhelm Wuellner (Berkeley: Center for Hermeneutical Studies, 1986), 11; cf. the similar comments in Parker, *John Calvin*, 105.

1536, and given also the nature of the dissonances identified by Wengert in their correspondence,[60] further examination of the relationship between the editorial strata of the *Institutes* and the successive editions of Melanchthon's *Loci* is probably necessary to the understanding of both documents. For in each work, alongside the desire for normative theological expression, there is also a profoundly occasional and contextual aspect that cannot be simply reduced to or elicited from its most pointed and polemical manifestations. And in that occasional and contextual aspect, there are clues to the progress of the exegetical and doctrinal conversation out of which the theology of the Reformers arose in its varied formulations.

60. See Wengert's essay in this volume.

7

Melanchthon's Rhetoric As a Context for Understanding His Theology

John R. Schneider

I. The Unknown Melanchthon

It is well enough known that Philip Melanchthon's standing as a teacher of Protestant doctrine was controversial during most of his lifetime, and that it has remained so in the centuries since his death. As Robert Stupperich wrote in his book, *Der unbekannte Melanchthon*, it is a bitter irony that the "most peaceable man of his age" somehow became "the most embattled."[1] So heavily did the endless controversies weigh upon Melanchthon that, by the end, he really did long to die, so that he might be set free from "the furies of theologians."[2] Afterwards, however, he was not set free—not in name and reputation, anyway. Ferocious battles between "Philippists" and "Gnesio-Lutherans" divided the movement for the next three generations.[3] In later times, historians waged intense debates over the interpretation of his doctrines and over the final legacy of his theology as a whole.

In his book, *Melanchthon: Alien or Ally?*, Franz Hildebrandt observed that what has made Melanchthon so controversial is the great extent to which he strove to integrate classical humanism into Protestantism.[4] For it seems that the many controversies that burned all around him in his lifetime—on free will and predestination, on justification, the eucharist

---

1. Robert Stupperich, *Der Unbekannte Melanchthon: Wirken und Denken des Praeceptor Germaniae in neuer Sicht* (Stuttgart: W. Kohlhammer, 1961), 9.

2. See text of the poem found near Melanchthon's deathbed, given in translation and discussed by E. Gordon Rupp, "Philip Melanchthon and Martin Bucer," in Hubert Cunliffe-Jones with Benjamin Drewery, eds., *A History of Christian Doctrine* (Philadelphia: Fortress Press, 1978), 378.

3. Robert Kolb, "Philip's Foes, but Followers Nonetheless," in M. Fleischer ed., *The Harvest of Humanism in Central Europe: Essays in Honor of Lewis W. Spitz* (St. Louis: Concordia, 1992), 159–78.

4. Franz Hildebrandt, *Melanchthon: Alien or Ally?* (Cambridge: Cambridge University Press, 1946).

and the adiaphora, among others—were, at bottom, also (and perhaps even more deeply) about the nexus of "faith and reason" underlying his approach to those doctrines. Indeed, the debates that have raged among scholars of Melanchthon have been mainly over that delicate seam which he wished to sew into the whole fabric of his theology. In that light, the impassioned, perennial question of Hildebrandt's title is as much a comment on the nature of Protestantism as it is on Melanchthon.

Indeed, none of the other major framers of Protestant teaching was so thoroughly immersed in Greek and Latin letters as Melanchthon was. Nor was any so naturally disposed to love them as gifts from God, or so masterly in cultivating them, as he was. To put it in perspective, as E. Gordon Rupp suggested, in Melanchthon we get some inkling of what might have happened had Erasmus himself become an evangelical.[5] But to invert the hypothesis, had Melanchthon remained Catholic, things would have been much easier for him. He might well have assumed one of those prestigious university chairs they offered him, and become known primarily as the successor to Erasmus as the foremost scholar of Europe. Historians would no doubt classify him, too, as one of those esteemed Catholic "reformers." However, as it happened, his unexpected destiny as midwife to the birth of Luther's cause put him in an almost impossible position. For in the earliest throes of its nativity, the evangelical movement was prone to ominous anti-intellectual and (its twin) antinomian eruptions. Melanchthon understood better than anyone did (on his own side, at least) that these precipitous pitfalls were always just one misstep off the sheer precipice of Luther's teachings on justification and Scripture. He knew from history and by instinct that, unlike souls, traditions do not live by "grace alone." To endure, and to become viable in the world, the "bread" of culture is needed. Melanchthon's burden thus was not merely to forge what was the first Protestant summary of the faith, as is commonly acknowledged. It was (more profoundly) to hammer out its very first model of human culture—in relation to that faith. Under the circumstances, then, we do not wonder that his thought has been so difficult to understand, or that it has been controversial for so long.

Making matters still more difficult, however, is the way in which Melanchthon's theology developed. From about 1527 onward, he began to make revisions that seemed to certain contemporaries to be dramatic departures from the original teachings of Luther and from his own earlier

5. Rupp, 374.

professions. These changes became manifest in his most important dog-matic work, the *Loci communes theologici,* which he subjected to successive revisions from the first edition in 1521[6] to the last one in 1559.[7] In the earliest one, Melanchthon came out boldly for the Wittenberg theology. In the introduction to that monumental work, a young and remarkably self-assured Melanchthon issued those now-famous and oft-quoted little manifestos against conventional methods in the schools: "the mysteries of heaven ought to be worshiped rather than investigated," he wrote; and, again: "to know Christ is to know his *benefits.*"[8] Moreover, his handling of that cluster of connected themes—original sin, election, law, grace and justification, was unequivocally in line with Luther's. And sprinkled throughout the work was a fresh recognition, on his part, of the pretense of philosophers, the limits of human reason and the grave dangers of transgressing them.[9]

When we turn to the last editions, however, it almost seems that an-other person wrote them. To begin, the author gives a rigorous argu-ment for *including* the very doctrines of God, the Trinity and the Incar-nation that he had so forcefully warned about early on.[10] Moreover, his handling of predestination was modified now to bring human freedom, dignity and value into balance with the negative evangelical claims on the powers of sin, and on the bondage of the will.[11] Furthermore, he now stressed the value of philosophy on all sorts of levels—including proofs from nature that God exists.[12] And the entire style of the last writings is markedly more pedestrian, making its tone seem many years removed from those first high-spirited beginnings, when everything had seemed so fresh and full of promise.

Among scholars, the most common explanation for the changes has been that there was truth, more or less, in the objection of his critics that

---

6. In Latin we recommend the edition in MSA II/1, 15–185. For the 1521 edition in translation, see William Pauck, tr./ed., *Melanchthon and Bucer,* The Library of Christian Classics, XIX (Philadelphia: The Westminster Press, 1959).

7. For the 1559 edition in Latin, MSA II/1, 186–388. For the 1555 edition in trans-lation, Clyde L. Manschreck (ed., tr.), introduction, Hans Engelland, *Melanchthon on Christian Doctrine: Loci Communes of 1555* (Grand Rapids, MI: Baker Book House, 1965).

8. See Pauck, 21, translation of Melanchthon's oft-cited words: "Mysteria divinitatis rectius adoraverimus, quam vestigaverimus." Also, 21: "cognoscere Christum, eius beneficia cognoscere est" (italics ours).

9. See, for example, ibid., 19–20.

10. See Manschreck, xlv–li.

11. Ibid., 51–69.

12. Ibid., 5–10.

he had given away his first principles—that Melanchthon was neither a very strong man, nor thus a very great thinker. Historians have almost universally understood him as a person who never quite found his most basic place to stand, trying as he did (so they say) to straddle high fences. In the context of his biography, they have supposed (for various reasons) that his earliest humanism was straightforwardly Erasmian. Thus, his adoption of Luther's theology in the autumn of 1518 seems to have been a sudden conversion from one worldview to (at its core) the direct opposite. From this perspective, the natural explanation for the later changes is that he never quite really was the author of his own professed convictions. Rather, he inherited them from admired others—first Erasmus, then Luther—and he never really understood the dialectical conflict that thus existed deep inside him. Then, when things got difficult, as they did, Melanchthon resorted, as people often do, to older habits. The inner conflict became manifest in the ambivalence of his later thought.[13] The title of Sperl's influential book, *Melanchthon zwischen Humanismus und Reformation*, summarizes the categories and general thesis of this common (and largely negative) assessment.[14] It seems that Melanchthon lived in suspension "between" two antithetical realms, thus never finding rest in either one.

The role of Melanchthon's theology in the great debate between Protestant Modernists of the nineteenth century and their antagonists is useful as a point of reference for our own proposals. For this debate typifies the general picture of Melanchthon that has become commonplace. Modernists like Albrecht Ritschtl appealed constantly to the early slogans on method as laying precedent for their own attack on the metaphysics of orthodoxy.[15] They generally disregarded the older Melanchthon as having given way to the countervailing "intellectualism" that crept in from his pre-Lutheran past (and was indicative of his less-than-Luther-sized stature). As Troeltsch wrote, the final harvest of this fateful

13. On this view of Melanchthon's development being marked by "conversions" and sudden "breaks" and syntheses (rather than deliberate reflection), see Timothy J. Wengert, *Philip Melanchthon's* Annotationes in Johannem *in Relation to its Predecessors and Contemporaries*, Travaux d'Humanisme et Renaissance 220 (Geneva: Droz, 1987), 56–57.

14. Adolf Sperl, *Melanchthon zwischen Humanismus und Reformation: Eine Untersuchung über den Wandel des Traditionsverständnisses bei Melanchthon und die damit zusammenhängenden Grundfragen seiner Theologie,* Forschung zur Geschichte und Lehre des Protestantismus, 10, XV, (Munich: Chr. Kaiser, 1959).

15. For appeals to Melanchthon's principles as anti-metaphysical, see Albrecht Ritschl, *The Christian Doctrine of Justification and Reconciliation* (Clifton, NJ: Reference Book Publishers, 1966), 396.

"first Protestant dogmatics" was really nothing more than to have offered "a theology of definitions."[16] As part of his powerful rebuttal of these theologians (and most deeply Schleiermacher, whom they followed), Barth ignored the obvious absurdity of the appeal itself and focused rather (again) upon the underlying hermeneutical problem of "faith and reason" in Melanchthon. Barth singled him out (in spite of the fact that Modernists appealed almost as often to Luther) as having implanted that deadly Ciceronian seed which now grew those twin deadly fruits of the modern age—"anthropocentricism" and "natural theology." The theology of the older Melanchthon was, to Barth, thus merely evidence in support of his revived Gnesio-Lutheran argument.[17] Melanchthon had corrupted the pure biblical Word by adding to it "the word of man." In the wider literature, while historians appreciate Melanchthon's manifest contributions to church, school and society, their understanding of his theology as a whole has been, until quite recently, almost universally one or another version of that dialectical sort. His work in theology has been noticed considerably less for its normative power than for the perennial problems of "Christ and culture" that it provokes.

The obvious influence of humanism on his theology, with the apparently uneven course of his evolution, does make the evangelical integrity of the whole very difficult to discern, much less to clarify. However, when one considers just how disciplined, careful and scrupulous Melanchthon always was with language (that this was his genius, in fact), and how very dutiful he was as a person, it is perhaps not surprising that scholarship might make the progress it has been making toward a more favorable image. One element of this change is a renewed focus on Melanchthon's beginnings. For, contrary to the view that he adopted Erasmus's philosophy wholesale, it seems certain now that Melanchthon, during his years as student and teacher in Tübingen (1512–1518), had already forged his own unique brand of humanism. And while Erasmus inspired him in the broadest sense (as he did all the young scholars), the most fundamental influences came from others (as will be noted), whose ideas he used and shaped with an originality that was largely unnoticed by historians.[18] But

16. Ernst Troeltsch, *Vernunft und Offenbarung bei Johann Gerhard und Philip Melanchthon* (Göttingen: Vandenhoeck & Ruprecht, 1891), 59.

17. Karl Barth, *Protestant Theology in the Nineteenth Century: Its Background and History* (Valley Forge: Judson Press, 1973), 76, 579.

18. On the very basic differences between Melanchthon and Erasmus, see especially Manfred Hoffman, "Rhetoric and Dialectic in Erasmus's and Melanchthon's Interpretation of John's Gospel," in Timothy Wengert and M. Patrick Graham, eds., *Philip Mel-*

furthermore, this peculiar humanism was much more solidly on track with what he discovered Luther doing in Wittenberg than was previously understood. Although there was much in Luther's vision that was new and astonishing to him, it also seems that the substance of his Christian humanism (and not just the linguistics of it) prepared him, to an extent that is extraordinary, for receiving Luther's vision as his own. It thus also equipped him, without any lapse of time whatsoever, to begin giving Luther's insights the hermeneutical structure and theological form they were lacking. So it was that, in almost no time at all (which is otherwise impossible to explain), Melanchthon emerged as Luther's advocate, and the primary public voice of early Lutheranism, on an international stage.[19]

When one first becomes aware of these beginnings, a fresh image does begin to come clear. That "unknown Melanchthon" suggested by Stupperich's title emerges from the evidence as a figure of measurably greater vision, accomplishment and stature than he has generally been given credit for in the histories.

II. Dialectics and Human Discovery

The most complete statement and application of this earliest philosophy is contained, not in a work of metaphysics or ethics, but in the books of rhetoric Melanchthon wrote while he was teaching at Tübingen. He had completed all but the final touches on his *De rhetorica libri tres* during his last year in Tübingen.[20] It came from the printer in January 1519.[21] As with his formal dogmatic work, the *Loci communes*, Melanchthon revised his *Rhetoric* in successive editions. They constitute phases that are somewhat in parallel to the course of his development in theology.[22] And there are, likewise, not dissimilar debates concerning what the progressive changes signified. Moreover, Melanchthon considered *De rhetorica* to be

anchthon (1497–1560) and the Commentery (Sheffield: Sheffield Academic Press, 1997), 48–78.

19. John Schneider, *Philip Melanchthon's Rhetorical Construal of Biblical Authority: Oratio Sacra* Texts and Studies in Religion. vol. 51, (Lewiston /Queenston/ Lampeter: The Edwin Mellen Press), 1990, 97–99.

20. See Schneider, "The Hermeneutics of Commentary: origins of Melanchthon's Integration of Dialectic into Rhetoric," in Wengert and Graham, *Melanchthon and the Commentary*, 20–47, esp. references on 22–23.

21. *Philippi Melanchthonis De rhetorica libri tres*, Wittenberg, 1519.

22. The best survey of the editions, if not the substance of their evolution, is in Joachim Knappe, *Philipp Melanchthons 'Rhetorik'*, Rhetorik-Forschungen, 6 (Tübingen: Niemeyer, 1993).

something much greater and more profoundly important than a mere lexicon, or manual of techniques and commonplaces on eloquence. The most complete recent studies agree that *De rhetorica* was in fact a systematic work of philosophy, or better, hermeneutics.[23] In its conception the writing was something very like what Ernesto Grassi deemed "rhetoric as philosophy," in reference to Florentine humanists such as Mirandella and Ficino.[24] Like theirs, Melanchthon's rhetoric was a challenge to the abstract, foundational rational systems that flourished in the schools of his time.

Melanchthon came to his philosophical position naturally. Fatherless at ten, his male mentors were all scholars who venerated Italian letters, and who passionately believed that ancient models of composition were linked inseparably to the discovery of truth. But furthermore, these "forerunners of the Reformation," to use Oberman's phrase, were all convinced that such models were the structures which enabled truth to take shape in the form of truly human civilization.[25] For all of them, to bring these arts to society north of the Alps was less a career in studies than it was a spiritual mission. It even included re-christening—a kind of scholars' baptism. When the boy Philip Schwarzerd (who learned the Latin and Greek languages as if he had been born to them) brilliantly performed a play (*Henno*) at the Pforzheim grammar school in the presence of his famed great-uncle John Reuchlin, the esteemed man renamed him "Melanchthon."[26] Now he, too, was an apostle of this missionary movement that wished to hitch Pegasus, as it were, to the oxcart of the world.

Of all the many stimuli and influences upon him at this formative time, two stand out as by far the most powerful (and neither was Erasmus). The one was a book on dialectic, by the Dutch humanist John Agricola (1444–1485), which his older acquaintance Joachim Oecolampadius, no doubt sensing its timeliness and propriety for the younger man's formation, presented to him sometime in 1516 [27] Agricola (known as "the educator of Germany") named the work, *De inventione dialectica*, and we shall discuss its provocative title just below. The second influence, how-

23. See esp. Wengert, *Annotationes*, and Schneider, *Oratio Sacra*.

24. Ernesto Grassi, *Rhetoric as Philosophy: The Humanist Tradition* (University Park: The Pennsylvania State University Press, 1980).

25. On Melanchthon's first teachers, Schneider, *Oratio Sacra*, 13–50.

26. On this episode and its spiritual significance, Maurer, *Der junge Melanchthon zwischen Humanismus und Reformation* (Göttingen: Vandenhoeck & Ruprecht, 1967–69), I, 20–21.

27. Schneider, *Oratio Sacra*, 34.

ever, was an early Medieval commentary on the philosophy of Aristotle by one Themestius.[28] Melanchthon discovered this text while taking a course in dialectics from his colleague and mentor Franz Stadianus. The theories advanced in both these works were similar in substance, and Melanchthon made them the foundations on which he would erect a theory of his own—a rhetorical theory which he believed would revolutionize the art as it was taught in the schools.

The principal element of Agricola's book, as the title indicates, was that the art of dialectics must be formally reconnected with the art of rhetoric.[29] The main point of that linkage, which he believed was crucial to the great chain of ancient civilization, was the concept of "invention." Of course, as every student of rhetoric knows, "invention" is what one does in the initial stages of composition. It is a matter of "finding" the right forms for expressing whatever it is that one deems worth writing or speaking about. Agricola's point, however (and the notion that shaped Melanchthon forever after), was that "invention" is even more fundamentally the business of dialectics and dialecticians. This was most directly a challenge to colleagues in his own discipline, and only indirectly to rhetoricians. (Melanchthon would take up the torch in that realm.) In brief, the message was that dialecticians must not allow their craft to deteriorate, as they were prone to let it do, into disconnected games of logic. They must remain centered instead on the universal and perennial questions of meaning and purpose in human life. For the professor of dialectics, moreover, the proper place to begin was with the conventional method of applying standard "categories" of definition to one's chosen topic or theme. That way one forged something more than just a definition, and in doing so created the elementary stuff of a powerful oration—on death, for instance, or virtue. We cannot elaborate here, but the main idea of Agricola's humanism is clear enough. The use of traditional "categories," or "topics" in dialectics was envisioned as "invention" for building the framework of great composition.[30] Of all the ideas that shaped Melanchthon's early understanding of the world, before meeting Luther, this one was of absolutely first importance to the building of his own humanism and later theology.

But before going on, there was the influence of Aristotle also, through the commentary of Themistius. Melanchthon's letters and other written

28. Ibid., 29; on Themistius, Peter Mack, *Renaissance Argument: Valla and Agricola in the Traditions of Rhetoric and Dialectic* (Leiden: Brill, 1993), 135.

29. Mack, *Renaissance Argument*, esp., 320–33.

30. Ibid.

comments on this approach convey the sense of real astonishment he felt at believing he had uncovered something momentous.[31] In his inaugural speech at Wittenberg in 1518, he proclaimed, in contrast to the common understanding, that Aristotle's interest was not really in metaphysics at all, nor in abstract analytics and logic. On the contrary, his metaphysics, analytics, logic, ethics, politics—everything he wrote—served the aim of his rhetoric, which was to put truth in literary forms that would at last shape individuals and societies in the image of wisdom and virtue.[32] So captivated by these thoughts was Melanchthon, that when he came to Wittenberg his next major project was to have been to gather a team of experts—Reuchlin and Stadian among them—to manufacture a newly edited and glossed publication of Aristotle's writings.[33] Alas, the projected work never got going, for his life was rudely interrupted in 1519 by that small matter of his destiny with Luther. Nonetheless, the philosophical substance of his plan did come forth in his own rhetoric.

III. Dialectics and Rhetoric: the Hermeneutic's Human Purpose

We can but briefly look at the texts written by Melanchthon which give some light upon his progress on the way to his mature rhetoric. The main one is a very obscure declamation that it seems he gave in Tübingen sometime in 1517. Published in that year as *De artibus liberalibus*, it stands as a fairly comprehensive statement of his educational theory to that time.[34] For our present purpose, the declamation contains two key statements—one about dialectic, the other about rhetoric. The statements are important, because what would distinguish Melanchthon's rhetoric from all other models in his time (and perhaps in any time) is the thoroughly systematic integration of dialectics into it. The statement Melanchthon made about dialectics in the early oration, adumbrating his later method, was simply that it was "the mother of all the arts."[35] Secondly, though (no doubt making some brows furrow, not least his professor of rhetoric Heinrich Bebel), Melanchthon proceeded to state that rhetoric, on the other hand, was but "a part of dialectics."[36] We cannot go

31. Discussion and references in Schneider, *Oratio Sacra*, 45, 56.

32. Melanchthon's inaugural speech, in MSA, III, 29–42.

33. Ibid., 35–36.

34. This speech occurs in full, *ibid.*, 17–28. See discussion in Schneider, *Oratio Sacra*, 38–43.

35. Ibid., 21.

36. Ibid., 22. On Melanchthon's view of Bebel, Schneider, *Oratio Sacra*, 29 and refs., n.31.

into the discussions that have begun on the course of his developmental path in these matters. It should be noted, however, in view of certain opinions to the contrary, that the statements in the declamation of 1517 are not in the least inconsistent with the views Melanchthon would advance in *De rhetorica*, and thereafter.[37] For assuming, as one must, that the "rhetoric" he disparaged in the speech was none other than the "rhetoric" which he would in his own works disparage in the schools, nothing changed but the terms. In truth, the hallmark of his theory (as will be clear) was that dialectics (as understood by Agricola) was philosophy in its most concentrated, seminal form, and then that rhetoric must grow from them.[38] He simply restated these very points in the inaugural address he was to give at Wittenberg only a year or so later.[39] And all together, they remained at the innermost core of his rhetorical theory to the end.[40]

The preface to *De rhetorica*—a dedication to his fellow student Bernhard Maurus—made this theoretical purpose—and Melanchthon's sense of its historic significance—as clear as could be. As he put it, in recent decades the two arts have become separated, so that the one, dialectics, is now "artless," "a maimed and paltry thing."[41] The once-noble art of rhetoric, likewise, has become little more than a supercilious tool of politicians, a means for "writing insincere praises of princes."[42] Concerned about this disintegration of the academic mind, a very young Melanchthon now aimed to bring dialectic and rhetoric back together, and thus salvage education in the schools. His main premise was obviously derived from Agricola: the two arts are essentially the same, differing only on the methodological surface. As he phrased it: "the one [dialectic] navigates with its sails more tightly drawn; the other [rhetoric] meanders more freely." But otherwise, he wrote, "the argument is the same."[43]

---

37. Knappe, *Melanchthons 'Rhetorik,'* 6, in our view is entirely mistaken, because Knappe's view is typically (in regard to Melanchthon) semantically presumptive in judging this part of the speech as "völlig unhumanistisch." "Un-Erasmian" would be a better term for it, but that illustrates the underlying error, here.

38. Knappe's comment that "Mit seinem Wechsel nach Wittenberg änderte Melanchthon seine Auffassung," ibid., is entirely unwarranted and only exemplifies the casual manner in which such dramatic shifts are attributed to Melanchthon with changes of climate and heroes.

39. MSA, III, 35–37.

40. Contrary to Wilhelm H. Neuser, see Schneider, *Oratio Sacra*, 69 and refs., n. 50.

41. *Philippi Melanchthonis De rhetorica libri tres*, Wittenberg, 1519.

42. Ibid.

43. Ibid. brackets ours.

Added to this intuition, Melanchthon demanded complete focus upon the "common causes," as he called them.[44] Again, in carrying Agricola's vision forward, he thus strove to keep education firmly linked together with the deepest experiences his students would have in life.[45] For in Melanchthon's view, when rightly formed by language, human reflection on these human causes (*caussae* rather than mere *res*) gave otherwise mere speaking (*verba*) the power of true speech (*oratio*). It was in this context, primarily, that he also expressed his debt to Erasmus, who wisely trained students to keep a store of commonplaces, or *loci communes*, on hand to assist in this noble purpose.[46]

As is useful to note, in the introduction to his own dialectics (published in 1520), Melanchthon (following convention) summed up the essential elements of that discipline as being three: definition, division and argumentation.[47] The primary concept, again, was that of the "categories" or "topics" that one used as the framework for all three operations. Explicitly following Agricola, he noted that the first parts of this work were a kind of "invention."[48] In listing the "topics" to be used, we note the deliberate progression from terms of "essence" to those of "effect" in the world. As Agricola and (so he believed) Aristotle did, he thus understood both the "topics" and this natural progression as basic sources, from which all composition ought to flow, "as it were from springs."[49] Melanchthon imported all these ideas, most basically the last one, into the methods of his rhetoric.

The main receptor in rhetoric for the techniques of dialectics was his revised notion of the classical *genus demonstrativum*, which he indicated was to be the model for the other types. From this one, so reformed into an incarnation of dialectics, he wrote: "the others draw their waters."[50]

44. Ibid., B1r.

45. Ibid., Hans-Jörg Geyer somewhat usefully compares these "common causes," which Melanchthon here lists as including "virtues, fortune, death, wealth, letters and the like," to the "existentials" of Heidegger, for the idea is not only ethical, it is about the whole scope of human meaning and purpose. Geyer, *Von der Geburt des wahren Menschen: Probleme aus den Anfängen der Theologie Melanchthons* (Neukirchen: Neukirchener Verlag des Erziehungsvereins, GmbH, 1965), 52.

46. *De rhetorica*, E3r-E4v.

47. *Compendaria dialectica*, CR 20, 711.

48. Ibid., Also Mack, *Renaissance Argument*, discussion of Melanchthon's *loci dialectici*, 327–33.

49. CR 20, 749.

50. *De rhetorica*, A5r. Almost all of the book (84 percent) was devoted to integrating dialectics into the invention and disposition of rhetoric. See Knappe, *Melanchthons 'Rhetorik,'* 30.

Going into some detail on Aristotle's "categories" (expanding them for his rhetorical purposes from three to nine), he laid the groundwork for what was to follow. To summarize: using these "topics" in their progression to define and otherwise work up a truly meaningful subject (such as his example, "justice"), a writer could not but produce a natural flow in composition from logical clarity to logical power. What is more, however, the aforesaid logical forces served the larger purpose of the theme, whose power was *human*. For the imperative when all three elements— dialectic, rhetoric and the world order—meshed perfectly was, all at once, cognitive, affective and moral. It was in that comprehensive sense that he wrote, "thus, the entire oration is absolved."[51]

Two other interrelated items in his rhetoric must be noted: the concept of the *scopus dicendi*, and his theory of *confirmatio*. These of course are ordinary rhetorical concepts. What is remarkable, however, is the way Melanchthon shaped them. Writing on the *genus deliberativum*, he explained that the *scopus* (or *status caussae*) was "the principal and chief theme of which the controversy consists, and to which all the arguments of the oration have to be referred."[52] Erasmus, likewise, was well known for stressing the importance of having a *scopus*, or main "sighting," as he sometimes called it, in view at all times.[53] However, for Erasmus this was not a dialectical technique as it entirely was for Melanchthon.[54] Indeed, the latter believed the *scopus* must be more than just a point of orientation for the whole. For him, it most generally was the thesis, the terms of which must be handled dialectically, its proposition then placed within a rhetorical structure that made it the inference of one or more arguments. To Melanchthon, the best way of proving one's thesis—the most powerful technique of *confirmatio*—was to make it come out as the conclusion of a syllogism. Hence, for him, the traditional practice of disposition might best be shaping an entire speech into an expanded syllogistic form.[55] That way (so he believed) one achieved, through perfect logical clarity and arguments, absolute certainty of truth.

---

51. *De rhetorica*, A3r.

52. Ibid., F1v.

53. M. O'Rourke Boyle, *Erasmus on Language and Method in Theology* (Toronto/Buffalo: [University of Toronto Press], 1977), esp. 76–78.

54. Ibid., on Erasmus's way of relating parts to the whole: "[not] a progressive mathematics of meaning, as in dialectics." Also, M. Hoffman, "Rhetoric and Dialectic in Erasmus's and Melanchthon's Interpretation of John's Gospel," esp. 75–78.

55. *De rhetorica*, B1r; and esp. E5v-E5r, and G2v.

With these ideas in view, we can now turn to the emergence of Melanchthon's evangelical hermeneutics, and to the controversial levels of his theology.

IV. The Rhetoric of Paul, Holy Scripture and Christian Doctrine

In 1519 Melanchthon committed himself to theology in earnest. He began writing commentaries based on lectures—on Genesis, Matthew and, of course, Romans. Indeed, his dogmatic work grew directly from study of this epistle. Lectures matured into what was at first to become a commentary on Lombard's *Sentences*. However, the work ripened quickly into an introduction to Christian doctrine. The *Loci communes theologici* came out in 1521.[56] Careful examination of this work in context reveals the extent to which his rhetoric supplied the framework for his hermeneutics on every level. This is most apparent in the brief outline of Romans that he used in writing the dogmatic work. The mechanical details appear most conspicuously in the rhetorical delineation of Romans, which he had prepared as the skeleton for the *Loci communes*. First published by Ernst Bizer in 1966, it reveals in detail how he was using his rhetoric to construe and interpret this crucial text.[57]

Melanchthon deemed the epistle was itself a work of rhetoric—in the *genus didacticus (demonstrativum)*— offering an "argument" by means of which to understand (dually) "what the Gospel is, and what is the use of Christ."[58] Paul thus forged a "status or proposition," which is that "the highest righteousness is faith," and thus, following an *exordium*, he used scores of conventional devices to set up his argument.[59] In the fourth chapter, Paul clinched his thesis with a "confirmation" consisting of a deduction in seven parts.[60] In a later, similar draft, Melanchthon classified the epistle as belonging rather to the *genus iudicale* and as thus comprising "an exordium, narration, confirmation—aptly composed."[61] The narrative (chapters one through three) established axioms on sin, law and righteousness out of sacred revealed tradition. The "confirmation" (mainly chapter four) contained "six arguments," each one being a sim-

---

56. On the early outlines of the *Loci communes*, see esp. Ernst Bizer, ed., *Texte aus der Anfangzeit Melanchthons* (Neukirchen/Vluyn: Neukirchener Verlag des Erziehungsvereins, 1966).

57. Bizer, *Texte*, 20–30.

58. Ibid., 20.

59. Ibid., 20–23.

60. Ibid., 23.

61. Ibid., 97.

ple deduction from the axioms given to prove the thesis in question, that we are justified by faith, apart from works of the law.[62] As a teacher of doctrine, then, Melanchthon thus clearly believed that Paul followed the very same rules of composition that shaped the traditions of antiquity.

In the preface that Luther invited him to write for his *Operationes in Psalmos* (1519), Melanchthon made the larger hermeneutical implications of this view clear.

> I am not saying this: that not all the sacred and canonical books are to me of the same rank. But certain ones are generally read more often, and such is their composition that they are able to act as interpreters, or commentaries on the rest. For example, among the Pauline epistles, the one to the Romans is a scopus—an Attic Mercury—which points the way into the rest.[63]

By Paul's method, then, his *status caussae* in Romans created a kind of *scopus* for understanding the sense of Scripture as a doctrinal whole.

In two orations on Paul, which the faculty appropriately invited him to give in 1520, he developed these ideas further.

> For since, some volumes prescribe laws, others narrate the history of past deeds, our Paul, by a certain methodological disputation, examines those *loci* without which it will not have profited at all to have learned laws. Neither the predictions of prophets nor the Gospels' histories can be entered into unless you follow his commentaries . . . serving as a method.

> In brief, for the sake of our redemption, indeed, we would not have known Christ himself, had God withheld Paul from the world.

> In vain you will have learned the evangelical history, unless you observe the *scope* and *use* of the history as demonstrated by him. [For] what else does he do but bring light to all Scripture as by a certain method?[64]

These passages indicate (besides much else) that in 1520 Melanchthon had already received and shaped Luther's doctrinal notion of Scripture in rhetorical terms. He did not imagine Scripture, conceptually, as a single, uniform writing, but as being a kind of purposeful liter-

---

62. Ibid., 98–99.
63. WA 5, 24. On this preface, Schneider, *Oratio Sacra*, 99–104.
64. CR XI, 38. On these orations, given in 1520, Schneider, *ibid.*, 163–87.

ary tradition (similar to that of the classics), the deepest meaning and purpose of which was illumined by its greatest orators. Melanchthon's notion of Scripture (in the relevant doctrinal senses), then, had Paul's rhetoric as the literal *scopus* of the whole. In that deeper sense, it *was* the whole. But it also had the rest—the diverse laws, histories, sayings and songs—as parts that were always in a dynamic relation to the center. Thus Melanchthon gave quite a remarkable account of the sense, unity and diversity of the canon (we shall encounter his notion of Scripture's uniqueness in a moment). But furthermore, the passages also show that as a diverse but rhetorically unified whole, Scripture achieves that total complex of human purposes we encountered moments ago. Through Paul, it confronts human beings with both the scope (the "what") and the use (the "effects") of its great message. Further examination of Melanchthon's earliest theological writings reveals that this general vision of Scripture as *oration* (in his peculiar sense of that term)—oration that was *sacred*—was uppermost in his understanding of himself as a commentator and theologian. Both these ideas must now be kept in view as we seek to show their relevance to his principles of "faith and reason" in forging Protestant theology.

V. Understanding Melanchthon's Theology in the Context of His Rhetoric

Melanchthon's use of these rhetorical thought-forms as a kind of first Protestant hermeneutics is immensely important as context for understanding the contested parts of his theology. In this last section, but briefly and in outline, we shall focus on questions about the integrity (with regard to the fundamental of *sola scriptura*) of his dramatic decisions to expand his doctrines as he did, and to begin stressing the virtues of philosophy to Christians. We shall also suggest an approach to disputes (with regard to the fundamental of *sola gratia*) over revisions he made in handling the doctrine of election. And, to conclude, we shall make some observations about his (rhetorical) theory of truth and how it illumines his vision of theology and his final legacy as a teacher of Protestant doctrine.

First, let us consider the issue of the expansion of topics. As noted, Ritschl, Barth and many others (for different reasons) have judged this expansion as indicating a disunity of clear principle, and a trend of degeneration in Melanchthon's theology as a whole. Some scholars, such as Wolf and Fraenkel, working carefully with the theological texts, have disputed this judgment.[65] Our understanding of the hermeneutical principles that Melanchthon used in forming these texts strongly supports their defense. For very simply, in 1521 he was obviously quite affected by the fresh realization that theology had lost its topical compass. In his terms, scholastic theologians had lost sight of the *scopus* of theology—Paul's teaching on the "benefits of Christ." To Melanchthon's way of thinking, no greater formal error was imaginable, for without knowing the *scopus* (of any oration, much less God's) we are left completely clueless. In that circumstance, focusing on this or that part of the speech only makes matters worse, for we see them as fragments rather than as the parts of a larger whole that they are; and we import all the wrong meaning into them. In respect of the doctrines of God, Trinity and Incarnation, what could be more harmful than teaching about them (*Deus in se*) without reference to the very truths of our human purpose and destiny that this very God is most concerned to make known? It would be rather like studying one's benefactor's molecular composition instead of being interested foremost with his purposes. As Fraenkel rightly observed in Melanchthon, "the *loci praecipui* are the way to understanding the whole of Christian doctrine. They are not identical with the whole," and thus, on the eventual expansion to include the other topics: "This is an expansion within, not a transformation of the original doctrinal scheme."[66] Another way of stating the matter is that Melanchthon simply corrected the "invention" of theologians' rhetoric at the first, and completed its full "disposition" at the last. There was certainly nothing in the beginning to give warrant to Ritschl's appeal (to principles opposed to a real metaphysics), and Barth ought rather to have found in the ending something very like a precedent for his own Christ-centered Christian realism. It seems that Melanchthon's expansion of his dogmatics was not at all confused, or degenerative. It was rather the outgrowth and application of his very first principles toward completeness and maturity in doctrine.

Let us similarly consider the contrast between Melanchthon's earlier and later writing on philosophical wisdom and proofs of God's existence. In the early stages, he indeed placed his emphasis upon the failings and deadly dangers of philosophy, in contrast to Scripture and its Gospel. One could pick sentences like this one from almost any page of his essays

65. See Peter Fraenkel, *Testamonia Patrum: The Function of the Patristic Argument in the Theology of Philip Melanchthon* (Geneva: Droz, 1961), esp. 43–51 on the factors underlying the expansion, and for an analysis that independently supports our argument.

66. Ibid., 45.

of that time: "they are straying entirely from the path who think that the doctrines of the Christian life are helped by the literature of the philosophers."[67] He wrote with discernible passion that philosophers were "blind," that their writings were ineffective, and that he had personally incurred much damage to his soul in reading them.[68] In contrast, one could pick sentences like this second one from almost any page of his essays on the subject less than ten years later: "how great is the magnitude and power of the arts in doctrine."[69] That there was a reversal of his earlier strategy is obvious enough, but did the later statement also signify a contradiction of the evangelical principle underlying the earlier one? We think not.

For one thing, careful examination reveals that even in his most severe criticisms of philosophy were not as exclusionary as they might sound. For example, in his *Declumatiuncula* on Paul (1520) he wrote this typical statement: "Philosophers *also* [our emphasis] placed beatitude in perfect virtue and perpetual tranquillity of the soul."[70] In other words (in undertone) they had the right questions and larger sense of purpose. Furthermore, as he often noted (disparagingly), philosophers understood many good "laws for living," and they had among them many "fine examples."[71] What they did not understand was "whence they might find such a soul," for they did not have revealed to them, "the mystery hidden for so many ages—the benefits of Christ."[72] At first, Melanchthon's purposes clearly were to define precisely what it was that made philosophy inferior to Scripture, and then, in that light, to discriminate clearly between them. However, we see that both the definition he gave and the distinction he made left the way open, in principle, for that later strategy of integration. For the claim contained in his metaphor that philosophy was "blind" (rhetorically powerful as it was to his fellows) actually entailed the secondary one that philosophy "saw" basic things, especially in ethics, remarkably well. In view of his rhetorical concepts, it is not very hard to understand the agility of his thinking on the matter. Again, it was the *scopus* of Christian doctrine that counted as its essence, gave Scripture its qualities of unity, clarity and force—in sum, the most basic qualities contained in the expression, *sola scriptura*. Once made, however (espe-

67. MSA I, 34.
68. Ibid., 34–35; 41.
69. MSA III, 90.
70. MSA I, 32.
71. Ibid., 30.
72. Ibid., 32.

cially once the uniquely Christian oration was expanded to completion), there could be no principled objection to placing the "orations" of human culture in (emergency) service of Christ.

More complex and difficult to discern, however, is coherence of principle (*sola gratia*) in Melanchthon's last teachings on predestination. For his earliest handling of the subject seems to have been straightforwardly deterministic and dialectical enough. In contrast, by the latest editions, Melanchthon had expanded things to include an entire chapter in qualified defense of belief in human freedom in that context.[73] In this discussion Melanchthon is careful to reject two extremes—a kind of Stoicism (which he feared was incipient in the growing influence of certain forms of Calvinism), and an ancient Pelagianism (the trend in Rome).[74] In sum, Philip affirmed the sovereignty of divine grace, but also warned that however it all happens a human being is no "piece of wood or a stone," which God merely acts upon.[75] He liked to cite the words of Chrysostom: "God draws, but he draws the one who is willing."[76] In this fashion, Melanchthon believed he was clearly in line with the best authorities that had written on the matter (including Luther).[77]

The criticism that Melanchthon was a "synergist" (and closet Erasmian) has been widely argued, and the intricate particulars of that debate cannot detain us here. Nevertheless, if we consider merely that Melanchthon imagined divine communication as rhetoric, and if we also consider what he supposed rhetoric in this instance was, perhaps we can gain some understanding of why he saw no conflict with his earlier notions, or with Luther's. Very simply, to Melanchthon, successful rhetoric (with its dialectical core) did two things with respect to the human will. First it made the moral realities of a person's circumstances perfectly clear. At one and the same time, however, it also persuaded and (in a word) compelled the person, by intuition of judgment, to believe, and then to act. (Belief of this sort already was, in fact, the beginning of the action.) All this is wrapped together in Melanchthon's concept of truth, as actualized in rhetoric. The integration of dialectics thus spelled differences between him and Erasmus, not just in their humanism, but in the manner in which their respective humanisms would give shape to the intricacies of their doctrines of election. And it perhaps explains why he

73. See Manschreck, 51–69.
74. Ibid., 51 (on Stoicism), 58 (on Pelagius).
75. Ibid., 60.
76. Ibid.
77. Ibid., 68.

believed to the last that his position on human freedom was not, in the end, a departure from Luther's.

Melanchthon's concept of truth, in this form, is also very important as context for one last issue of concern. That is the reputation his theology has earned for what we may call its sense of vision and purpose—Melanchthon's understanding of himself and his mission. Troeltsch's phrase, "theology of definitions," sums up the general attitude of historians toward Melanchthon's place in history. He was to Luther what Boswell was to Johnson—a secretary and organizer of his master's ideas—but little more. Against this perception, it should suffice to consider again what Melanchthon's notion of definition was. For it was hardly that of a "Luther's lexicon," but was rather a dialectical and rhetorical notion with immense implications for human life. Properly formed "definitions" tapped into the greatest cosmic powers in the universe, and they unleashed those powers in the most perfect and humanly momentous manner possible. This rhetorical supposition was almost certainly behind what might otherwise seem a bland and pedestrian method in his *Loci communes*, particularly later on. Beginning always with the "what is it?" (*quid est?*), he progressed dutifully to the "What power?" (*quid vis?*) on each doctrine. While the result may have been excessively pedestrian, repetitive and a little dull (compared with the literary extravagances of a Luther or Calvin), we ought at the very least appreciate the vision at work. In its own terms, it was successful, and a good many people (including Luther and Calvin) found its harvest invaluable as a resource for their own lives and works.

In conclusion, in the context of his rhetoric, the general integrity of Melanchthon's theology as a whole begins to come into clearer light than otherwise. And his stature as a theologian of Protestantism and as a man of great ability and character only grows.

8

Melanchthon between Renaissance and Reformation: from Exegesis to Political Action[*]

Nicole Kuropka

Unexpected dimensions of Philip Melanchthon's powerful fusion of Renaissance and Reformation ideals become clear through the analysis of his rhetoric. In step with other humanists, Melanchthon turned away from scholastic speculations to the necessity of lucid speech. His orator is astute about current political affairs and intends to galvanize the audience rather than please them. Rhetoric thus aimed at public life resembles a northern version of Florentine civic humanism as characterized by Hans Baron.[1] Melanchthon held Florence in high esteem and singled it out as the hub of education: "Florence is entitled to be looked upon as the leader of Europe because this city was the first to welcome back the refugee scholars of Greek learning."[2] It is not mere chance that Melanchthon focused on Florence. Here the original languages and academic disciplines came to life again, a revival of basic linguistic skills to open up sources, which Protestant exegesis used so effectively. Melanchthon's rhetoric has the double aim of decoding sources and reforming politics, making linguistic faculties and political action two sides of the same coin. Previously, scholars have split this coin in halves. Theologians have emphasized the impact of rhetoric on biblical exegesis by arguing that Mel-

[*] I greatly appreciate Catherine A. Pomerleau's tireless help in polishing my English and discussing ideas.

1. Hans Baron, *The Crisis of the Early Italian Renaissance* (Princeton: Princeton University Press, 1968).

2. "Maximum beneficium . . . in universam Europam urbs Florentia contulit, cum primum graecarum literarum professores patria pulsos iussit ad se diverti. . . ." *In laudem novae scholae* (1526) CR 11, 109, 25–29. The most recent and specific work on Melanchthon's relations to the Italian humanists is Stefan Rhein, "'Italia magistra orbis terrarum.' Melanchthon und der italienische Humanismus," in *Humanismus und Wittenberger Reformation. Festgabe anläßlich des 500. Geburtstages des Praeceptor Germaniae Philipp Melanchthon am 16. Februar 1997*, ed. Michael Beyer et al., (Leipzig: Evangelische Verlagsanstalt, 1997), 367–88.

anchthon constructs Scripture as sacred rhetoric.[3] Renaissance scholars have characterized Melanchthon's revival of the classical ideal of rhetoric as aimed at political responsibility of decent citizens (*viri boni*) in public life (*res publica*).[4] In order to do justice to Melanchthon, we have to re-unite both sides and assess the implications of his policies for the general populace. Important points and revisions in the three versions of his textbook on rhetoric[5] guide us through his theory while his funeral orations for Frederick the Wise (d.1525) and Martin Luther (d.1546) demonstrate how Melanchthon applied this ideal to the key players of his time.

The opening sentences of Melanchthon's earliest book on rhetoric (1519) confirm the double purpose of exegesis and political activity: "Rhetoric is the art of speaking effectively. . . . For two reasons rhetoric holds a preeminent position among all academic fields: first, rhetoric is the operating principle behind all other disciplines and, second, it prepares the youth to determine public affairs."[6] Rhetoric is the foremost academic discipline because it equips one with the basic linguistic tools so essential for academic discourse. After a foundation in grammar and dialectic, rhetoric provides the student with the ability to understand, create and critique orations (*oratio*). For Melanchthon 'oration' is a broad term, encompassing both oral speeches and written texts from classical to biblical sources. His rhetoric supplies the basic components of such an oration: deciding on a genre (*genera causarum*)[7] and structure (*dispositio*),

3. Timothy J. Wengert, *Philip Melanchthon's "Annotationes in Johannem" in Relation to its Predecessors and Contemporaries* (Geneva: Librairie Droz, 1987); and John R. Schneider, *Philip Melanchthon's Rhetorical Construal of Biblical Authority: Oratio Sacra*, (Lewiston: E. Mellen Press, 1990). See also Kees Meerhoff, "The Significance of Philip Melanchthon's Rhetoric in the Renaissance," in *Renaissance Rhetoric*, ed. Peter Mack, (New York: St. Martin's Press, 1994), 46–62.

4. Olaf Berwald, *Philipp Melanchthons Sicht der Rhetorik*, (Wiesbaden: Harrassowitz, 1994) as well as J. R. McNeilly, "Melanchthon's Earliest Rhetoric," in *Rhetoric: A Tradition in Transition, in Honor of Donald C. Bryant*, ed. Walter R. Fisher (East Lansing, MI: Michigan State University Press, 1974), 33–48.

5. Joachim Knape's synopsis of the three versions provides an excellent overview about common features and differences: Joachim Knape, *Philipp Melanchthons 'Rhetorik'*. (Tübingen: M. Niemeyer, 1993), esp. 23–54.

6. "Rhetorica dicendi artificium. . . . Eam ob causam inter ingenuas artes vel primas tenuit, docebantur rhetorica pueri, partim quo haberent veluti organon quoddam, ad quod exigerunt reliquas disciplinas, partim quo de civilibus causis recte iudicare consuescerent." *De rhetorica libri duo* 1519, fol. a3[a], 1–9, this print in the 'Staatsbibliothek Nürnberg' is hereafter cited as *Rhetoric* 1519.

7. Melanchthon added to the three classical genre of demonstrative (*genus demonstrativum*), deliberative (*genus deliberativum*) and judicial (*genus judiciale*) the didactic

key words (*loci communes*) to grasp and memorize main issues, speaking style (*elocutio*) and ways to influence the emotions of the audience (*affectus*). Together these elements form a 'how to' guide for writing and understanding orations. Melanchthon demonstrates the application of rhetoric to his students in his lectures on classical authors and biblical books. Increasingly he interprets St. Paul as a rhetorician and claims that Paul's letters can only be fully understood by seeing how they fit into rhetorical conventions. In Romans Paul participates in the trial of human souls. It is a juridical speech arguing for justification based on faith alone and making the point that human works fail to achieve acquittal.[8] Accordingly, Paul structured this letter by moving from an introduction (*exordium*), to the exposition of the legal case (*narratio*) and finally to a presentation of relevant evidence (*confirmatio*).[9]

Melanchthon was acquainted with the use of the juridical genre through the humanistic tradition, but his application of juridical speech to solve theological issues reflects his experience as a leader of the reformation movement. In his earliest *Rhetoric* of 1519—most of which was written before his coming to Wittenberg—Melanchthon sticks to a narrow definition and includes only law cases and disputes as topics for this genre.[10] About a decade later he relates theological disputations to court procedures: theologians, as much as judges, strive to clarify ambiguous

---

genre which traditionally belonged to dialectic: "Vulgo tria numerant genera causarum. Demonstrativum, quo continetur laus et vituperatio. Deliberativum, quod versatur in suadendo et dissuadendo. Iudiciale, quod tractat controversias forenses. Ego addendum censeo διδασκαλικὸν genus, quod etsi ad dialecticam pertinet, tamen, ubi negociorum genera recensentur, non est praetermittendum . . ." *Elementorum rhetorices libri duo* (1531) CR 13, 421, 16–23, hereafter cited as *Rhetoric* 1531.

8. Justification based on faith alone became Melanchthon's prime example for the juridical genre: *Institutiones rhetoricae* 1521, fol. b4ᵇ, 7–10, manuscript in the Tübinger Universitätsbibliothek, hereafter cited as *Rhetoric* 1521; *Rhetoric* 1531, 431, 6–10. See also Timothy J. Wengert, "Philip Melanchthon's 1522 Annotationes on Romans and the Lutheran Origins for Rhetorical Criticism," in *Biblical Interpretation in the Era of the Reformation. Essays presented to David C. Steinmetz in Honor of His Sixtieth Birthday*, ed. R. A. Muller and J. L. Thompson, (Grand Rapids: Eerdmans, 1996), 118–40, here: 127–28; Rolf Schäfer, "Hermeneutik im Römerbrief-Kommentar von 1532," *ZThK* 60 (1963): 216–35.

9. Wilhelm Maurer, "Melanchthons Loci communes von 1521 als wissenschaftliche Programmschrift. Ein Beitrag zur Hermeneutik der Reformationszeit," *LJ* 27 (1960), 1–50; and Ernst Bizer, *Theologie der Verheißung. Studien zur Theologie des jungen Melanchthons (1519–1524)* (Neukirchen-Vlyun: Neukirchener Verlag des Erziehungsvereins, 1964), 134–35.

10. "Tertium genus causarum est, quod ad forum litesque pertinet, ac ob id iudiciale solet vocari, de quo mihi pauciora, sed tamen aliquid, dicenda sunt. . . ." *Rhetoric* 1519, fol. g1ᵇ, 34–36.

laws, to give practical advice and to untangle disputed issues. Whether lawyers must solve a murder in a courtroom or theologians have to clarify the right celebration of the Eucharist from the pulpit—the rhetorical equipment is the same on both stages.[11] The example of the juridical genre epitomizes Melanchthon's tendency to employ rhetoric for both politics and theology. Rhetoric is crucial to politicians for managing affairs of state and to theologians for dealing with church matters. His rhetorical models elucidate how programatically he relates rhetoric to the issues of state and church. From Virgil and Quintilian to Agricola and Erasmus, Melanchthon has a large variety of exemplary rhetoricians in his repertoire and explicitly refers his hearers to those models. Two masters of this art stand out: Cicero and Paul.

From the very beginning Cicero is the most prominent. Because this Roman orator mastered the rules of dialectic and offered brilliant examples of eloquence, students should focus their energy on Cicero's *De officiis*.[12] Melanchthon also directs the attention of his students to Cicero's speech for Milo, since this juridical work is a model of clarity[13] and provides the students with the ideal standard for defense[14] and praise.[15] Originally Paul stands in the shadow of the great master Cicero, but he gains ground in the later revisions. Melanchthon discovers the components for ideal rhetoric in Paul's letters: Paul is an expert in eloquence,[16] structural composition and the genres of oration.[17] Melanchthon not only holds the rhetorical ability of Cicero and Paul in high regard but also praises their moral values. He highlights the importance of Cicero by comparing his writings with the Bible. Whereas the Holy Scripture is the only basis for true religion, Melanchthon turns to Cicero on moral issues:

---

11. "Nam disputationes ecclesiasticae magna ex parte similitudinem quandam habent forensium certaminum. Interpretantur enim leges, dissolvunt ἀντινόμιας videlicet sententias, quae in speciem pugnare videntur, explicant ambigua, interdum de iure, interdum de facto disputant, quaerunt factorum consilia." *Rhetoric* 1531, 429, 25–31.

12. "Haec est, ni fallor, in methodo dialectica, tota inveniendi ratio, quam qui volet diligenter exercere, Ciceronis librum de Officiis in manus accipiat. . . . *Rhetoric* 1519, fol. b4ª, 20–22.

13. *Rhetoric* 1519, fol. g1ᵇ – g4ᵇ.

14. *Rhetoric* 1519, fol. f4ᵇ.

15. "Elegantissima est insinuatio in Milonia oratione M. Ciceronis. . . ." *Rhetoric* 1519, fol. d2ª, 33–34.

16. *Rhetoric* 1521, fol. d4ª, 25–26; e3ᵇ, 23–25.

17. "Iudiciale genus est quo controversiae, ac lites continentur. . . . Nam ut de civilibus negociis, ita iisdem fere locis de literatis causis disceptari potest, ut cum Paulus probat, non esse ex operibus iusticiam, . . ." *Rhetoric* 1521, fol. b4ᵇ, 5–10.

Cicero's writings are exemplary in their private and public ethics.[18] Due to the natural law inherent in all human beings Melanchthon can adopt Ciceronian ethics. As Paul teaches, humankind is endowed with knowledge of the law (Rm. 2.14–15). God invested all people with a conscience that calls every step in life to account.[19] Even more, human abilities are not limited to discerning good; we are also equipped with reason. Melanchthon calls the enlightenment which people can acquire through reason 'philosophy,'[20] a term which covers all fields of scientific and social observations as well as ethics.[21] Knowledge of philosophy is not only essential for public duties but even more for theology; only after mastering the skills for textual analysis provided by philosophy can theologians open up the holy writings.[22] Even though theology depends on philosophical methods, the distinction between the two is crucial.[23] Philosophy errs in three points: knowledge about God, the teaching of justification and the overestimation of human abilities.[24] Although the Gospel exceeds

18. "Verum ego religionem ex divinis literis censeo hauriendam esse. De civilibus moribus malim audire Ciceronem. . . ." *De praefatione in officia Ciceronis* (1525), CR 11, 88, 6–8.

19. "Imo Gentes etiam habuerunt legem, hoc est notitiam naturalem de moribus discernentem honesta et turpia. . . . Ac Paulus erudite ratiocinatur, quod Gentes habeant legem, ac simul declarat, quid sit lex naturae; habent conscientiam accusantem et excusantem, id est, discernentem honesta et turpia, . . ." *Commentarii in epistolam Pauli ad Romanos* (1540), CR 15, 577, 33–40. Hereafter cited as *Romans*.

20. Günter Frank, *Die theologische Philosophie Philipp Melanchthons (1497–1560)*. (Leipzig: Benno, 1995) gives a thorough analysis of Melanchthon's multi-dimensional view of philosophy.

21. "Philosophia, quatenus est scientia loquendi et rerum naturalium et civilium morum et ea tantum de rebus naturalibus ac moribus civilibus, affirmat ac docet, quae certa ratione comprehendit." *Melanchthons Werke in Auswahl. 4: Frühe exegetische Schriften*, gen. ed. Robert Stupperich, vol. ed. Peter F. Barton (Gütersloh: Gerd Mohn, 1963), 230, 12–15, hereafter called MSA 4.

22. "Nam in ea sum plane sententia, ut qui velit insigne aliquid, vel in sacris vel foro conari, parum effecturum, ni animum antea humanis disciplinis (sic enim philosophiam voco) prudenter, et quantum satis est, exercuerit." *De corrigendis adolescentiae studiis* (1518), CR 11, 22, 30–34. "Verum quod ad sacra attinet, plurimum refert quomodo animum compares. Nam si quod studiorum genus, sacra profecto potissimum ingenio, usu et cura opus habent." Ibid. 23, 25–29.

23. Cf. Hans Scheible, "Melanchthon zwischen Luther und Erasmus," in *Renaissance-Reformation. Gegensätze und Gemeinsamkeiten*, ed., A. Buck, (Wiesbaden: O. Harrassowitz, 1984), 155–80.

24. "Quando autem ratio seu philosophia Dei voluntate iudicat, tum fere errat." MSA 4, 238, 3–4. "Secundo, errat philosophia de iustificatione, si statuat coram Deo satis esse civilem iustitiam." Ibid, 239, 9–10. "Tertio fallitur philosophia, cum putat rationem satis habere virium ex sua natura contra vitia, nec videt opus esse Spiritu sancto . . ." Ibid, 240, 7–9.

philosophy, philosophy is an irreplaceable gift of God. Theology does not relate to the details of daily life and so would not suffice to maintain life in the world. Philosophy is absolutely essential for social and cultural life since it includes medicine for health, geometry for architecture and civil law for government.[25] Melanchthon stresses the importance of government. He is convinced that Paul sides with him in arguing that society requires government and is in need of public servants.[26] In Romans 13 Paul teaches the divinely ordained relation of state and church. The Gospel approves all existing state systems and creates neither alternative constitutions nor new civil laws. That the church must exist in the state has far-reaching consequences for Christians. Christians are not exempted from fulfilling their duties as loyal citizens,[27] since they are standing before God and in the world. By emphasizing Cicero's *De Oratore* as a guide to governing, Melanchthon places a high responsiblity on rulers.[28] Thus Melanchthon promotes rhetoric in the service of theology, philosophy, and education as facets of public life. The first goal of rhetoric is to provide the linguistic abilities to understand and consider scholarly issues critically. Rhetoric as an analytical tool benefits scriptural exegesis especially, yet the ability to communicate is for Melanchthon the key to all politically responsible life—as theologian, politician, judge or citizen.

The significance of rhetoric for state and church is made manifest through Melanchthon's funeral orations for Frederick the Wise[29] and

25. "Philosophia vero est doctrina vitae corporalis: sicut vides medicinam valetudini servire, mores civiles communi hominum tranquillitati et iudiciis exercendis: deinde alias artes aliorum usuum causa repertas esse. Geometria metitur corpora, in emendo, venendo, in aedificando. Arithmetica contractus et magnam partem societatis humanae gubernat." MSA 4, 241, 31–242, 3.

26. "Paulus magistratuum autoritatem praedicat, cum gladii usum ordinationem Dei vocat, et magistratum Dei ministrum." *De legibus* (1525), CR 11, 69, 10–12.

27. "Deinde meminerint [i.e. lectores] Evangelium non constituere aliam politiam mundanam, sed approbare omnium gentium politias, ac leges de rebus civilibus,. . . ." *Romans*, 710, 8–11.

28. "Nam cum oratio nascatur ex rerum cognitione, erit inops orator sine harum rerum scientia. Et cum orator maxima reipublicae consilia gubernet, opus est ei ad sapienter dicendum et iudicandum omnium illarum maximarum artium scientia. Nam existere aliquos tales rerumpublicarum gubernatores necesse est omnibus aetatibus." *M. T. Ciceronis de oratore libri tres* (1541) CR 16, 689, 17–23.

29. *De Friderico Electore*, CR 11, 90–98. Hereafter quoted as *Fridericus*. Cf. Eberhard Winkler, "Melanchthons lateinische Leichenrede auf Kurfürst Friedrich den Weisen" *Zeitschrift für Religions- und Geistesgeschichte* 18 (1966): 33–42; and Ingetraut Ludolphy, *Friedrich der Weise. Kurfürst von Sachsen 1463–1525* (Göttingen: Vandenhoeck & Ruprecht, 1984).

Martin Luther.[30] When Frederick the Wise died on May 5, 1525, his citizens could look back at a long reign by their prince. After the division of Saxony into an electoral and a ducal territory, Frederick had led electoral Saxony through economic troubles and the crises of the early Reformation in his principality and the Empire. Melanchthon himself witnessed the last eight years of Frederick's reign and drew on this experience for his analysis. The political consequences of the death of this prince were unpredictable; there was reason to fear the worst. Electoral Saxony lost a statesman of classical dimensions, ruling with eloquence, wisdom and diplomacy. This characterization pervades the whole oration, and Melanchthon expounds on this portrayal from three different perspectives: politics, church and education.

According to Melanchthon, Frederick was a better ruler than Cicero. Cicero—the perfect Roman orator—did not succeed as a statesman. He suppressed a civil revolt ruthlessly and thereby abandoned his ideal of trusting in the power of rhetoric. Frederick, on the other hand, protected his country from war with diplomacy and eloquence.[31] He responded to mobilization and warmongering in his own state with a policy of peace: "Just as in hazardous storms a steersman requires astounding vigilance and incredible efforts to protect his ship, likewise seeking peace in tough times demands an outstanding character."[32]

Melanchthon's oration sparkles to convince his audience of the superiority of peace-bringing eloquence and persuasiveness over bellicose policies.[33] If the commoners could understand the advantages of peace, they would have a higher esteem for Frederick and deep gratitude for the thirty peaceful years in Saxony under his reign. They would under-

---

30. My primary source is not the long version of the *Corpus Reformatorum*, which is the product of Joachim Camerarius' revision but Melanchthon's original, shorter speech reprinted in Siegfried Bräuer, "Die Überlieferung von Melanchthons Leichenrede auf Luther" in *Humanismus und Wittenberger Reformation*. 185–252, hereafter called Bräuer, "Leichenrede". See also James Michael Weiss, "Erasmus at Luther's Funeral: Melanchthon's Commemorations of Luther in 1546," *SCJ* 16 (1985): 91–114.

31. "Verius hic de se praedicare possit [i.e. Fridericus]: Cedant arma togae, quam Cicero, qui motum in Republica civilem armis crudelius etiam quam res poscebat, vindicavit." *Fridericus* 92, 17–20.

32. "Porro quemadmodum periculosis tempestatibus sine summa vigilantia, summoque labore navem servare incolumem gubernator non potest, ita tam duro tempore pacatam tenere provinciam tot annos, non est vulgaris ingenii opus." *Fridericus* 92, 20–25.

33. "Ad vulgus in maiore admiratione sunt, clariusque cernuntur bellicae virtutes, et pluris fit miles aliquis athletico robore, quam moderatus et placidus civis." *Fridericus* 91, 27–30.

stand that God could not provide for this state better than with such a virtuous leader.[34] Frederick, with his politics of peace, is a Christian ruler.[35] He fulfilled Christ's prophecy that the peaceful and meek would inherit the earth. In addition, Frederick was concerned about the Christian religion in his state. He sought dialogue with theologians but was always concerned to avoid scholastic quarrels because God's Word and not reason was his guiding principle.[36] He built churches, introduced Protestant liturgies and called the best theologians into his state.[37] This last point leads to Frederick's accomplishments in the realm of education. Frederick served his state by founding a university in Wittenberg and advanced the cause of education in electoral Saxony. Eager to find scholarly truth, Frederick stands above the mass of coarse rulers, who flee learning more than poisoned snakes.[38]

There is an enormous contextual leap from 1525 to Melanchthon's funeral oration for Luther in 1546. The Protestants had survived because they were an important source of financial support for Emperor Charles V in the midst of ever-shifting imperial foreign policy. The Augsburg Diet (1530) had drawn lines between Protestants and Roman Catholics, so that even successive religious councils could not generate any lasting agreement. After the resolution of the troubles plaguing Charles V's foreign policies, the emperor had a free hand to tackle the Protestant problem—war was in the air. This atmosphere is reflected in Melanchthon's oration. He worries that the Protestant factions will splinter without the unifying presence of their most important teacher and leader.

Melanchthon devotes his oration to Luther's achievements as a servant of the church within the state and is generous in his praise. The many virtues enumerated in his speech can be summarized as 'Luther the perfect orator'. Melanchthon highlights Luther's linguistic and persuasive gifts. Luther's treatises and his translation of the Bible are testimonies to posterity of his eloquence: his German translation opened the

34. ". . . nihil a Deo melius, nihil utilius, nihil divinius his regionibus dari potuisse, quam talem principem tam pertinaciter fugitantem bella." *Fridericus* 92, 32–34.

35. "Divina enim praeconia etiam meretur, nam cum mundus imperii possessionem vi atque armis defendi debere existimet, Christus contra pronunciat beatos esse mites et a saevitia alienos, eisque possessionem terrae pollicetur." *Fridericus* 93, 18–23.

36. "Dicebatque optare se ut de sacris ex solo Dei verbo iudicaretur." *Fridericus* 94, 1–2.

37. ". . . templa condidit, ceremonias invexit, accersivit undecunque qui sacra docerent." *Fridericus* 93, 36–37.

38. "Praetereo iam quod schola constituta sensit, quantum adferat Rebuspublicis scientia literarum, quas vulgus principum odit cane peius et angue." *Fridericus* 94, 46–49.

Old and New Testament to lay readers. Christians could then easily grasp the Gospel—the translation was clearer than earlier biblical commentaries.[39] Due to Luther the clarity of Scripture was shining once more: Luther illuminated true penance, Paul's teaching on the justification of the sinner, which spells the difference between Law and Gospel and establishes the haven in which believers can find consolation for their despairing souls.[40] Melanchthon does not hesitate to rank Luther with the greatest men in the history of the church. Since the creation of the world, God appointed instructors for his church, and Luther is included in the list of church teachers ranging from Adam to the fourteenth-century mystic, Johann Tauler.[41] Moreover, Luther exceeds statesmen like Solon or Augustus, since true church leaders are more important than even the greatest governors in history.[42] Here we encounter the image of Luther as the flawless orator. In Luther natural gifts combined with lifelong training; he steadily improved his rhetorical abilities to reach the peak of expression and eloquence. For Melanchthon this characterization would have been wanting and horribly incomplete if he had not gone on to speak about Luther's actions in the public domain. In the service of the church Luther never lost sight of public life: "In his writings, Luther taught and supported other God-given offices and public life as no one ever did before."[43] More than anyone before him, Luther expounded the difference between spiritual and civil justice. His dedication to the Gospel never allowed Luther either to ignore the differences between state and church affairs or to disdain the state. In fact Melanchthon is particularly quick to reject the accusation that Luther

39. ". . . vertit in linguam Germanicam prophetica et Apostolica scripta, tanta perspicuitate, ut haec ipsa versio plus lucis adferat lectori, quam plerique commentarii." Bräuer, "Leichenrede" 211, 43–45.

40. "Lutherus veram et necessariam doctrinam patefecit; fuisse enim tenebras in doctrina de poenitentia densissimas, manifestum est. His discussis ostendit, quae sit vera poenitentia, et quis sit portus, quae firma consolatio mentis quae expavit sensu irae Dei. Illustravit Pauli doctrinam quae ait, fide iustificari hominem. Ostendit discrimen Legis et Evangelii, Justitae Spiritus, et politiciae." Bräuer, "Leichenrede" 211, 29–33.

41. Bräuer, "Leichenrede" 211, 4–17. The largest part of Melanchthon's list contains biblical people. Among the post-biblical are only: "Polycarpus, Irenaeus, Gregorius Neocaesariensis, Basilius, Augustinus, Prosper, Maximus, Hugo, Bernardus, Taulerus, et alibi alij." Ibid, 211, 14–15.

42. "Fuerint sane magni viri Solon, Themistocles, Scipio, Augustus, et similes, qui magna imperia vel constituerunt vel rexerunt: tamen longe inferiores sunt his nostris ducibus Esaia, Baptista, Paulo, Augustino, Luthero. Haec vera discrimina intelligere nos in Ecclesia decet." Bräuer, "Leichenrede" 211, 21–23.

43. "Monstravit et alia vera officia Deo grata, et vitam civilem ita ornavit et munivit, ut nullius unquam literis ita ornata et munita sit." Bräuer, "Leichenrede" 211, 40–41.

lacked interest in politics: "Luther did not turn a blind eye to the state as many think . . . rather he was very concerned with state affairs and exercised a political savvy in assessing all the players around him."[44]

Melanchthon describes both Luther and Frederick as perfect orators but omits the traditional features of a laudation.[45] He remains silent about their lineage, youth and education and instead highlights their particular service for public life in state and church. These eulogies on the ideal theologian and statesman are not mere artistic monuments to be admired for their form. Both orations had their origins in times of political crises due to the loss of a significant leader. The peace-securing elector Frederick passed away during the spreading peasants' revolts. The theology-refining Luther died on the eve of confessional wars. In these unstable moments, Melanchthon presents the ideal of education securing theology and politics, exhorting his audience—who were listening to the funeral ceremony or would read the orations later[46]—to follow the models of Frederick and Luther in their daily lives.

Melanchthon devoted his own lifework to carrying out this Christian civic humanism. Throughout his life he not only was active in politics and theology but strove to make education available for the general populace. The founding and reforming of new schools testify to these goals of widespread impact and to up-to-date education.[47] Melanchthon's call in words and deeds for general education gained him the title 'teacher of the Germans' (*Praeceptor Germaniae*), but not everybody was affected by this call. Work on visitations has shown that the Reformers' educational goals were not achieved to their satisfaction, leaving uneducated people in Germany for generations.[48] The success of Melanch-

---

44. "Nec erat ut multi putant, negligens in consideranda Republica. . . . Sed et Rempublicam norat, et omnium cum quibis vivebat sensus ac voluntates sagacissime perspiciebat." Bräuer, "Leichenrede" 213, 9–11.

45. *Rhetoric* 1531, 448, 10–25.

46. Various Latin and German reprints of Luther's funeral oration and Melanchthon's second oration on Frederick in 1551 attest to the fact that these orations could reach a broader audience beyond only the Latin-speaking mourners present, cf. Bräuer, "Leichenrede" 186–209.

47. Cf. Hans Scheible, "Melanchthons Bildungsprogramm," *BPKG* 53 (1986) 181–95 and Markus Wriedt, "Die theologische Begründung der Schul- und Universitätsreform bei Luther und Melanchthon," in *Humanismus und Wittenberger Reformation.* 155–84.

48. Gerald Strauss, *Luther's House of Learning. Indoctrination of the Young in the German Reformation* (Baltimore: John Hopkins University Press, 1978); and Susan C. Karant-Nunn, "The Reality of Early Lutheran Education. The Electoral District of Saxony – a Case Study," *LJ* 57 (1990): 128–46, 143.

thon's ideal that education should be extended to the general population cannot be judged by the degree to which it was achieved during his lifetime, since he contributed to a longterm expansion of education. Throughout his life, he still had to contend with people who had not yet entered the circle of "the educated." One group among them, the peasants, grabbed the Bible and weapons to defend their cause. Just before Frederick's death Melanchthon saw the consequences of peasant uprisings. Traveling to Eisleben for the opening of a new school, he found the beginning of the first term delayed by the unrest.[49] A few months later Melanchthon wrote a refutation of the peasants' demands, in which he deals predominantly with the importance of obedience to rulers and securing peace but also mentions in passing the education of peasants. Melanchthon hopes that if the peasants in revolt are properly instructed they will see and understand their mistakes.[50] Education will lead to a better understanding of Scripture and obedient subjects. In the same way he concludes with the demand to the rulers to ensure the provision of schools and training for the youth.[51] On the other hand, Melanchthon interprets the peasants' revolt as the encroachment of uneducated rustics into a political sphere, which rightfully belongs to rulers, and so he disregards their concern.

> The demands of the peasants have no validity. Indeed, it would be necessary for such rugged and uneducated people as the Germans are to have less freedom than they do. Joseph ruled Egypt with a firm hand to keep a tight rein on it. But our rulers allow the people all disruption, demand only money but do not keep discipline, from which great disorder follows.[52]

49. Hans Scheible, *Melanchthon. Eine Biographie* (München: Verlag C. H. Beck, 1997), 79.

50. *Confutatio Articulorum Rusticanorum* (1525), CR 20, 643, 4–23. Hereafter cited as *Confutatio*. See also Walter Zöllner, "Melanchthons Stellung zum Bauernkrieg," in *Philipp Melanchthon 1497–1560*, vol. 1, *Philipp Melanchthon. Humanist, Reformator, Praeceptor Germaniae*, ed. Melanchthon-Komitee der deutschen Demokratischen Republik, (Berlin: Akademie-Verlag, 1963) 174–89.

51. *Confutatio* 662, 34–37.

52. "Darumb hat das zu mutten der bawrn keyn scheyn. Ja es wer von nötten, das eyn solch wild ungezogen volck, als teutschen sind, noch weniger freyheyt hette, dann es hat. Joseph hat Aegypten hart beschwert, das dem volck der zam nicht zu weyt gelassen wurde. Aber unsere herschafften gestatten dem volck allen mutwillen, nehmen nur gelt von yhn, da neben halten sie es yn keyner zucht, daraus volgt grosser unradt." *Confutatio* 655, 31–38.

Melanchthon's political rhetoric should not be evaluated only from the positive goal of improving education, but also from a negative perspective, too: as Melanchthon strives to eradicate illiteracy through the extension of schools, he simultaneously legitimates the subjugation of the uneducated. What does the new educational ideal mean for the developing Reformation, which was breaking the shackles of the papacy and tradition by proclaiming the priesthood of all believers? In 1960 Hans Ahrbeck advanced the thesis: "The Protestants had to abandon the dangerous principle of the priesthood of all believers. . . . The authority of the Catholic Church had to be replaced by the authority of scholarly disciplines."[53] The fusion of renaissance and reformation thought paved the way for a new hierarchy in the Protestant Church. The religious power of the priesthood of all believers did not remain for long in the hands of the laity, since the ideal of the educated Christian snatched it away from the lay folk and transferred it to university lecture halls and church pulpits. Thus, the reforming movements of the commoners had to face a new authority which did not hesitate to advocate the use of force to sustain its position just as the medieval Church had done before.

After recognizing that Melanchthon and other humanists highlighted the civic responsibility of rulers and subjects, one should consider these humanists' preferred political approach, and its implications. In the case of Melanchthon, the ideal of education leads to moral and obedient subjects, confirming princely rule. Only by considering the range of views on education will we discover the extent to which the goals of humanists and Protestant educational programs justified, subverted or refashioned the current political order.

---

53. "Man mußte das gefährliche Prinzip des allgemeinen Priestertums aufgeben. . . . An die Stelle der Autorität der katholischen Kirche mußte die Autorität der Wissenschaft treten." Hans Ahrbeck, "Melanchthon als Praeceptor Germaniae," in *Philipp Melanchthon. Forschungsbeiträge zur vierhundersten Wiederkehr seines Todestages dargegeben in Wittenberg 1960,* ed. Walter Elliger, (Göttingen: Vandenhoeck & Ruprecht, 1960), 133–48, 141.

Bibliography

Primary Sources

Die Amerbachkorrespondenz. Edited by Alfred Hartmann and Beat Rudolf Jenny, Basel: Universitätsbibliothek, 1942–

Barth, Peter and Niesel, Wilhelm (eds) *Joannnis Calvini Opera Selecta.* Munich: Kaiser, 1952

Baum, G., Cunitz, E., Reuss, E. (eds) *Ioannis Calvini Opera Quae Supersunt Omnia.* 59 vols, Brunswick: Schwetschke, 1863–1900

Die Bekentnissschriften der evangelisch-lutherischen Kirche. 4th ed. Göttingen: Vandenhoeck and Ruprecht, 1959; 10th ed. Göttingen: Vandenhoeck and Ruprecht, 1986

Bergendorff, Conrad (ed.) *Luther's Works.* Philadelphia: Muhlenberg, 1958

Beza, Theodore *Tractationes Theologicae.* 3 vols, Geneva: 1570–1582

Bindseil, Heinrich (ed.) *Philippi Melanchthonis epistolae, iudicia, consilia, testimonia aliorumque ad eum epistolae quae in Corpore Reformatorum desiderantur.* Halle, Schwetschke, 1874.

Bizer, Ernst (ed.) *Texte aus der Anfangzeit Melanchthons.* Neukirchen: Neukirchener Verlag des Erziehungsvereins, 1966

Bullinger, Heinrich *Decades.* Cambridge: Cambridge University Press, 1849–52

Calvin, John *Catechismus, sive christianae religionis institutio.* Basle: 1538

―――. *Catechismus, sive christianae religionis institutio...Catechism or Institution of the Christian Religion.* Translated by Ford Lewis Battles, 4th ed., Pittsburg: Pittsburg Theological Seminary, 1976

―――. *Christianae religionis institutio, totam fere pietatis summam, et quicquid est in doctrina salutis cognitu necessarium, complectens: omnibus pietatis studiosis lectu dignissimum opus, ac recens editum.* Basel: Platter and Lasius, 1536

―――. *Epitre a tous amateurs de Jésus-Christ: Préface à la traduction française du Nouveau Testament par Robert Olivetan (1535)...avec Introduction sur une édition française de l'Institution dès 1537.* Edited by Jacques Pannier, Paris: Fischbacher, 1929

―――. *Institutio christianae religionis nunc vere demum suo titulo respondens.* Strasbourg: Wendelin Rihel, 1539

―――. *Institutio christianae religionis nunc vere demum suo titulo respondens.* Strasbourg: Wendelin Rihel, 1543

————. *Institutes of the Christian Religion*. (1536 version) Translated and annotated by Ford Lewis Battles, rev. ed., Grand Rapids: Eerdmans, 1986

Castellio, Sebastian *Concerning Heretics*. Edited by Roland Bainton, NewYork: Octagon Books, 1965

Concordia Triglotta: Libri symbolici Ecclesiae Lutheranae, Germanice-Latine-Anglice. St Louis: Concordia Publishing House, 1921

Luther, Martin. *Luthers Werke. Kritische Gesamtausgabe. Briefwechsel*. 18 vols. Weimar: H. Böhlau, 1930–85

————. *Luthers Werke. Kritische Gesamtausgabe [Schriften]* 65 vols. Weimar: H. Böhlau, 1883–1993

Melanchthon, Philip *Examen...qua commendatur ministerium Evangelii*. Wittenberg, 1556

————. *ad impios articulos bavariae Inquisitionis*. Wittenberg, 1559

————. *Melanchthons Briefwechsel: Kritische und kommentierte Gesamtausgabe*. Edited by Heinz Scheible. 10 vols. to date. Stuttgart-Bad Cannstatt: Frommann-Holzboog, 1977–

————. *Melanchthons Werke in Auswahl. [Studienausgabe]* Edited by Robert Stupperich. 7 vols. Gütersloh: Gerd Mohn, 1951–75

Nicolaides, Wenceslaus *Cantiones evangelicae...quae in ecclesiis Boemicis...canuntur*. Wittenberg: Rhau, 1554

Pauck, Wilhelm (ed.) *Melanchthon and Bucer*. Library of Christian Classics, Vol. 19. Philadelphia: Westminster Press, 1969

Reid, J. K. S. (ed.) *Calvin: Theological Treatises*. Philadelphia: Westminster Press, 1954

Reu, Johann M. (ed.) *Quellen zur Geschichte des kirchlichen Unterrichts in der evangelischen Kirche Deutschlands zwischen 1530 und 1600*. Vol. 1/1 Hildesheim: Georg Olms, 1976

Rilliet, Albert and Dufour, Théophile (eds) *Le Catéchisme français de Calvin, publié en 1537, réimprimé pour la première fois*. Geneva: H. Georg, 1878

Schaff, Philip (ed.) *Creeds of Christendom*. 3 vols. Reprint Grand Rapids: Baker, 1990

Sebastiani Castellionis Dialogi III. Aresdorffi: 1578

Staehelin, Ernst (ed.) *Briefe und Akten zum Leben Oekolampads, zum vierhundertjährigen Jubiläum der Basler Reformation*. 2 vols, Leipzig: Heinsius, 1927–34

Tappert, Theodore G. (ed. and translator) *The Book of Concord*. Philadelphia: Muhlenberg, 1959

Ursinus, Zacharias *Tractationes theologicarum*. Vol. 1, Neustadt: Harnisch, 1584

Verzeichnis der im deutschen Sprachbereich erschienen Drucke des XVI. Jahrhunderts. Stuttgart: Hiersemann, 1983–

Secondary Sources

Ahrbeck, Hans 'Melanchthon als Praeceptor Germaniae.' In *Philipp Melanchthon. Forschungsbeiträge zur vierhundertsten Wiederkehr seines Todestages dargegeben in Wittenberg, 1960*, edited by Walter Elliger, Göttingen: Vandenhoeck & Ruprecht, 1960

Althaus, Paul *The Ethics of Martin Luther*. Philadelphia: Fortress Press, 1972

Autin, Albert *L'Institution Chrétienne de Calvin*. Paris, Société Française d'Editions littéraires et techniques, 1929

Baker, J. Wayne *Heinrich Bullinger and the Covenant: The Other Reformed Tradition*. Athens, Ohio: Ohio University Press, 1980

Baron, Hans *The Crisis of the Early Italian Renaissance*. Princeton: Princeton University Press, 1955

Barth, Karl *Protestant Theology in the Nineteenth Century: Its Background and History*. Valley Forge: Judson Press, 1973

Battles, Ford Lewis 'Calculus Fidei.' In *Interpreting John Calvin*, edited by Robert Benedetto, Grand Rapids: Baker Book House, 1996

Benoit, Jean-Daniel 'The History and Development of the *Institutio*: How Calvin Worked.' In *John Calvin*, edited by G. E. Duffield, Appleford: Sutton Courtney Press, 1966

Bentley, Jerry H. *Humanists and Holy Writ: New Testament Scholarship in the Renaissance*. Princeton: Princeton University Press, 1983

Berwald, Olaf *Philip Melanchthons Sicht der Rhetorik*. Wiesbaden: Harrassowitz, 1994

Bierma, Lyle D. *The Doctrine of the Sacraments in the Heidelberg Catechism*. Studies in Reformed Theology and History, New Series. Princeton: Princeton Theological Seminary, forthcoming

Bietenholz, Peter *Basle and France in the Sixteenth Century. The Basle Humanists and Printers in Their Contacts with Francophone Culture*. Geneva: Librairie Droz, 1971

———. *Contemporaries of Erasmus: a Biographical Register of the Renaissance and Reformation*. 3 volumes, Toronto: University of Toronto Press, 1986

Bizer, Ernst *Theologie der Verheissung. Studien zur Theologie des jungen Melanchthons (1519–1524)*. Neukirchen-Vluyn: Neukirchener Verlag des Erziehungsvereins, 1964

Boehmer, Edward *Bibliotheca Wiffeniana. Spanish Reformers of two centuries from 1520. Their Lives and Writings*. Reprint, New York: B. Franklin, 1962

Bouwmeester, G. *Zacharias Ursinus en de Heidelbergse Catechismus*. The Hague: Willem de Zwijgerstichting, 1954

Bouwsma, William J. 'Calvinism as *Theologia Rhetorica*.' In *Calvinism as Theologia Rhetorica*, edited by Wilhelm Wuellner, Berkeley: Center for Hermeneutical Studies, 1986

Boyle, M. O'Rourke *Erasmus on Language and Method in Theology*. Toronto: University of Toronto Press, 1977

Brändly, W. 'Oswald Myconius in Basel.' *Zwingliana* 11 (1959)

Bräuer, Siegfried 'Die Überlieferung von Melanchthons Leichenrede auf Luther.' In *Humanismus und Wittenberger Reformation. Festgabe anlässlich des 500. Geburtstages des Praeceptor Germaniae Philipp Melanchthon am 16. Februar 1997*, edited by Michael Beyer et al., Leipzig: Evangelische Verlagsanstalt, 1997

Büsser, Fritz 'Die Bedeutung des Gesetzes.' In *Handbuch zum Heidelberger Katechismus*, edited by Lothar Coenen, Neukirchen: Neukirchener Verlag, 1963

———. 'Elements of Zwingli's thought in Calvin's *Institutes*.' In *In Honor of John Calvin, 1509–1564*, edited by Edward J. Furcha, Montreal: McGill University, 1987

———. 'Zwingli als Exegete: A contribution to the 450th anniversary of the death of Erasmus.' In *Probing the Reformed Tradition: Historical Studies in honor of Edward A. Dowey, Jr*, edited by B. Armstrong and E. McKee, Louisville: Westminster/John Knox Press, 1989

Burchill, Christopher 'On the Consolation of a Christian Scholar: Zacharias Ursinus (1534–83) and the Reformation in Heidelberg.' *Journal of Ecclesiastical History* 37 (1986)

Burnett, Amy Nelson 'Simon Sulzer and the Consequences of the 1563 Strasbourg Consensus in Switzerland.' *Archiv für Reformationsgeschichte* 83 (1992)

Chrisman, Miriam *Lay Culture, Learned Culture: Books and Social Change in Strasbourg, 1480–1599*. New Haven: Yale University Press, 1982

Clemen, Otto 'Briefe aus Basel an Melanchthon.' In *Kleine Schriften zur Reformationsgeschichte*, edited by Ernst Koch, Leipzig: Zentralantiquariat der DDR, 1987

————. 'Vier Briefe des Buchdruckers Johann Oporin an Kaspar Peucer.' In *Kleine Schriften zur Reformationsgeschichte*, edited by Ernst Koch, Leipzig: Zentralantiquariat der DDR, 1987

Collange, J. F. 'Philippe Melancthon et Jean Sturm, humanistes et pédagogues de la Réforme.' *Revue d'Histoire et de Philosophie Religieuse* 68 (1988)

Doumergue, Emile *Jean Calvin: Les hommes et les choses de son temps.* Lausanne: G. Bridel, 1902

Ebrard, Johannes H. A. *Das Dogma vom heiligen Abendmahl und seine Geschichte.* 2 vols, Frankfurt: Zimmer, 1846

Edwards, Mark U. *Luther and the False Brethren.* Stanford: Stanford University Press, 1975

Egli, Emil 'Biblianders Leben und Schriften.' In *Analecta Reformatoria*, edited by Emil Egli, Zurich: Zürcher & Furrer, 1901

Engelland, Hans *Melanchthon on Christian Doctrine: Loci Communes of 1555.* Edited, translated, with an introduction by Clyde Manschreck, Grand Rapids: Baker Book House, 1965

Farmer, Craig S. 'Eucharistic Exhibition and Sacramental Presence in the New Testament Commentaries of Wolfgang Musculus.' In *Wolfgang Musculus (1497–1563) und die oberdeutsche Reformation*, Edited by R. Dellsperger, R. Freudenberger, and W. Weber, Berlin: Akademie Verlag, 1997

Felici, Lucia *Tra riforma ed eresia. La Giovinezza di Martin Borrhaus (1499–1528).* Florence: L. S. Olschki, 1995

Fischer, Danièle 'Calvin et la Confession d'Augsbourg.' In *Calvinus ecclesiae Genevensis custos*, edited by Wilhelm Neuser, Frankfurt am Main: Peter Lang, 1984

Franekel, Peter *Testimonia Patrum: The Function of the Patristic Argument in the Theology of Philip Melanchthon.* Geneva: Droz, 1961

Frank, Günter *Die Theologische Philosophie Philipp Melanchthons (1497–1560).* Leipzig: Benno, 1995

Gamble, Richard '*Brevitas et facilitas*: Toward an Understanding of Calvin's Hermeneutic.' *Westminster Theological Journal* 47 (1985)

Ganoczy, Alexandre *The Young Calvin.* Translated by D. Foxgrover and W. Provo, Philadelphia: Westminster Press, 1987

Geiger, M. *Basel im Zeitalter der Orthodoxie.* Basel, 1958

Gerrish, Brian A. 'Sign and Reality: the Lord's Supper in the Reformed Confessions.' In *The Old Protestantism and the New: Essays on the Reformation Heritage*, edited by Brian Gerrish, Chicago: University of Chicago Press, 1982

Geyer, Hans-Jörg *Von der Geburt des wahren Menschen: Probleme aus den Anfängen der Theologie Melanchthons*. Neukirchen: Neukirchener Verlag des Erziehungsvereins, 1965

Good, James I. *The Heidelberg Catechism in Its Newest Light*. Philadelphia: Publication and Sunday School Board of the Reformed Church in the United States, 1914

———. *The Origin of the Reformed Church in Germany*. Reading, PA: Daniel Miller, 1887

Gooszen, Maurits 'Inleiding.' In *De Heidelbergsche Catechismus: Textus Receptus met Toelichtende Teksten* Leiden: Brill, 1890

Gordon, Bruce 'Calvin and the Swiss Reformed Churches.' In *Calvinism in Europe 1540–1620*, edited by A. Duke, G. Lewis and A. Pettegree, Cambridge: Cambridge University Press, 1994

Grassi, Ernesto *Rhetoric as Philosophy: The Humanist Tradition*. University Park: The Pennsylvania State University Press, 1980

Guggisberg, Hans R. *Sebastian Castellio 1515–1563. Humanist und Verteidiger der religiöser Toleranz*. Göttingen: Vandenhoeck and Ruprecht, 1997

Guggisberg, Kurt *Bernische Kirchengeschichte*. Bern: P. Haupt, 1958

Henss, Walter *Der Heidelberger Katechismus im konfessionspolitischen Kräftespiel seiner Frühzeit*. Zurich: Theologischer Verlag, 1983

Heppe, Heinrich 'Der Character der deutsch-reformierten Kirche und das Verhältniss derselben zum Luthertum und zum Calvinismus. *Theologische Studien und Kritiken* 23 (1850)

———.*Geschichte des deutschen Protestantismus in den Jahren 1555–1581*. 4 vols, Marburg: Elwert, 1852–59

Hesselink, I. John *Calvin's Concept of the Law*. Allison Park, PA: Pickwick, 1992

———. *Calvin's First Catechism: A Commentary*. Louisville: Westminster/John Knox Press, 1997

———. 'Development and Purpose of Calvin's Institutes.' *Reformed Theological Review* 24 (1965)

———. 'The Law of God.' In *Guilt, Grace and Gratitude: A Commentary on the Heidelberg Catechism* edited by Donald J. Bruggink, New York: Half Moon, 1963

Hickman, James T. 'The Friendship of Melanchthon and Calvin.' *Westminster Theological Journal* 38 (1976)

Higman, Francis 'The Question of Nicodemism.' In *Calvinus Ecclesiae Genevensis Custos*, edited by Wilhelm Neuser, Frankfurt am Main: Peter Lang, 1984

Hildebrandt, Franz *Melanchthon: Alien or Ally?* Cambridge: Cambridge University Press, 1946

Hoffmann, Manfred 'Rhetoric and Dialectic in Erasmus's and Melanchthon's Interpretation of John's Gospel.' In *Philip Melanchthon (1497–1560) and the Commentary*, edited by Timothy Wengert and M. Patrick Graham, Sheffield: Sheffield Academic Press, 1997

————. *Rhetoric and Theology: The Hermeneutic of Erasmus*. Toronto: University of Toronto Press, 1994

Hollweg, Walter 'Die beiden Konfessionen Theodor von Bezas: Zwei unbeachtete Quellen zum Heidelberger Katechismus.' In *Neue Untersuchungen zur Geschichte des Heidelberger Katechismus* Neukirchen: Neukirchener Verlag, 1961

Karant-Nunn, Susan 'The Realigy of Early Lutheran Education. The Electoral District of Saxony - A Case Study.' *Lutherjahrbuch* 57 (1990)

Kawerau, Gustav *Johann Agricola von Eisleben: Ein Beitrag zur Reformationsgeschichte*. Berlin: Wilhelm Hertz, 1881

Keen, Ralph *A Checklist of Melanchthon Imprints Through 1560*. St Louis: Center for Reformation Research, 1988

Kisch, Guido *Melanchthons Rechts- und Soziallehre*. Berlin: Walter de Gruyter, 1967

Klooster, Fred H. *The Heidelberg Catechism: Origin and History*. Grand Rapids: Calvin Theological Seminary, 1982

————. *A Mighty Comfort: The Christian Faith According to the Heidelberg Catechism*. Grand Rapids: CRC Publications, 1990

————. 'The Priority of Ursinus in the Composition of the Heidelberg Catechism.' In *Controversy and Conciliation: The Reformation and the Palatinate, 1559–1583*, edited by D. Y. Hadidian, Allison Park, PA: Pickwick, 1986

Knappe, Joachim *Philipp Melanchthons 'Rhetorik'*. Tübingen: Niemeyer, 1993

Koch, Ernst 'Auseinandersetzungen um die Autorität von Philipp Melanchthon im Kursachsen im Vorfeld der Konkordienformel von 1577.' *Lutherjahrbuch* 59 (1992)

Köhler, Walther *Zwingli und Luther: Ihre Streit über das Abendmahl nach seinen politischen und religiösen Beziehungen*. Quellen und Forschungen zur Reformationsgeschichte 6, Gütersloh: Bertelsmann, 1924

Köstlin, Julius 'Calvin's Institutio nach Form und Inhalt, in ihrer geschichtlichen Entwicklung.' *Theologische Studien und Kritiken* 41 (1868)

Kok, Joel Edward 'The Influence of Martin Bucer on Calvin's Interpretation of Romans 7: 14–23' PhD Dissertation, Duke University, 1993

Kolb, Robert 'Historical Background of the Formula of Concord.' In *A Contemporary Look at the Formula of Concord*, edited by Robert Preus and Wilbert Rosin, St Louis: Concordia Press, 1978

————. 'Philip's Foes, but Followers Nonetheless.' In *The Harvest of Humanism in Central Europe: Essays in Honor of Lewis W. Spitz*, edited by M. Fleischer, St Louis: Concordia, 1992

————. 'Teaching the Text: The Commonplace Method in Sixteenth Century Lutheran Biblical Commentary.' *Bibliothèque d'Humanisme et Renaissance* 49 (1987)

Kutter, Markus *Celio Secundo Curione. Sein Leben und sein Werk (1503–1569)*. Basel: Helbing & Lichtenhahn, 1955

Lang, August *Der Heidelberger Katechismus und vier verwandte Katechismen* Leipzig: Deichert, 1907

————. 'The Sources of Calvin's *Institutes* of 1536.' *Evangelical Quarterly* 8 (1936)

Lefranc, Abel *Calvin et l'éloquence française*. Paris: Fischbacher, 1934

Leith, John H. 'Calvin's Theological Method and the Ambiguity in his Theology.' In *Reformation Studies: Essays in Honor of Roland H. Bainton*, edited by Franklin H. Littell, Richmond: John Knox, 1962

Leu, Urs *Conrad Gesner als Theologe. Ein Beitrag zur Zürcher Geistesgeschichte des 16. Jahrhunderts*. New York: Peter Lang, 1990

Ludolphy, Ingetraut *Friedrich der Weise. Kurfürst von Sachsen 1463–1525*. Göttingen: Vandenhoeck & Ruprecht, 1984

Maag, Karin *Seminary or University? The Genevan Academy and Reformed Higher Education, 1560–1620*. Aldershot: Ashgate Publishing Company, 1995

MacCulloch, Diarmaid *Thomas Cranmer. A Life*. New Haven: Yale University Press, 1996

Mack, Peter *Renaissance Argument: Valla and Agricola in the Traditions of Rhetoric and Dialectic*. Leiden: Brill, 1993

Manschreck, Clyde *Melanchthon, the Quiet Reformer*. New York, Abingdon Press, 1958

Mathers, Constance J. 'Enzinas' In *Oxford Encyclopedia of the Reformation*, edited by Hans Hillerbrand, 4 vols, New York: Oxford University Press, 1996

Maurer, Wilhelm *Der junge Melanchthon zwischen Humanismus und Reformation*. Göttingen: Vandenhoeck & Ruprecht, 1967–68

———. 'Melanchthon's Loci communes von 1521 als wissenschaftliche Programmschrift.' *Lutherjahrbuch* (1960)

McGrath, Alister E. *A Life of John Calvin: A Study in the Shaping of Western Culture*. Cambridge, MA: Basil Blackwell, 1990

McNeilly, J. R. 'Melanchthon's Earliest Rhetoric.' In *Rhetoric: A Tradition in Transition, in Honor of Donald C. Bryant*, edited by Walter R. Fisher, East Lansing, MI: Michigan State University Press, 1974

Meerhoff, Kees 'The Significance of Philip Melanchthon's Rhetoric in the Renaissance.' In *Rhetoric: A Tradition in Transition, in Honor of Donald C. Bryant*, edited by Walter R. Fisher, East Lansing: Michigan State University Press, 1974

Meylan, Edward F. 'The Stoic Doctrine of Indifferent Things and the Conception of Christian Liberty in Calvin's *Institutio Religionis Christianae*.' *Romanic Review* 28 (1937)

Müller, E. F. Karl *Die Bekenntnisschriften der reformierten Kirche*. Leipzig, Deichert, 1903

Muller, Richard *Christ and the Decree: Christology and Predestination in Reformed Theology from Calvin to Perkins* Durham, NC: Labyrinth, 1986

———. *Post-Reformation Dogmatics*. Volume 1. Grand Rapids: Baker Book House, 1987

———. ' "Scimus enim quod les spiritualis est": Melanchthon and Calvin on the Interpretation of Romans 7:14–23.' In *Melanchthon and the Commentary*, edited by M. Patrick Graham and Timothy J. Wengert, Sheffield: Sheffield Academic Press, 1997

Neuser, Wilhelm *Die Abendmahlslehre Melanchthons in ihrer geschichtlichen Entwicklung (1519–1530)*. Neukirchen-Vluyn: Neukirchener Verlag, 1968

———. *Calvins Beitrag zu den Religionsgesprächen von Haguenau, Worms und Regensburg*. Neukirchen: Erziehungsverein, 1969

———. 'The Development of the *Institutes* 1536–1559.' In *John Calvin's Institutes: his opus magnum. Proceedings of the second South American Congress for Calvin Research July 31-August 3, 1984*, edited by B. J. van der Walt, Potchefstroom: Potchefstroom University for Christian Higher Education, 1986

———. 'Die Väter des Heidelberger Katechismus.' *Theologische Zeitschrift* 35 (1979)

———. 'Die Versuche Bullingers, Calvins und die Strasburger, Melanchthon zum Fortgang von Wittenberg zu bewegen.' In *Gesammelte Aufsätze zum 400. Todestag*, 2 vols, edited by U. Gäbler and E. Herkenrath, Zurich, Theologischer Verlag, 1975

Nevin, John W. *The Commentary of Dr. Zacharias Ursinus on the Heidelberg Catechism.* Translated by G. W. Willard, Grand Rapids: Eerdmans, 1954

———. 'Doctrine of the Reformed Church on the Lord's Supper.' *Mercersburg Review* 2 (1850)

Niesel, Wilhelm *The Theology of Calvin.* Translated by Harold Knight, London: Lutterworth, 1956; reprinted Grand Rapids: Baker Book House, 1980

Nijenhuis, Willem *Calvinus oecumenicus: Calvijn en de eenheid der kerk in het licht van zijn briefwisseling.* S'Gravenhage: Martinus Nijhoff, 1959

Oelrich, Karl Heinz *Der spätere Erasmus und die Reformation.* Münster: Aschendorff, 1961

Ogonawski, Zbigniew 'Faustus Socinus, 1539–1604.' In *Shapers of Religious Traditions in Germany, Switzerland and Poland, 1560–1600*, edited by Jill Rait, New Haven: Yale University Press, 1981

Olin, John C. (editor) *John Calvin and Jacopo Sadoleto: A Reformation Debate.* New York: Harper, 1966

Quere, Ralph Walter 'Christ's Efficacious Presence in the Lord's Supper: Directions in the Development of Melanchthon's Theology after Augsburg.' *The Lutheran Quarterly* 29 (1977)

———. *Melanchthon's Christum Cognoscere. Christ's Efficacious Presence in the Eucharistic Theology of Melanchthon.* Nieuwkoop: de Graaf, 1977

Packer, James I. 'Calvin the Theologian.' In *John Calvin: A Collection of Essays*, edited by Gervase Duffield, Grand Rapids/Appleford: Eerdmans/Sutton Courtney Press, 1966

Pannier, Jacques 'Notes historiques et critiques sur un chapitre de l'*Institution* écrit à Strasbourg (1939).' *Revue d'Histoire et de Philosophie Religieuses* (1934)

Parker, T. H. L *Calvin: An Introduction to His Thought.* First American Edition, Louisville, KY: Westminster/John Knox Press, 1995

———. *Calvin's New Testament Commentaries.* Second Edition, Louisville: Westminster/John Knox Press, 1993

———. *John Calvin.* Tring: Lion, 1977

———. *John Calvin: A Biography.* Philadelphia: Westminster, 1975

Peter, Rodolphe and Gilmont, Jean-François *Bibliotheca Calviniana. Les oeuvres de Jean Calvin publiées au xvie siècle: Ecrits théologiques, littéraires et juridiques.* 2 vols, 1532–1564, Geneva: Librarie Droz, 1991–94

Peter, Rodolphe 'Calvin, traducteur de Mélanchthon.' In *Horizons européens de la Réforme en Alsace*, edited by Marijn de Kroon and Marc Lienhard, Strasbourg: Istra, 1980.

Rhein, Stefan 'Italia magistra orbis terrarum.' In *Humanismus und Wittenberger Reformation. Festgabe anlässlich des 500. Geburtstages des Praeceptor Germaniae Philipp Melanchthon am 16. Februar 1997*, edited by Michael Beyer et al., Leipzig: Evangelische Verlagsanstalt, 1997

Richards, George W. *The Heidelberg Catechism: Historical and Doctrinal Studies.* Philadelphia: Publication and Sunday School Board of the Reformed Church in the United States, 1913

Ritschl, Albrecht *The Christian Doctrine of Justification and Reconciliation.* Clifton, NJ: Reference Book Publishers, 1966

Rohls, Jan *Theologie reformierter Bekenntnisschriften.* Göttingen: Vandenhoeck & Ruprecht, 1987

Rupp, E. Gordon 'Philip Melanchthon and Martin Bucer.' In *A History of Christian Doctrine*, edited by H. Cunliffe-Jones and B. Drewery, Philadelphia: Fortress Press, 1978

Schäfer, Rolf 'Melanchthon's Hermeneutik im Römerbrief-Kommentar von 1532.' *Zeitschrift für Theologie und Kirche* 60 (1963)

Schaff, Philip 'The Friendship of Calvin and Melanchthon.' *Papers of the American Society of Church History.* 4 (1892)

———. 'Geschicht...des Heidelberger Katechismus.' *Zeitschrift für die historische Theologie* 3 (1864)

———. *History of the Christian Church.* 7 vols. New York: Scribner's, 1903

Scheible, Hans 'Luther and Melanchthon.' *Lutheran Quarterly* 4 (1990)

———. 'Melanchthons Bildungsprogramm.' *Blätter für Pfälzische Kirchengeschichte* 53 (1986)

———. *Melanchthon: eine Biographie.* Munich: Verlag C. H. Beck, 1997

———. (editor) *Melanchthon in seinen Schülern*, Wolfenbütteler Forschungen 73. Wiesbaden: Harrassowitz Verlag, 1997

———. 'Melanchthon zwischen Luther und Erasmus.' In *Renaissance-Reformation. Gegensätze und Gemeinsamkeiten*, edited by August Buck, Wiesbaden: O. Harrassowitz, 1984

———. 'Wolfgang Musculus und Philipp Melanchthon.' In *Wolfgang Musculus (1497–1563) und die oberdeutsche Reformation*, Edited by R. Dellsperger, R. Freudenberger, and W. Weber, Berlin: Akademie Verlag, 1997

Schenk, Wilhelm 'Erasmus und Melanchthon.' *Heythrop Journal* 8 (1967)

Schneider, John 'The Hermeneutics of Commentary: origins of Melanchthon's Integration of Dialectic into Rhetoric.' In *Philip Melanchthon (1497–1560) and the Commentary*, edited by Timothy Wengert and M. Patrick Graham, Sheffield: Sheffield Academic Press, 1997

————. *Philip Melanchthon's rhetorical construal of Biblical authority: Oratio Sacra*. Lewiston: Edwin Mellen Press, 1990

Schoeck, R. J. *Erasmus of Europe: Prince of Humanists 1501–1536*. Edinburgh: Edinburgh University Press, 1993

Seeberg, Reinhold *Text-book of the History of Doctrines*. Translated by Charles E. Hay, Grand Rapids: Baker Book House, 1977

Selderhuis, Herman J. 'Die Loci Communes des Wolfgang Musculus: Reformierte Dogmatik anno 1560' In *Wolfgang Musculus (1497–1563) und die oberdeutsche Reformation*, Edited by R. Dellsperger, R. Freudenberger, and W. Weber, Berlin: Akademie Verlag, 1997

Sperl, Adolf *Melanchthon zwischen Humanismus und Reformation: Eine Untersuchung über den Wandel des Traditionsverständnisses bei Melanchthon und die damit zusammenhängenden Grundfragen seiner Theologie*. Munich: Chr. Kaiser, 1959

Staedtke, J. 'Konrad Gesner als Theologe.' *Gesnerus* 23 (1965)

————. 'Der Zürcher Prädestinationsstreit von 1560.' *Zwingliana* 9 (1953)

Staehelin, Ernst *Das theologische Lebenswerk Johannes Oekolampads*. Quellen und Forschungen zur Reformationsgeschichte 21, Leipzig: Heinsius, 1939

Steinmann, Martin *Johannes Oporinus, ein Basler Buchdrucker um die Mitte des 16. Jahrhunderts*. Basel/Stuttgart: Helbing & Lichtenhahn, 1967

Strauss, Gerald *Luther's House of Learning: Indoctrination of the Young in the German Reformation*. Baltimore: Johns Hopkins University Press, 1978

Stupperich, Robert *Melanchthon*. Translated by Robert H. Fisher, London: Lutterworth, 1965

————. *Der Unbekannte Melanchthon: Wirken und Denken des Praeceptor Germaniae in neuer Sicht*. Stuttgart: W. Kohlhammer, 1961

Sturm, Erdmann *Der junge Zacharias Ursinus: Sein Weg vom Philippismus zum Calvinismus* Neukirchen: Neukirchener Verlag, 1972

Sudhoff, Karl *C. Olevianus und Z. Ursinus: Leben und ausgewählte Schriften*. Elberfeld: Friedrichs, 1857

Taplin, Mark 'Bernardino Ochino and the Zurich Polygamy Controversy of 1563.' M. Litt dissertation, University of St Andrews, 1995

————. 'The Italian Reformers and the Zurich Church.' PhD dissertation, University of St Andrews, 1998

Teuteberg, René 'Simon Grynaeus.' In *Der Reformation verpflichtet: Gestalten und Gestalter in Stadt und Landschaft Basel aus fünf Jahrhunderten*, edited by Rudolf Suter and René Teuteberg, Basel: Christoph Merian Verlag, 1979

Thommen, Rudolf *Geschichte der Universität Basel, 1532–1632*. Basel: Detloff, 1889

Thompson, Bard and Bricker, George H. (eds) *The Mystical Presence and Other Writings on the Eucharist*. Philadelphia: United Church, 1966

Thompson, Bard 'The Palatinate Church Order of 1563.' *Church History* 23 (1954)

———. 'Reformed Liturgies: An Historical and Doctrinal Interpretation of the Palatinate Liturgy of 1563, Mercersburg Provisional Liturgy of 1858, Evangelical and Reformed Order of 1944, and Their Sources' B. D. Thesis, Union Theological Seminary, New York, 1949

Troeltsch, Ernst *Vernunft und Offenbarung bei Johann Gerhard und Philip Melanchthon*. Göttingen: Vandenhoeck & Ruprecht, 1891

Van't Spijker, Willem 'The Influence of Luther on Calvin According to the *Institutes*.' In *John Calvin's Institutes: his opus magnum. Proceedings of the second South American Congress for Calvin Research July 31–August 3, 1984*, edited by B. J. van der Walt, Potchefstroom: Potchefstroom University for Christian Higher Education, 1986

Venema, Cornelius P. 'Heinrich Bullinger's Correspondence on Calvin's Doctrine of Predestination 1551–1553.' *Sixteenth Century Journal* 17 (1986)

Visser, Derk *Zacharias Ursinus: the Reluctant Reformer - His Life and Times*. New York, United Church, 1983

Volz, Hans 'Beiträge zu Melanchthons und Calvins Auslegungen des Propheten Daniel.' ZKG 67 (1955/6)

Wallace, Ronald S. 'Calvin's Approach to Theology.' In *The Challenge of Evangelical Theology: Essays in Approach and Method*, edited by Nigel Cameron, Edinburgh: Rutherford House, 1987

Warfield, Benjamin B. 'On the Literary History of Calvin's Institutes.' In John Calvin's *Institutes of the Christian Religion*, translated by John Allen, Philadelphia: Presbyterian Board of Christian Education, 1936

Weisman, Christoph *Eine Kleine Biblia: Die Katechismen von Luther und Brenz*. Stuttgart: Calver, 1985

Weiss, James Michael 'Erasmus at Luther's Funeral: Melanchthon's Commemorations of Luther in 1546.' *Sixteenth Century Journal* 16 (1985)

Wendel, François *Calvin: the Origins and Development of His Religious Thought*. Translated by Philip Mairet, New York: Harper & Row, 1963

Wengert, Timothy 'Adiaphora.' In *Oxford Encyclopedia of the Reformation*, edited by Hans Hillerbrand, 4 vols, New York: Oxford University Press, 1996

———. 'Caspar Cruciger (1504–1548): The Case of the Disappearing Reformer.' *The Sixteenth Century Journal* 20 (1989)

———. 'The Day Philip Melanchthon got mad.' *Lutheran Quarterly* 5 (1991)

———. 'Georg Major (1502–1574): defender of Wittenberg's Faith and Melanchthonian Exegete.' In *Melanchthon in seinen Schülern*, Wolfenbütteler Forschungen 73. Hans Scheible (editor), Wiesbaden: Harrassowitz Verlag, 1997

———. *Human Freedom, Christian Righteousness: Philip Melanchthon's Exegetical Dispute with Erasmus of Rotterdam*. New York: Oxford University Press, 1997

———. *Law and Gospel: Philip Melanchthon's Debate with John Agricola of Eisleben over* Poenitentia. Grand Rapids: Baker Book House, 1997

———. 'Luther and Melanchthon, Melanchthon and Luther.' *Luther-Jahrbuch* 65 (1998)

———. 'The Origins of the Third Use of the Law: Philip Melanchthon's Commentary on Colossians (1534).' Paper presented at the annual Sixteenth Century Studies Conference, San Francisco, CA October 1995

———. *Philip Melanchthon's* Annotationes in Johannem *in Relation to its Predecessors and Contemporaries*. Travaux d'Humanisme et Renaissance 220, Geneva: Librairie Droz, 1987

———. 'Philip Melanchthon's 1522 Annotations on Romans and the Lutheran Origins of Rhetorical Criticism.' In *Biblical Interpretation in the Era of the Reformation: Essays presented to David C. Steinmetz in honor of his sixtieth birthday*, edited by R. A. Muller and J. L. Thompson, Grand Rapids: W. B. Eerdmans, 1996

———. '"With Friends Like This...": The Biography of Philip Melanchthon by Joachim Camerarius.' In *The Rhetorics of Life-Writing in Early Modern Europe: Forms of Biography from Cassandra Fedele to Louis XIV*. Edited by Thomas F. Mayer and D. R. Woolf, Ann Arbor: University of Michigan, 1995

Williams, G. H. *The Radical Reformation*. 3rd Edition, Kirksville: Sixteenth Century Journal Publishers, 1992

Winkler, Eberhard 'Melanchthons lateinische Leichenrede auf Kurfürst Friedrich den Weisen.' *Zeitschrift für Religions- und Geistesgeschichte* 18 (1966)

Wriedt, Markus 'Die theologische Begründung der Schul- und Universitätsreform bei Luther und Melanchthon.' In *Humanismus und Wittenberger Reformation. Festgabe anlässlich des 500. Geburtstages des Praeceptor Germaniae Philipp Melanchthon am 16. Februar 1997*, edited by Michael Beyer et al., Leipzig: Evangelische Verlagsanstalt, 1997

Zöllner, Walter 'Melanchthons Stellung zum Bauernkrieg.' In *Philipp Melanchthon 1497–1560*, vol 1: *Philipp Melanchthon. Humanist, Reformator, Praeceptor Germaniae*, edited by the Melanchthon-Komitee der deutschen Demokratischen Republik, Berlin: Akademie-Verlag, 1963

Zuck, Lowell H. 'Heinrich Heppe: a Melanchthonian Liberal in the Nineteenth-Century German Reformed Church' *Church History* 51 (1982)

Index